ALLYN AND BACON'S COLLEGE LATIN SERIES

UNDER THE GENERAL EDITORSHIP OF

CHARLES E. BENNETT AND JOHN C. ROLFE

T. MACCI PLAVTI

CAPTIVI

WITH INTRODUCTION AND NOTES

BY

HERBERT C. ELMER

CORNELL UNIVERSITY

ALLYN AND BACON

Boston and Chicago

Norwood Press
J. S. Cushing & Co. — Berwick & Smith
Norwood Mass. U.S.A.

PREFACE.

THE text of the present edition of the *Captivi* may by some, perhaps, be considered ultra-conservative. I still hold, and more firmly than ever, the view expressed in my edition of the *Phormio* of Terence, that the testimony of the manuscripts is invariably entitled to more consideration than arbitrary "corrections." Again and again has it been demonstrated that manuscript readings, which to our imperfect vision seemed impossible, represent after all what was originally written in ancient texts. Even while the present volume is in preparation, there appears in the *Rheinisches Museum* an article by Birt, wherein he makes it seem probable that scores of manuscript readings in Plautus which editors have considered certainly corrupt, and which most of them have taken it upon themselves to "emend," are correct as they stand. Many other supposedly corrupt manuscript readings in Plautus have, during the last few years, been vindicated by the work of Leo, Skutsch, and other investigators. When our fallibility of judgment on such matters is being demonstrated afresh, even as we go to press with our new editions, does it not become us to treat the text with the utmost caution and to cherish an increasing respect for manuscript traditions? In establishing the text I have been guided by the principle that, before an editor is justified in introducing any conjecture unsupported by ancient testimony, the following conditions must exist: (1) it must be positively proved by careful investigation that the ancient testimony, if any exists, cannot possibly be correct; (2) the conjecture ·must have been sanctioned by the consensus of all competent critics. Until these requirements are met, all conjectures should be confined to critical notes. It is better to leave a passage unintelligible, with the certain imprint of the centuries upon it, than, at the risk of continuing the work of the corrupting hands that have wrought before us, to introduce mere conjectures that are not of such a nature as to command general acceptance. While, therefore, I believe I have duly considered all the important suggestions that have been made in recent years so far as they bear upon the text of the *Captivi*, and while I have mentioned many of these in my critical notes, I have introduced but few of them into my text. Such textual criticism as I have allowed myself to indulge in has been systematically excluded from the main commentary and relegated to an Appendix, which is also utilized for the citation of authorities for statements made in my notes, where such citation seemed desirable.

In preparing the book I have had access to all important editions of the *Captivi* ; but I have consulted most frequently those of Brix-Niemeyer, Goetz and Schoell, Hallidie, Leo, Lindsay, Morris, and Sonnenschein. To all of these I hereby acknowledge my indebtedness for valuable help. I am further indebted to Messrs. B. H. Sanborn & Co. for their courtesy in allowing me to embody in the present volume a few pages from the Introduction to my edition of the *Phormio*, of which they are the publishers.

I must also express to Professor E. W. Fay, of the University of Texas, Professor Gonzalez Lodge, of Bryn Mawr College, and Professor J. C. Rolfe, of the University of Michigan, my gratitude for their kindness and generosity in devoting time and labor to reading the proof sheets and for many valuable suggestions. I owe most, however, to Professor C. E. Bennett, who has subjected every page of both my manuscript and the proof sheets to the most searching criticism, and suggested numerous improvements. Many of the merits which I hope the present volume may be found to have are in no small degree due to his scholarly touch.

H. C. ELMER.

ITHACA, May, 1900.

INTRODUCTION.

I.

A SKETCH OF THE HISTORY OF GREEK AND ROMAN COMEDY.

1. THE ORIGIN OF THE GREEK DRAMA.

1. The Greek drama had its origin in the village festival that was wont to be held each year at the vintage time in honor of Dionysus, the god of wine, the bringer of good cheer. Dionysus, in the popular fancy, was supposed to have wandered through the world, accompanied by a band of satyrs and nymphs, spreading his worship among men, encountering countless dangers and hardships in his progress, now falling into the hands of pirates and thrown into chains, now aiding the gods in their war with the giants, now being torn to pieces at the command of the jealous Hera, but springing up again with new life, and finally triumphing over all obstacles and bringing joy and blessing to all mankind. It was customary among the country folk, when they gathered in the grapes, to celebrate the adventures of this god, whose bounty they were about to enjoy. One member of the company would impersonate the god himself, and the others would act the part of his attendant satyrs; and the story of the god's adventures would thus, in a rude and impromptu fashion, be enacted. Some parts of this story were bright and gay, while others were sad and tragic; and it was in these rude attempts

to represent its different aspects that both comedy and
tragedy had their origin.   Tragedy, however, was earlier
than comedy in reaching maturity.

2. The Early Greek Comedy.

2. The word "comedy" (κωμῳδία) means literally the "song
of revelry" (κῶμος, ᾄδειν), or possibly the song of the κώμη,
i.e. " village song."   The Dorians, and especially one **Susa-
rion** (about 580 B.C.), seem to deserve the credit of having
first dramatized the rude dialogue in which comedy had its
origin, and of having given it something like a literary form.
The principal representative, however, of that branch of literature, before it reached the perfection it attained during
the period of Pericles, was **Epicharmus**, a contemporary of
Aeschylus.   But comedy did not reach any high degree
of development until it was taken up by the master artists
of Athens in the time of Pericles.   The conditions of Greek
life at this period were peculiarly favorable for developing
this branch of writing.   The intellectual activity and the
highly developed political life of the times worked together
to bring it rapidly to a position of great importance and influence.   **Cratinus, Eupolis,** and **Phrynichus** are the first to be
mentioned as writers of the old Attic comedy; but these are
of little importance in comparison with **Aristophanes,** who
appeared upon the scene in the latter part of the fifth century B.C. (444–388) and became by far the most important
representative of the old school.   It lies, of course, in the
nature of comedy to depict the gay and humorous; and
at the time with which we are now dealing, the keen
and absorbing interest taken by all classes in politics gave
direction to the popular comedy.   Public men and affairs
formed its material.   These were subjected to that keen wit
with which the Athenians, above all others, were endowed.
With reference to form and technique, it was natural enough

that comedy should for the most part be modelled on the lines marked out by writers of tragedy, which already existed in a highly developed form.

The unfortunate result of the Peloponnesian War, which broke the self-conscious vigor of Athens, forms a turning-point in the history of Attic comedy. With the disappearance of eager participation of the people in public affairs, died out also their interest in them; other and narrower interests — above all, material interests — began to engross their attention. They had been wont to spare neither pains nor expense in organizing, equipping, and training a chorus as an essential feature of every play. But now, while they still continued for a time to furnish the chorus, they no longer felt the old pride in providing it with an elaborate outfit, or in training it when equipped; and their growing indifference ultimately resulted in its being given up altogether. In fact, the Plutus of Aristophanes, the latest of the eleven plays of that author which have been preserved to us, shows that a decided change in this respect has already taken place. In lieu of choral parts having an organic connection with the play, is found between the acts a song that has no such connection.

3. THE LATER GREEK COMEDY.

3. The new Attic comedy, which does not appear fully developed till the latter part of the fourth century, is almost wholly severed from all connection with public life, and shows, in comparison with the old comedy, a lack of variety in the subjects treated, and a lack of the old boldness in handling materials. Comedy now is a tame society play, dealing merely with the manners and customs of family life. The abuses practised in public life no longer receive notice even by so much as an allusion. At the same time personal attacks upon individuals have ceased; only typical charac-

ters, such as bragging soldiers, sponging parasites, and inso-
lent sycophants, are held up to ridicule. As compensation
for this narrower range of subjects, appears invention of new
situations and of amusing complications out of which the
same ever-recurring characters have to extricate themselves.
In this respect the fruitful, untiring genius of the poets of
the new comedy challenges our admiration, though our esti-
mate of them is based upon mere fragments from their plays
and upon Latin plays that are modelled after them.

Among the poets of the new Attic comedy, of whom there
were more than sixty, the most distinguished in the judgment
of antiquity was **Menander** (342–290 B.C.). Next to him,
Philemon, Diphilus, Philippides, Posidippus, and **Apollodorus**
of Carystus are to be named as the favorite writers of
comedy. Of the original productions of these poets only a
few fragments have come down to us. We have, however,
Latin adaptations from some of their plays in the two great
comic poets of Rome, **Plautus** and **Terence.**

Of course the transition from the old to the new comedy
was a gradual one. It extended over a period of fifty years,
from the Plutus of Aristophanes (presented first in 408 and
again — this time in a revised form and without chorus and
parabasis — in 388) to about the time of the Macedonian
sovereignty (338). The best known poets of this period are
Antiphanes and **Alexis.** Whether we should look upon this
so-called **middle comedy** as forming a distinct type by itself
may be questioned; but at any rate the division into the
old and the new is an important one, and each of these two
classes is marked by well-defined characteristics.

The new comedy, in its development, coincides with the
political decline of Greece and with the gradual decay of
her art. As compared with the old comedy, it shows in
many respects unmistakable retrogression. As a natural
result, however, of the conditions already indicated, it is free
from that distinctly local coloring, which makes even a play

of Aristophanes often unintelligible to one who is not familiar with the condition of affairs in Athens at the time the
play was written; it has the cosmopolitan character which
becomes, during the fourth and third centuries before Christ,
more and more noticeable in Greek life. It was owing to
this peculiar cosmopolitan character that the new comedy,
about the middle of the third century before Christ, found
a welcome in Rome — a city highly developed politically,
but as yet without a literature. That the comic poets of
Rome chose the material for their translations and adaptations exclusively from the new (and the so-called middle)
comedy is not, then, due wholly to the fact that that kind of
writing was still flourishing when Roman literature began.

4. ROMAN COMEDY.

4. The ancient Romans, like the Italians of to-day, had,
as one of their notable characteristics, a fondness for the
dramatic, and especially for the comic. Vergil, in *Georg.*
II. 385–396 (cf. Hor. *Ep.* II. 1. 139 ff.), pictures the gayeties
of rural festivals, at which improvised jests, in rude verse,
were exchanged in animated dialogue. These **versus Fescennini**, as they are commonly called (probably after the town
of Fescennia), had no literary importance; but still we see
in them germs similar to those from which the Greeks developed their artistic comedy. It is interesting also to note
that a process of development seems to have set in on
Roman, much as it did on Greek, soil. As a demand was
felt for something less rude than these *versus Fescennini*, a
form of representation arose for which preparation was
made beforehand, and less was intrusted to improvisation.
To add to the interest of the entertainment, the verses were
now accompanied by music and dancing, and the whole
performance in this improved form took the name of **Satura**.
These performances, if we may accept the common view

regarding the meaning of the term *saturae*,[1] seem to have been devoid of any connected plot, but they demanded a certain amount of care and skill on the part of the performers, and accordingly a class of people began to devote special attention to acting as a profession. We must of course look upon these *saturae* (of which the contents were of a purely local character, and the structure even yet not artistic) as entirely different from the Greek comedies, as far as their contents and their structure were concerned. A nearer approach to dramatic form was made in the **fabulae Atellanae**, so called because they are said to have originated in the Campanian town of Atella. The *fabulae Atellanae* were broad farces in which figured stock characters analogous to the clown, pantaloon, and harlequin of a modern pantomime. Rude as all these performances were, they nevertheless awakened in the Roman public an interest in dramatic representations. Under favorable circumstances they might have developed into an artistic drama that would have been truly Roman in thought and feeling.

5. But there now appeared on the scene an influence that was destined to dominate the whole course of Roman literature. After the war with Pyrrhus, the Romans came into closer contact with the Greek cities of southern Italy and Sicily, and had their attention called to the creations of Greek genius. They never recovered from the spell that was thus cast about them. Instead of attempting to create a literature of their own along independent lines, they now devoted themselves chiefly to copying the masterpieces of Greece. The first fruits of this new influence were seen in mere translations and adaptations from the Greek. The comedies that were thus translated, or adapted, are called

---

[1] In an interesting paper on "The Dramatic Satura and the Old Comedy at Rome" (*Amer. Jour. Phil.* Vol. XV.), Hendrickson expresses the view that *satura* in Livy (7. 2) is merely the designation of an assumed Roman parallel to the old Greek comedy.

fabulae palliatae, from the Greek cloak (*pallium*) worn by
the actors, to distinguish them from the **fabulae togatae** in
which Roman manners were represented. The first writer
to be mentioned in this connection is **Livius Andronicus,** who
was born at Tarentum about 284 B.C. After the capture of
his native city in 272 B.C., he became the slave of M. Livius
Salinator, who, charmed by the talents of the young man,
soon afterwards gave him his freedom. In 240 Livius was
engaged to produce, as one of the attractions of the *ludi
Romani,* two Latin plays, a tragedy and a comedy, adapted
from Greek originals. Such dramatic entertainments had
for a long time been regularly given in the original Greek
in the towns of southern Italy, and so were more or less
familiar to the Romans. These performances found such
favor at Rome that from this time on they became a regular
part of the games. Livius Andronicus must then be looked
upon as having introduced **a new era** for the Roman stage.
In Livy the historian (7. 2), the existence of a connected
plot and the systematic arrangement of the contents are
designated as the features that distinguished the new drama
from the old *satura.* It was further distinguished by the
employment of Greek metres and by differences in the form
of representation. Only a few fragments of the plays of
Livius have come down to us. We know, however, that he
was held in so great esteem at Rome that, in honor of him,
the temple of Minerva on the Aventine was appropriated to
the use of *scribae et histriones,* who organized themselves
into a sort of poets' guild.

6. Another writer, likewise active in both tragedy and
comedy, was **Cn. Naevius,** a native of Campania, born about
265 B.C. Being a Latin by descent, he took part in the
First Punic War, a conflict which he afterward described
in Saturnian verse. After 235 B.C. we find him noted at
Rome as a fiery and popular poet, especially in the field of
comedy. Fragments of thirty of his comedies have come

down to us. The violent attacks which he made on the
highest families of Rome led to his imprisonment and later
to his banishment. He died in exile in 201 B.C., or, according to some authorities, a little later.

7. T. Maccius Plautus was a writer of comedies only.
We have preserved to us only the most meagre details
regarding his life. An uncertainty exists even about his
name. It was long supposed to have been M. Accius
Plautus. Ritschl (1806–1876) attempted [1] to prove that it
was T. Maccius Plautus, and his conclusions have been
commonly accepted by scholars; but it has recently been
demonstrated [2] that the question as to his name cannot yet
be considered definitely settled. We know that he was
born at Sarsina, a small village in Umbria, about 254 B.C.
On coming to Rome, [3] probably at an early age, he found
employment at the hands of certain theatrical managers.
What he saved from his earnings here he subsequently lost
in foreign speculation, after which he returned penniless to
Rome and was compelled to earn his bread at hard labor in
a mill, — a duty generally reserved for the lowest slaves.
His employment in the theatre, however, had interested
him in the stage, and he resolved to turn to account the
knowledge this experience had given him. He accordingly
found time, even amid the unfavorable conditions surround-
ing him, to write comedies, and in a short time he became
the most popular of comic poets. His death came in 184
B.C., but the popularity of his plays remained undimin-
ished; and when, after the middle of the second century
B.C., it became customary, instead of presenting new plays,

---

[1] *Parerga*, p. 3.

[2] Leo, *Plautinische Forschungen* (Berlin, 1895), pp. 72 ff. Compare also Cocchia in the *Rivista di Filologia*, XIII. pp. 97 ff., and
Hülsen in *Berl. Phil. Wochenschrift*, VI. pp. 419 ff.

[3] The account here given of the early life of Plautus is the usual
one, but few of the details are certain.

to bring the old again and again upon the stage (see p. xx), the comedies of Plautus long continued to be among the chief attractions of the theatre. So great indeed was his popularity that plays of other writers were frequently given out under his name, in the hope of insuring for them a more cordial welcome. That he was fully conscious of the hold he had upon the sympathies of the people is shown by the epitaph, still preserved, which he himself wrote for his own tomb. It is as follows: —

> Postquam est mortem aptus Plautus, comoedia luget
> Scaena est deserta ac dein risus, ludus iocusque
> Et numeri innumeri simul omnes collacrumarunt.

(After Plautus succumbed to death, Comedy put on mourning, the stage was left unoccupied, then Laughter, Mirth, and Merriment, and Verses numberless, all with one accord burst into tears.)

8. To Plautus at one time were ascribed one hundred and thirty plays. In iii. 3. 1, Gellius records an assertion of Varro that twenty-one of these plays were admitted by all to be genuine productions of Plautus. These so-called[1] *fabulae Varronianae* were probably the plays that have come down to us, viz. —

Amphitruo,	*Epidicus,*	*Poenulus,*
Asinaria,	*Bacchides,*	*Persa,*
Aulularia,	*Mostellaria,*	*Rudens,*
Captivi,	*Menaechmi,*	*Stichus,*
Curculio,	*Miles Gloriosus,*	*Trinummus,*
Casina,	*Mercator,*	*Truculentus,*
Cistellaria,	*Pseudolus,*	

and the *Vidularia,* of which only a few fragments remain. A few others of the one hundred and thirty plays may have

---

[1] The term *fabulae Varronianae* is really a misnomer, as it implies that Varro passed judgment upon the plays to which he referred, whereas he merely recorded that *consensu omnium Plauti esse censebantur.*

been genuine productions of Plautus, but most of them were undoubtedly the works of some inferior poet or poets. While all of the twenty plays preserved to us are *fabulae palliatae*, Plautus treated his Greek originals with considerable freedom, and never hesitated to introduce distinctly Roman allusions, and to recast in a mould of his own the material offered him by his original, wherever he thought that by such recasting he could add to the humor or interest of the play. For the points of contrast between Plautus and Terence in this and other respects, see p. xix ff. As already indicated, the popularity of Plautus among his contemporaries was unrivalled. On the subsequent history of his plays, and the judgment of posterity regarding them, see Chapter II., below, p. xx.

9. Q. Ennius is chiefly noted for his epic poem called *Annales*, — in which he related, in eighteen books, the entire history of Rome from the earliest times down to his own, — for his *saturae*, and his tragedies. But he also attempted comedy, and so deserves mention here. He was born at Rudiae in Calabria, in 239 B.C. In 204 he was brought by the quaestor M. Porcius Cato from Sardinia to Rome, where he seems to have lived in moderate circumstances as teacher of Greek and as stage poet. In 184 B.C. he received the right of Roman citizenship, which he lived to enjoy for fifteen years. None of his comedies have come down to us — not even in fragments of any importance.

10. The next poet worthy of mention in this connection is **Statius Caecilius**, who enjoyed an enviable reputation among the ancients as a writer of *palliatae*, and who was an important forerunner of Terence. An Insubrian by birth, he came to Rome about 194 B.C., probably as a captive taken in war. Later, however, he was given his freedom. His first attempt at comedy failed, and was not even heard to the end by the impatient audience; but he toiled on till he won literary fame and a name among comic poets second only, as yet, to that of Plautus. He died soon after Ennius, with whom in life he had been on the most intimate terms.

11. Publius Terentius Afer was born at Carthage, about 190 B.C.[1] At an early age, he came to Rome as a slave of the senator Terentius Lucanus. His master, struck by the talent and the prepossessing appearance of the boy, not only caused him to be carefully educated, but also gave him his freedom. The associations to which he had been accustomed in the house of his master made it easy for him to keep up his connections with the nobility of Rome, and certain prominent members of this nobility became his firm friends. Chief among these were Scipio Africanus (the younger), C. Laelius, and L. Furius Philus.

12. The literary tendency of the times, as well as his own inclination, led the poet to devote his activity to the *fabula palliata*. Terence produced his first comedy, the *Andria*, at the *ludi Megalenses*, in April, 166 B.C. The aediles, who had charge of the games, had some misgivings about allowing the presentation of a play by an entirely unknown poet. He was accordingly induced to submit his play first to the older poet Caecilius, for approval. Regarding the meeting between these two poets, the following story is told. Terence found Caecilius at dinner, and, as the caller was meanly dressed, he was given a seat on a bench near the couch on which the great author was reclining, and was then given permission to read what he had written. After the first few verses had been read, Caecilius was so captivated by the young man's talents that he invited him to a place beside him upon the couch. He then listened attentively and with unbounded admiration to the remainder of the play.

---

[1] The date generally given is 185, in accordance with Suetonius, in his *vita Terenti;* but H. Sauppe (*Nachr. d. Gött. ges.*, 1870, pp. 111 ff.) has made this date seem very improbable.

13. The order of presentation of the plays of Terence, during the lifetime of the poet, may be seen from the following table: —

Andria	at the *ludi Megalenses*,			166 B.C.
Hecyra[1]	"	"	"	165 B.C.
Heauton timorumenos	"	"	"	163 B.C.
Eunuchus	"	"	"	161 B.C.
Phormio	"	"	*Romani*,	161 B.C.
Hecyra	"	"	*funerales* of Aemilius Paulus, 160 B.C.[2]
Adelphoe	"	"	" of Aemilius Paulus, 160 B.C.
Hecyra	"	"	*Romani*, 160 B.C.[3]

14. It is not to be wondered at that the earliest writers, in adapting the productions of foreign genius to Roman ears, should give them something of a native character, and we accordingly find that all the plays of Plautus bear Latin titles (*Asinaria, Aulularia, Captivi,* etc.), except in plays like the *Amphitruo* and the *Epidicus*, where the title is taken from the Greek name of a person in the play. Attention has already been called to the fact that the plays of Plautus abound in Roman allusions. Later, however, as the influence of Greek culture came to be more widespread, there was an ever-increasing tendency to make the Latin plays more nearly like the Greek from which the plots were taken. Indeed, the contemporaries of Terence, among them his chief adversary, Luscius Lanuvinus, made it a point of attack that he sometimes departed so far from his Greek original as to weave into the general plot of his drama such scenes from other Greek comedies as particularly struck his fancy. This process of combining parts of different plays into one was maliciously called *contaminatio*. Except in this one respect,

---

[1] This attempted presentation, however, proved a failure; and tradition accordingly assigns the *Heauton* to the second place, the *Eunuchus* to the third, etc.

[2] Second unsuccessful presentation.

[3] Third, and successful, presentation.

Terence has followed his Greek originals very closely, and the Roman allusions, which are so common in Plautus, are almost entirely wanting in Terence.

15. All six plays of Terence met with great applause from the public, though the *Hecyra* was not received with favor until the third attempt to present it.

16. After the third production of the *Hecyra*, in 160 B.C., Terence left Rome for Greece, probably to acquire a more intimate knowledge of the life and customs of the people of that country. In the following year, 159 B.C., the poet died, while on the point of returning to Rome with translations which he had recently made of other comedies.

17. The last writer of *palliatae* who is of sufficient importance to call for notice here was **Turpilius**, who was a contemporary of Terence and who lived till 103 B.C. Thirteen titles of plays written by him are known to us, but only a few fragments of the plays themselves are preserved. Judging from these fragments, his style was livelier than that of Terence, and of a more popular character.

18. It will be seen from this brief sketch of Roman comedy that the two names that stand out in high relief among Rome's comic poets are those of Plautus and Terence. While these two poets both alike represent the class of comedy known as *fabulae palliatae*, and while they take as their models Greek poets of the same school and the same period, they present, nevertheless, with reference to each other, many sharply contrasted characteristics. Plautus wrote for the crowd, and his language is that of the street and the barber shop ; Terence wrote primarily for the cultured few, and his language is that of the salon. The wit of Plautus, while often coarse and obscene, is fresh, original, sparkling, spontaneous, and is a bid for a loud laugh ; that of Terence is more refined, studied, subdued, and usually expects hardly more than a smile. Plautus, while under restraint, as an imitator of models necessarily is, displays,

nevertheless, abundant creative fancy, and frequently startles
one with clever originalities.   Terence is satisfied with fidelity to his Greek model, departing from it rarely, and only
when he feels that his artistic purpose requires it.   Plautus
is given to exaggerated puns, striking effects, sharp contrasts.   Terence aims at truth, accuracy, and artistic finish.
The style of Plautus is reckless and extravagant, of the do-
all and dare-all sort, and his words are often imported from
the Greek or manufactured to suit the occasion.   The style
of Terence is more sober and sedate, and his words are
those sanctioned by good Latin usage.   Plautus can inflict
upon an individual such a name as Vaniloquidorus Virginis-
vendonides Nugiepiloquides Argentumexterebronides Te-
digniloquides Nummosexpalponides Quodsemelarripides
Nunquameripides (*Pers.* 702); Terence would consider
such word-making beneath his dignity.   Plautus aimed at
making fun, sacrificing or subordinating everything to
this one purpose ; Terence aimed at drawing a true picture
of Greek life in the purest colloquial Latin, so far, at any
rate, as Greek life was correctly portrayed in the poets from
whom he drew his material.   In general, the excellences of
Plautus are largely such as depend upon spontaneity of
genius ; those of Terence are the result of thought and
study and painstaking in reproducing, in the most artistic
form, the excellences of his Greek models.

II.

HISTORY OF THE TEXT OF PLAUTUS.

19. After the death of Terence, the writing of *fabulae
palliatae* almost ceased.[1] In the absence of new productions, the custom now began of presenting again upon the

---

[1] Turpilius probably ceased writing at an early date (Ritschl,
Parerga, p. 188, Rem.).

stage the plays of former poets. It was but natural that many changes should be made in these old plays to make them better suited to the altered conditions under which they were to be reproduced. The text of Plautus has suffered not a little by the arbitrary changes that were made for such purposes. His plays continued to be put on the stage for a long time after the poet's death, and there can be no doubt that they are preserved to us in the form which they received to fit them for these later reproductions. Some of the **prologues** now prefixed to the plays may have been written for performances given about the middle of the first century B.C.[1] To about the same time probably belong the **acrostic arguments,** or metrical summaries, prefixed to all the plays of Plautus except the *Bacchides*. For the **non-acrostic arguments,** which belong to a later period, see p. xxiii. As early as the second half of the second century B.C., scholars began, in imitation and emulation of the Greek grammarians, to turn their attention to the study of *fabulae palliatae*. The texts of the comedians were brought together in suitable form for reading, special care being taken to preserve, as far as possible, different readings wherever such existed. Notes, too, on the history of the different plays were collected and arranged in a connected manner. Lastly, Roman scholars wrote various treatises on the scenic and linguistic peculiarities of the old comedians, and on other topics of interest to the student of literature. Among these were **L. Accius** (the famous writer of tragedy), **Porcius Licinus, Volcacius Sedigitus, L. Aelius Stilo, Aurelius Opilius, Q. Cosconius, Serv. Clodius,** and, above all, **M. Terentius Varro,** whose works, distinguished as they were for their learning and practical wisdom, formed the chief source of information for the historians of literature. The material for these

---

[1] See, however, for a discussion of the date of composition of the prologues, Leo, *Plautinische Forschungen*, pp. 170 ff.; Trautwein, *de prologorum Plautinorum indole atque natura* (Berlin, 1890).

works was drawn from the actors' copies of the plays, so
far as they could be procured, and from the records of
magistrates regarding the productions of plays brought out
under their supervision. Consideration for the convenience
of the reader led to the practice of indicating at the beginning of each scene the characters who take part in that
scene, and of dividing plays into acts (see p. xxx). But,
after a time, interest in the performances of the early
drama began to flag, and in the Augustan period not merely
had such performances ceased to be popular, but so little
interest was felt in Plautus himself that his plays now
found but few readers, and the copies produced during this
period were carelessly and indifferently made. Many of
the corruptions in the text undoubtedly date from this
period of indifference. It was during this period, also, that
the plays became separated from one another, each going
its own way through the hands of copyists, and each meeting with its own fate. This independent circulation of
individual plays accounts in part for the marked differences
in the condition of the texts. Some plays passed through
the hands of very careless and ignorant copyists, and are
still full of the corruptions they then received; others fell
into worthier hands, and have come down to us in a more
satisfactory form; but all alike were less carefully treated
than would have been the case if a livelier and a more
general interest had been felt in the author. This period
of indifference toward, and neglect of, the plays of Plautus
lasted till about the second half of the first century A.D.

20. At that time there arose a famous scholar and literary critic, **Marcus Valerius Probus,** who interested himself
in the critical study of Rome's greatest poets. It is certain
that he revised the works of Lucretius, Vergil, and Horace.
Possibly also, as Leo[1] assumes, he made a collection, from

---

[1] *Plautinische Forschungen*, pp. 21 ff.

all quarters, of the scattered and neglected plays of Rome's greatest comedian, Plautus. At any rate, some such collection must have been made by some one at about this time. There is, however, no reason to suppose that it consisted only of the twenty-one plays now assigned to Plautus. It is probable that other plays were extant and were included in the collection, and that another grammarian published a critical edition of twenty-one of these plays, including in this *corpus* only such as Varro had said (see p. xv) were admitted by everybody to be undoubtedly genuine productions of Plautus. After publication, such an edition must have become the basis of all Plautine study, an assumption which accounts for the fact that all the other plays became scattered again and were gradually lost. The text of Plautus must, by this time, have become very corrupt. To render it readable, many arbitrary alterations were undoubtedly made; to render it intelligible, frequent comments and glosses were added. In this way numerous interpolations crept in, and the text became still further corrupted. It should be noticed, however, that the corruptions dating from this period are chiefly due to a lively interest in the plays, while the earlier corruptions above referred to (p. xxii) were due to carelessness and neglect.

21. The second century A.D. was characterized by a display of erudition, and a popular field for such display was that offered by archaic Latin. Great zeal was shown in the study of the early poets. The principal representative of the learning of this period is **C. Sulpicius Apollinaris**. It is possible that the **non-acrostic arguments** (see p. xxi) were written by this critic. Plautus was, however, doomed to be forgotten again. In the Middle Ages he seems to have been practically unknown. Hrotswitha von Gandersheim, an imitator of Terence, who flourished in the latter half of the tenth century, knows nothing of him. At the beginning of the fifteenth century all but eight of the plays were still unknown. These eight were *Amphitruo, Asinaria, Aulula-ria, Captivi, Curculio, Casina, Cistellaria,* and *Epidicus,* and these are preserved in a large number of extant manuscripts, dating from the fourteenth and fifteenth centuries. A manuscript (D), containing some of these eight plays and also the remaining twelve, was found in Germany about 1428, and is now in the Vatican at Rome. It dates from the twelfth century. The oldest manuscript (A) of Plautus now extant, and indeed one of the oldest Latin manuscripts preserved to us, was discovered by Cardinal Mai in 1815, in the Ambrosian library at Milan, and is known as the *Ambro-sian palimpsest.* It was written in the fourth or fifth century, and is of course of great importance in establishing the text, though it lacks the *Amphitruo, Asinaria, Aulularia,* and *Cur-culio* entirely, and preserves the other plays in a more or less incomplete form. Two other manuscripts (B and C) were used by Camerarius in the sixteenth century, one of these (B, of the eleventh century) containing all of the twenty plays, the other (of the twelfth century) only the last twelve. A collation of a very important manuscript — viz. the one used by Turnebus, a famous French scholar of the sixteenth century — has recently been discovered by Lindsay.[1]

22. Somewhat more than forty years after the discovery of the manuscript containing the twelve lost plays, appeared the first complete printed edition of Plautus,[2] that of Georgius Merula, published in Venice in 1472. From that time on there was an almost constant succession of editions of either a part or the whole of Plautus, until toward the end of the seventeenth century. Then interest in Plautine studies again died out and during the

---

[1] Sonnenschein, however (*Class. Rev.* for May, 1899), expresses doubt as to whether Lindsay's discovery really represents the readings of the *codex Turnebi.*

[2] There was, however, a somewhat earlier edition of the other eight plays.

whole of the eighteenth century practically nothing of any importance was done in this field.   The beginning of the present century was marked by the appearance of Bothe's edition (1809–11) in four volumes, the last consisting of a commentary of 872 closely printed pages.   The activity thus renewed has continued till the present time, and has resulted in the appearance of numerous important editions and volumes of Plautine studies, culminating with the completion, in 1896, of the monumental critical edition of Goetz and Schoell, and that of Leo.   For further information and enumeration of important editions see, for instance, Ritschl's *Opuscula*, II. pp. 34 ff.; Teuffel-Schwabe, *Geschichte der Römischen Literatur* (translated by Warr), §§ 97 and 99.

III.

DRAMATIC ENTERTAINMENTS, THE ACTORS, THE STAGE, ETC.

23. It should be noted that, for some time after Livius Andronicus, dramatic performances in Rome were given only at the *ludi Romani* or *maximi* (in September) under the supervision of the curule aediles.   Somewhat later they formed a part likewise of the *Megalesia* (in April), given under the direction of the curule aediles, of the *ludi plebei* (in November), given by the plebeian aediles, and, after 211 or 212 B.C., of the *ludi Apollinares* (in July), given by the *praetor urbanus*.   To the officials who conducted the games, a specified sum of money was furnished by the state, for the purpose of defraying the expense attending the occasion. In the course of time, as the games took on a more elaborate character, the sum donated by the state had to be increased repeatedly, and even then those who took them in charge frequently found it necessary to make liberal contributions

from their own private means.   Besides the games that were
thus celebrated on behalf of the state, there were also others
given on extraordinary occasions, viz. *ludi funebres* (or *fune-
rales*), in honor of celebrated men, those accompanying dedi-
cations and triumphs, and those given as votive offerings.

24. Down to 174 B.C. the dramatic performances took
place near the temple of the deity chiefly concerned in the
festivities.[1]   Permanent theatres of stone, such as were later
built on a scale of great grandeur, were as yet unknown.
When a play was to be produced, a wooden stage was erected
for the purpose, and then taken down after the performance.
This stage was ordinarily built near the foot of some hill,
or slope, so that the rising ground might afford convenient
seats for the spectators, while those in front would not
obstruct the view of those in the rear.   On such a slope the
people assembled under the open sky.   As no seats were
provided for their accommodation, they usually sat, or
reclined, upon the ground.   The more fastidious sometimes
had stools brought for them from their homes, although
this was looked upon as a mark of effeminacy and was
even forbidden.   In 179 B.C., a stage of stone was erected
near the temple of Apollo, but this was of small dimensions
and was probably intended for use only at the *ludi Apollinares.*   Five years later, arrangements were made, on the
part of the state, for the building of a substantial, permanent stage,[2] but this, if it was actually built, seems
soon to have disappeared.   In 146 B.C., L. Mummius built
a complete theatre, provided with rows of seats, but this
was of wood, and was taken down after each performance.
Finally, in 55 B.C., was dedicated the stone theatre of Cn.
Pompeius, the first permanent theatre erected in Rome.   It

---

[1] Funeral games (perhaps also the *ludi Romani*) took place in the
forum.   That the *ludi Apollinares* at least, in the beginning, were
given in the Circus Maximus, is clear from Liv. 25. 12, 14.

[2] Ritschl, *Parerg.* p. 227.

is said to have been capable of accommodating forty thousand spectators.[1]

25. The dramatic performances usually took place between *prandium* (about twelve o'clock) and *cena* (after three o'clock), so that when we consider the other amusements that formed a part of the day's exercises, it seems hardly possible that more than one play could, as a rule, have been presented on any one day. Later, in Cicero's time, the custom of giving these performances in the early morning was introduced.

26. When a play was to be given, the fact was announced by a crier (*praeco*), that the people might assemble at the proper place. Immediately before the performance began, there was a *tituli pronuntiatio*, an announcement of the subject of the play; but sometimes the prologue itself conveyed to the audience their first information regarding the subject of the play and the name of the poet. The actors were slaves, or, in later times, freedmen, this profession being considered beneath the dignity of free-born men. The *dominus*, or general manager of the troupe was a freedman, who also took part in the acting and was sometimes called the *actor* (i.e. *par excellence*). At first, poets were wont to bring out their plays themselves, hiring slaves and freedmen for the purpose, but this practice ceased at an early date, and, as early as Plautus, the poet himself was no longer *actor* also. The *Stichus* of Plautus, for instance, according to the *didascalia*, was brought out by T. Publilius Pellio, who is severely criticised by the poet himself (*Bacch.* 214 f.) for the manner in which he put the *Epidicus* on the stage.

27. To the theatrical managers (*domini*) application was made by those who wished to give dramatic entertainments.

---

[1] Lanciani (*The Ruins and Excavations of Ancient Rome*, p. 459) gives the number of *loca* as 17,580.

The poets had business relations, for the most part, only with these managers, who bought, or rejected, their plays, and who accordingly were very influential in determining the fate, and encouraging the development, of poetic talent. In exceptional cases, however, the givers of the games, as they were men of experience in such matters and naturally felt great interest in the success of the performances, had a voice in the selection of the plays to be presented. All financial risk attending the presentation of a play was borne by the theatrical manager. As it was of great importance to the givers of the games that the people should be pleased with the amusements provided for them at such great expense, a reward was offered to the *dominus*, varying in amount according to the success of the play given by him.[1] This of course was calculated to secure the choice of the best possible play and to assure its presentation in the best possible manner. The *dominus* on his part was accustomed, after a successful performance, to reward the deserving actors of his company with a banquet. Cf. Plaut. *Cist.* 785; *Rud.* 1418 ff.

28. As regards the external equipment necessary for the dramatic performances, this was provided by contractors (*conductores;* cf. Plaut. *Asin.* Prol. 3), under the supervision of those who gave the games.[2]

29. Among the Greeks, the number of actors allowed upon the stage at any one time was limited. This was not the case among the Romans, as there could be any number of actors which convenience might dictate. The *dominus gregis* did not, of course, care to increase the number un-

---

[1] The assertion of Mommsen, *Röm. Gesch.* I.[8] p. 889, that the poets received their reward only when the play did not prove a failure, has not been substantiated.

[2] The costumes of the actors were provided by the *choragus*, whom Mommsen (*Röm. Gesch.* I. p. 886) regards as identical with the *dominus gregis*.

necessarily, on account of the additional expense, preferring rather to produce a play with a few superior actors than with a larger number of indifferent ones. The Latin *fabula palliata* resembled the later period of the new Greek comedy in having no chorus. In exceptional cases, there seems to have been something similar to it, probably in imitation of the Greek original, e.g. the chorus of fishermen in Plaut. *Rud.* (vs. 290 ff.); but this was placed, not in the orchestra, but upon the stage. There is nothing of the kind, however, in Terence.

30. Female characters were, until comparatively late times (cf. Donatus on *And.* IV. 3. 1), impersonated by male actors in female dress.

31. The custom of using masks seems to have been introduced, soon after Terence, by the theatrical managers, Cincius Faliscus and Minucius Prothymus. Up to that time actors depended for their effects upon wigs and rouge.

32. The plot in a *fabula palliata* is invariably laid in a Greek town or colony, usually in Athens. When the action was supposed to be taking place in a town, the *proscaenium* represented an open street in that town. The background was ordinarily formed by three private houses, corresponding to the three entrances to the royal palace as represented on the stage in Greek tragedy ; in place of one of these was sometimes the front of a temple, when the character of the play made such a building necessary. Narrow alleys also opened from the back of the stage into the street (cf. *Phorm.* 891 f.). Upon the stage stood, according to Donatus, two altars — one on the right dedicated to Liber, another on the left, dedicated to the deity chiefly concerned in the festivities of which the production of the play formed a part. On this point, however, there are differences of opinion.[1]

---

[1] See Dziatzko's note, in the *Einleitung* to his *Phormio*, p. 25 (Dziatzko-Hauler, p. 36).

On the right (from the point of view of the spectators) the
street was supposed to lead to the forum and the interior of
the town; on the left, to the harbor and foreign countries.

IV.

DIVISION OF PLAYS INTO ACTS AND SCENES.

33. A division of dramas into acts was already known in
the time of Plautus and Terence, but it does not as a rule
seem to have been clearly marked by the writers themselves. It was left rather to the discretion of the theatrical
manager to introduce intermissions at suitable places in the
play. This is perhaps the reason why the manuscripts, at
least all the oldest of them, have no division into acts.
Definite divisions were, however, established by the grammarians and the commentators of antiquity (though these
sometimes differ among themselves), and five was settled
upon as the proper number of acts for a drama (cf. Horace,
A. P. 189 f.).

34. The division into scenes, on the other hand, is very
old. It was customary to place before each scene a complete list of all the characters to appear in that particular
scene. In the copies which formed the basis of our manuscripts, each character who had anything to say was de-
noted by a letter of the Greek alphabet, which letter served
also in the text to designate that character. For the division into scenes, two principles seem to have been followed
in our manuscripts. According to one of these, a new
scene is formed by the exit or the entrance of a single
actor. Exceptions to this rule are formed by cases in which
a person leaves the stage only for a moment, or in which the
persons who remain behind have little to say, and that of
no importance, until the entrance of another actor, or other

actors, and the opening of a new scene (e.g. *Phorm.* 219, 778, 816). According to the other principle, a new scene is indicated only where the change of actors introduces an important turn in the plot.

V.

THE METRES OF PLAUTUS AND THE APPROPRIATENESS OF DIFFERENT METRES TO DIFFERENT MOODS.

35. The metres found in Plautus are chiefly iambic, trochaic, anapaestic, cretic, and bacchic. A peculiarity of iambic, trochaic, and anapaestic verses is that they are, at least in Greek poetry, measured by dipodies, i.e. pairs of feet, instead of by single feet, each dipody having one main and one subordinate ictus. Accordingly, a verse of four feet is called a dimeter (instead of a tetrameter), one of six feet a trimeter (instead of a hexameter), etc. Frequently, however, and especially with reference to early Latin poetry, these verses are called *quaternarii, senarii*, etc., names given them solely with reference to the number of feet contained in each, the distinctions between the odd and the even feet having been, for the most part, lost sight of by early Latin poets.

36. The verse of the early poets has always presented many difficulties. Even in the time of Cicero the most common and least difficult of these metres — namely the iambic *senarius* — was apparently but little understood.[1] After a time the plays came to be actually written as so much continuous prose. In most of our manuscripts of them, no attempt is made to divide the text into verses at

---

[1] Cf. Cic. *Orator*, 55, 184 : *At comicorum senarii propter similitudinem sermonis sic saepe sunt abiecti, ut non numquam vix in eis numerus et versus intellegi possit.*

all. The same is true of all the early editions prior to that of Pylades (1506). It is only during the present century that most of the laws governing these early metres have been discovered. Even yet many difficulties remain, and it is frequently impossible to determine definitely the character of individual verses or the points at which verse-division should be made. In the *Captivi*, for instance, there are twenty verses (212, 232–234, 497–515, 836) which the recent critical edition of Goetz and Schoell makes no attempt to assign to definite metres. On account of the difficulties of Plautine and Terentian metres, it has, since the time of Bentley, been customary for each editor to mark the main, or primary, ictuses in each verse, in order to indicate what seems to him individually, or to editors generally, the proper scansion.

37. For the proper understanding of the classification and discussion of metres about to be given, the following definitions should be noted : —

(*a*) **arsis**, used in this book to indicate the unaccented part of a foot.

(*b*) **thesis**, used in this book to indicate the accented part of a foot. (See, however, note on p. xlv.)

(*c*) **diaeresis**, that sort of division (within a verse) which is caused by the coincidence of the end of a word with the end of a foot, e.g. in the verse —

Ĭtĕ dŏ|mŭm sătŭ|rāe uĕnĭt | Hḗspĕrŭs | ĭtĕ că|pēllāe,

there is diaeresis after *uenit* and again after *Hesperus*.

(*d*) **hiatus**, the coming together of two vowels (each with its own natural quantity), caused by the non-elision of a final vowel before a word beginning with a vowel or *h* (but see Introd. § 74).

(*e*) **semi-hiatus**, the occurrence of a final *long* vowel, or a diphthong, before a word beginning with a vowel or *h*, with the result that the long vowel or diphthong is *shortened* but *not elided;* e.g. *quĭ aget* in —

Quĭă prī̆|mās pār|tīs quī̆ ă̆|gĕt, ĭs ĕ̆|rīt Phŏ̄r|mĭŏ̄.

(*f*) **syllaba anceps**, *the uncertain syllable*, a term given to the final syllable of a verse for the reason that this sylla-ble may, in any Latin verse, be either long or short, re-gardless of the theoretical requirements of the metre.

(*g*) **clausula**, *the close*, a short verse used to end a series of longer verses, always with the same rhythm as the preceding verse and subject to the same metrical treat-ment as the complete verses of the same rhythm.

38. The metres of Plautus, so far as they are found in the *Captivi*, may be divided into the following varieties : —

[*N.B.* — *Whenever two short syllables are substituted for an accented long syllable of the normal foot, the accent falls on the first short syllable, e.g. _ ∠ becomes _ ◡́◡, ◡◡◡́◡; ∠ _ becomes ◡́◡ _, ◡́◡◡◡; ∠◡ becomes ◡́◡◡; ◡∠ becomes ◡◡́◡, etc. In what is said below regarding the association of the several metres with different moods, it will of course be understood that the charac-teristics mentioned are not always prominent. The moods indicated are, in each case, to be regarded merely as those most frequently asso-ciated with the verse.*]

1. IAMBIC.

39. In all iambic verses, any one of the following feet is allowed as a substitute for the pure iambus, ◡ ∠: (*a*) ana-paest, ◡◡ ∠; (*b*) spondee, > ∠; (*c*) tribrach, ◡ ◡́ ◡; (*d*) dactyl, > ◡́ ◡; (*e*) proceleusmatic, ◡◡ ◡́ ◡. It should be noticed, however, that, in an acatalectic verse, the last foot is invariably a pure iambus (with the privilege of course, of the *syllaba anceps*).[1]

---

[1] See Introd. § 37 (*f*).

40. Iambic Senarius (Trimeter Acatalectic). — The caesuras may be classified as follows, in the order of their frequency: (*a*) the so-called penthemimeral, after the arsis of the third foot, e.g.[1] ∪ ⸗ ∪ ∠ ∪ ∥ ⸗ ∪ ∠ ∪ ⸗ ∪ ⸌ ; (*b*) the hepthemimeral, after the arsis of the fourth foot, e.g. ∪ ⸗ ∪ ∠ ∪ ⸗ ∪ ∥ ∠ ∪ ⸗ ∪ ⸌, in which case there is often diaeresis after, or a secondary caesura in, the second foot.

41. In connection with this verse, the following peculiarities call for notice: (1) an anapaest is seldom allowed immediately after a dactyl, or a tribrach; (2) when a proceleusmatic is used, its ictus-syllable nearly always begins a word, and the ictus and word-accent, with rare exceptions, coincide. The proceleusmatic is most common in the first foot; it is rare in the fifth foot.

42. Nearly all the plays of Plautus open with *iambic senarii*. This is the verse of ordinary narrative or dialogue, sometimes also of soliloquy, and seems the one best adapted for making the audience acquainted with the general situation. Its movement may be illustrated by the following lines: —

" The tempest nears us ; darkly rolls the angry sea ;
  The thunder mutters ; lightnings leap from cloud to cloud."

As the plot develops, the metre changes to suit the varying moods of the characters.

43. Iambic Octonarius (Tetrameter Acatalectic). — The caesura of this verse falls into two classes: (*a*) It may be after the fifth arsis, i.e. ∪ ⸺ ∪ ∠ ∪ ⸗ ∪ ∠ ∪ ∥ ⸗ ∪ ∠ ∪ ⸗ ∪ ∠ ; (*b*) it may be at the end of the fourth foot, e.g. ∪ ⸗ ∪ ∠ ∪ ⸗ ∪ ⸌ ∥ ∪ ⸗ ∪ ∠ ∪ ⸗ ∪ ⸌, in which case the fourth foot is treated like the final foot of the

---

[1] In what follows, the primary ictus is represented by *''*, and the secondary by *'*.

verse, i.e. it must be a pure iambus (with the privilege of the *syllaba anceps*), and hiatus is sometimes allowed after it.

44. The anapaest is never (or very rarely) allowed in this verse after a tribrach or a dactyl.

45. *Iambic octonarii* are suited to an animated, impassioned mood. Compare: —

"And furious every charger neighed to join the dreadful revelry."

46. Iambic Septenarius (Tetrameter Catalectic), called *septenarius* because only seven feet are complete, though it really contains seven and a half feet. — The caesura is (*a*) usually after the fourth foot, which then presents the same peculiarities of treatment as the *octonarius* under similar conditions; (*b*) sometimes after the arsis of the fifth foot.

47. *Iambic septenarii*, which in Latin occur only in comic poets, are found chiefly in serio-comic strains. Compare: —

"A captain bold of Halifax, who lived in country quarters."

48. Iambic Quaternarius (Dimeter Acatalectic), rare in Plautus (see verse 197). — This verse is usually employed as a *clausula* in connection with *octonarii* and *septenarii*.

49. The movement of this verse is illustrated by the first and third verses of the following stanza: —

> The rív|ers rúsh | intó | the seá,
>   By castle and town they go;
> The wínds | behínd | them mér|rilý
>   Their noisy trumpets blow.

50. Iambic Ternarius (Dimeter Catalectic). — This verse is used as a *clausula* (see verse 784).

51. Iambic Monometer Hypercatalectic (i.e. a monometer + another syllable). — Two such monometers are found together in verse 215[b], for which the scheme is —

$$\smile\ \overset{\prime\prime}{-}\ \smile\ \overset{\prime}{-}\ |\ \_ \qquad \_\ \overset{\prime\prime}{-}\ \smile\ \overset{\prime}{-}\ |\ \_$$

2. Trochaic.

52. Any one of the substitutes allowed in iambic verses for the pure iambus may, except as indicated below, also stand here for the pure trochee, $\angle \cup$, the metrical accent being, however, in all cases, upon the first syllable of the foot.

53. Trochaic Octonarius (Tetrameter Acatalectic). — This verse is used only in lyric parts of the plays, in connection with other verses, to form special rhythmic systems.

54. The caesura is (*a*) usually after the fourth foot, from which foot the dactyl is then excluded; (*b*) sometimes in the fourth or fifth foot. In this verse a tribrach, a spondee, or an anapaest is allowed even in the eighth foot.

55. *Trochaic octonarii* are peculiar to those parts of a scene that are intended to be sung. The movement of this verse may be illustrated by the following : —

"Beams of moon, like burning lances, through the tree-tops flash and glisten."

56. Trochaic Septenarius (Tetrameter Catalectic), called *septenarius* because only seven feet are complete, though it really contains seven and a half feet. — This is a favorite verse with Plautus. The caesura may be (*a*) after the fourth trochee, in place of which a dactyl is not then admissible; (*b*) after the fifth arsis, generally with a minor caesura after the fourth thesis or the third arsis. In this verse, as in iambic verse, an anapaest is very rare immediately after a dactyl. The seventh foot is commonly kept pure, though a tribrach or a dactyl is occasionally found. The last syllable of the verse may, as usual, be either long or short.

Trochaic septenarii are suited to a somewhat more quiet, peaceful frame of mind. Compare : —

"Tell me not in mournful numbers, life is but an empty dream."

57. Trochaic Tripody Acatalectic. — This is perhaps illustrated in verse 207[b]. If the scansion is correctly indicated in the text, the scheme is —

$$\overset{\prime\prime}{-}\,\cup\,\angle\,\cup\,\overset{\prime}{\mathcal{C}}\,\cup\,\cup$$

3. ANAPAESTIC.

58. In an anapaestic verse, any one of the following feet is allowed as a substitute for the pure anapaest, $\cup\,\cup\,\angle$: (*a*) spondee, $\_\angle$; (*b*) dactyl, $\_\mathcal{C}\,\cup$; (*c*) proceleusmatic, $\cup\,\cup\,\mathcal{C}\,\cup$. But the final thesis of an acatalectic verse cannot be resolved into short syllables.

59. Anapaestic Octonarius (Tetrameter Acatalectic). — In this verse there is regularly diaeresis after the fourth foot, where hiatus and *syllaba anceps* are then allowed as at the end of a verse.

60. Anapaestic Septenarius (Tetrameter Catalectic), called *septenarius*, because only seven feet are complete, though it really contains part of another foot. — The characteristics of the seven feet are in general the same as those of corresponding feet in the *octonarius*.

61. Anapaestic Quaternarius (Dimeter Acatalectic). — This occurs in verse 206[a], for which the scheme is —

$$\cup\,\cup\,\overset{\prime\prime}{-}\,\_\,\overset{\prime}{\mathcal{C}}\,\cup\,\_\,\overset{\prime\prime}{-}\,\_\,\angle$$

4. CRETIC.

62. For the normal cretic, $\overset{\prime\prime}{-}\,\cup\,\angle$, may be substituted (*a*) the first paeon, $\overset{\prime\prime}{-}\,\cup\,\mathcal{C}\,\cup$; (*b*) the fourth paeon, $\mathcal{C}\,\cup\,\cup\,\angle$; (*c*) the molossus, $\overset{\prime\prime}{-}\,>\,\angle$; (*d*) the choriambus, $\overset{\prime\prime}{-}\,\cup\cup\,\angle$; (*e*) the ionic a minore, $\mathcal{C}\,\cup\,>\,\angle$; (*f*) the ionic a maiore, $\overset{\prime\prime}{-}\,>\,\mathcal{C}\,\cup$.

63. Cretic Tetrameter Acatalectic. — In this verse the first paeon, probably the ionic a maiore, and (with rare ex-

ceptions) the molossus, are excluded from the final foot.
The normal scheme is

$$\text{⸖} \cup \angle \mid \_ \cup \angle \mid \text{⸖} \cup \angle \mid \text{⸖} \cup \angle .$$

Cretic Dimeter Acatalectic. — This verse presents the same
peculiarities as the tetrameter.

5. Bacchic.

64. For the normal bacchius, $\cup \text{⸖} \angle$, may be substituted
(*a*) the fourth paeon, $\cup \, \mathcal{C} \cup \angle$; (*b*) the second paeon, $\cup \text{⸖} \mathcal{C} \cup$;
(*c*) the molossus, $> \text{⸖} \angle$; (*d*) the ionic a minore, $\backsim \text{⸖} \angle$;
(*e*) the choriambus, $> \mathcal{C} \cup \angle$; or (*f*) the ionic a maiore,
$> \text{⸖} \mathcal{C} \cup .$

65. **Bacchic Tetrameter.** — A caesura is commonly found
after the second or third iambus and occasionally diaeresis
after the second bacchius (see G.-L. 812). The normal
scheme is

$$\cup \text{⸖} \angle \mid \cup \text{⸖} \angle \mid \cup \text{⸖} \angle \mid \cup \text{⸖} \underset{\cup}{\angle}.$$

6. Compound Verses.

66. **Cretic Dimeter + Trochaic Dipody Acatalectic.** — The
normal scheme is $\text{⸖} \cup \angle \mid \text{⸖} \cup \underset{\cup}{\angle} \parallel \text{⸖} \cup \angle \cup$. In the *Captivi*
this is found only in verse 214.

67. Metres other than those above described are comparatively rare in Plautus; and as they are not found in the
Captivi, they do not concern us here.

68.   Table of Metres of the Captivi.

1-194 . . iambic senarii.	198–199. . . . iambic octonarii.
195–196 . iambic octonarii.	200 . . . . iambic septenarius.
197. . . . iambic dimeter acatalec-	201 . . . . (?)
tic.	202 . . . . iambic senarius.

203. . . . iambic octonarius.

204. . . . cretic tetrameter (incomplete).

205. . . . cretic tetrameter acatalectic.

206ᵃ . . . anapaestic dimeter acatalectic.

206ᵇ . . . cretic tetrameter acatalectic.

207 . . . cretic dimeter acatalectic.

207ᵇ . . . trochaic tripody acatalectic.

208–209. trochaic octonarii.

210–211. cretic tetrameters acatalectic. (For a different division, see Goetz & Schoell.)

212. . . . iambic dimeter catalectic.

213. . . . cretic tetrameter acatalectic.

214. . . . cretic dimeter acatalectic + trochaic dipody acatalectic.

215ᵃ . . . anapaestic dimeter acatalectic.

215ᵇ . . . two iambic monometers hypercatalectic.

216–222. cretic tetrameters acatalectic.

223. . . . iambic septenarius.

224. . . . no verse with this number appears in the text, owing to the manner of verse-division adopted.

225. . . . iambic octonarius.

226–230. bacchic tetrameters acatalectic.

231. . . . iambic septenarius.

232. . . . trochaic septenarius.

233. . . . iambic dimeter catalectic.

234. . . . iambic dimeter acatalectic.

235–239. cretic tetrameters acatalectic.

240–241. trochaic octonarii.

242–360. trochaic septenarii.

361–384. iambic senarii.

385–497. trochaic septenarii.

498–515. uncertain.

516–524. iambic octonarii.

525. . . . iambic senarius.

526–529. trochaic septenarii.

530. . . . iambic senarius.

531. . . . trochaic septenarius.

532. . . . iambic senarius.

533. . . . iambic octonarius.

534. . . . trochaic septenarius.

535. . . . trochaic octonarius.

536–540. iambic octonarii.

541–658. trochaic septenarii.

659–767. iambic senarii.

768–769. trochaic septenarii.

770–771. iambic octonarii.

772. . . . trochaic septenarius (?).

773. . . . iambic octonarius.

774–775. trochaic septenarii.

776–780. iambic octonarii.

781–783. bacchic tetrameters.

784. . . . iambic dimeter catalectic.

785–790. bacchic tetrameters (some of them imperfect).

791–832. trochaic septenarii.

833–834. iambic octonarii.

835. . . . cretic tetrameter acatalectic.

836. . . . (?)

837. . . . iambic septenarius.

838–839. . . .	trochaic septenarii.	922–927. . . .	bacchic tetrameters acatalectic.
840.	(?)	928–929. . . .	trochaic octonarii.
841–908. . . .	trochaic septenarii.	930–1036 . . .	trochaic septenarii.
909–921. . . .	iambic octonarii.		

VI.

DIFFERENCES IN THE MANNER OF RENDERING VARIOUS RHYTHMS; MUSICAL ACCOMPANIMENT, ETC.

69. A change in the character of the verse was often accompanied also by a corresponding change in the manner of presenting the scene. With reference to the differences in the manner of presentation, the various parts of a play are to be divided into three distinct classes : —

70. (1) Those composed of ordinary narrative, or dialogue, written in **iambic senarii**, without musical accompaniment.

(2) Those merely recited to the accompaniment of the flute, written in **trochaic** or **iambic septenarii** and in **iambic octonarii**.

(3) Those of a purely lyric nature, sung to a set tune with flute accompaniment, written in varying metres — including those under (2), — but commonly characterized by the presence of **trochaic octonarii**.[1]

71. In the text editions of antiquity, letters were added to the superscriptions of different scenes to indicate the manner in which they were to be rendered, and these marks are still distinguishable in some of the manuscripts of Plautus. These show that the last two kinds of scenes, (2) and (3) above, as they were both accompanied by music,

---

[1] The rules governing the change of verse in these parts have not yet been discovered. K. Meissner, in *Fleckeisen's Jahrbücher für Philologie und Pädagogik* (1884), attempts to show that they are divided into strophes. See also Schlee, *de vers. in cant. Ter. cons.* (Berlin, 1879).

were marked with the letter *C.*, i.e. **canticum**; the first kind (1), with the letters *DV.*, i.e. **diuerbium**, spoken dialogue, without musical accompaniment. In the editions of Terence, as may be seen from Donatus, scenes of a purely lyric character were marked *M.M.C.* (perhaps an abbreviation for *modi mutati cantici*); those merely recited with musical accompaniment, simply *C.* (though this rests upon the opinion of Ritschl, Donatus giving us no information on this point); those consisting of ordinary dialogue, *DV.*[1]

72. Sometimes there was music also before the beginning of the play (before the prologue) and between the acts. The music for the plays of Plautus and Terence seems to have been composed entirely by slaves. The music was given by a single flute-player (*tibicen*), probably by the composer himself, with a double flute, or, perhaps we might say, clarinet, as the instrument bore a greater resemblance to it than to our flute. It was played by blowing into both tubes at the same time. From the *didascaliae* we learn of four different kinds of these instruments: *tibiae pares*, in which the two pipes were of equal length; *tibiae impares*, in which they were of unequal length; *tibiae serranae*, of which but little is known, though they were probably of equal length;[2] and *duae dextrae tibiae*, in which the two tubes were of equal length and identical in key and note.

Regarding the last-mentioned *tibiae*, we are told by Varro that the right tube was for leading (*tibia incentiua*), the left for accompanying (*tibia succentiua*). We have no further knowledge regarding the difference between the various kinds of these instruments; but we may be certain that the choice of instrument depended upon the character of the

---

[1] Indications of this system of marking are preserved in the *Phormio* of Terence, before Act II. Scene 4 ; see *Rh. Mus.* XXIX. 54.

[2] On the character of the music used in the plays, see Howard on the Αὐλός, or Tibia, in the *Harvard Studies in Classical Philology*, IV. (1893).

play. In the case of the *Heauton timorumenos*, we know from the *didascalia* that instruments were changed in the course of the play itself.

73. An important difference between the practices of the ancient and of the modern stage may be inferred from Livy, 7. 2, 8 ff. It is here recorded that, from the time of Livius Andronicus, throughout the whole period when Roman comedy was at its height, the lyrical parts were sung by a person especially selected for the purpose and stationed near the flute-player, while the actors meanwhile were wont merely to act silently, in a manner suitable to the words thus sung.

VII.

PROSODY.

The prosody and the language of Plautus differ far more from those of the later classical authors, than do those of Terence, though there were only a few years between the two writers. Peculiarities of this nature will be pointed out in detail in the notes. The more important of these, however, may well find a place in this introduction.

1. PECULIARITIES OF INDIVIDUAL SYLLABLES AND COMBINATIONS.

74. Initial **h** is capable of preventing the elision of a preceding final syllable ending in a vowel or *m*, and of making a long syllable after a preceding final consonant.[1]

75. **L** or **r**, added to a mute, does not make a long syllable, e.g. *pătrem* (never *pātrem*). Later, such syllables might be pronounced long (i.e. *pat-rem*) or short (i.e. *pa-trem*).

---

[1] See Birt in *Rhein. Mus.* for 1899, pp. 40 ff.

76. The **final s** of words ending in *ĭs* and *ŭs* did not necessarily make a long syllable before a following consonant. Before a vowel it was probably sometimes elided, just as final *m* was (see notes on verses 466, 532, 691, and App. thereon). As late as the boyhood of Cicero, final *s* was often very faintly pronounced, e.g. *satĭ(s) uerborum* in 125 (instead of *satĭs uerborum*), *magĭ(s) noscas* in 290 (instead of *magĭs noscas*).

77. Final *ĕ* in the following words might apparently be treated as a silent letter:[1] *ille, inde, quippe, unde, nempe,* and probably some others occasionally; e.g. *esse,* and imperatives like *mitte, dice;* cf. —

Men. 57, *Ĕpĭdámnĭen|sĭs ĭll(e) quēm dū|dūm dĭxĕrăm*
Poen. 2, *Ĭnd(e) mĭ prĭncĭpĭ|ūm cắpĭ(am) ēx ēā | trăgŏēdĭā*
Mil. 922, *Nēmp(e) tū nŏuĭ|stĭ mĭlĭtēm, | mĕ(um) ĕrŭm? — Rŏgā|rĕ*
     mĭrūmst.

In the interrogative particle **-ne** this final *ĕ* was not merely often silent, but it was often omitted even in writing; e.g. *certon* (for *certone*) in 643, *uiden* (for *uidesne*). The disappearance of final *e* is further illustrated in *hic* for *hice, horunc* for *horunce, dic* for *dice,* etc.

78. The dissyllabic vowel combinations **ea, eha, ei, ehi, eo, eu, ia, ie, ii, ihi, io, iu, oi, ohi, ui, ua, ue, uo,** are often slurred together into a single syllable by *synizesis,* e.g. *eadem, eam, mea, mei, ei, rei, eodem, meos, eum, gratĭam, dĭe, dĭu, otĭo, proĭnde, fuĭsse, duĕllum, duăs.*[2]

---

[1] It has been customary to explain the metrical phenomena connected with these words by supposing the first syllable to be treated as short, e.g. *ĭllĕ, ĭndĕ,* etc. ; but see Skutsch, *Studien zur Plautinischen Prosodie* (Leipzig, 1892), pp. 30ff. Skutsch, however, was in part anticipated in his theory by Wase, Weise, Bothe, and Ritschl.

[2] In the case of *ia, ie, ii, io, iu* and *ui, ua, uo,* the pronunciation above referred to was facilitated by the fact that *i* and *u* before a vowel had a tendency to take on a consonantal character.

79. A similar phenomenon, apparently, is found in the monosyllabic use of the words **eius, huius, quoius** ($e\widehat{i}us$, $hu\widehat{i}us$, $quo\widehat{i}us$); cf. 39, 106, 107, 289, 641.

80. The forms of **aio** are freely handled, and present the following peculiarities: $\breve{a}it$ (592), $\bar{a}it$ (365), $\bar{a}in$ (*Am.* 284), $\widehat{a}ibat$ (561), $\widehat{a}iebatis$ (676), $\breve{a}is$ (613).

81. In certain words, a **u** that was, in later times, consonantal appears as a vowel; e.g. *reliquos* is regularly tetrasyllabic in Plautus and Terence (i.e. *relic̆ŭŏs*), *larua* is regularly trisyllabic (i.e. *larŭă*); cf. *solŭō*, *silŭă*, etc., in later poets.

82. The following vowels and syllables, commonly short in classical poetry, are sometimes long in Plautus: —

(*a*) **a** in the nominative singular of masculine proper names of the first declension; e.g. *Am.* 439, *Sosiā*.

(*b*) Final **e** of the infinitive; e.g. *Truc.* 425, *darē*; *Mil.* 848, *promerē*.

(*c*) Final **e** in the ablative of the third declension, e.g. 914, *carnē*; *Ps.* 616, *militē*.

(*d*) Final **o** in *modo* (the adverb), e.g. 458, *As.* 5, 869, 876, etc.; and in *ego*.

(*e*) **-at, -et, -it** in the third person singular present of verbs of the first, second, and fourth conjugations [1] and **-it** of the perfect (all originally long); e.g. 11, *negāt*; 196, *decēt*; 350, *scīt*; 9, *uendidīt*; 34, *emīt*; *Am.* 643, *uicīt*; *Mil.* 214, *astitīt*; *Ps.* 311. Similarly, in the final syllable of subjunctive forms and of the imperfect indicative, the vowel was originally long.

(*f*) **-ar, -or** in the first person passive of verbs; e.g. *Am.* 559, *loquār*; *Capt.* 1023, *regrediōr*; and **-or** in the nominative singular of nouns and adjectives (comparative degree), e.g. *sorōr*, *uxōr*; *longiōr*, *stultiōr*.

---

[1] Final *-īt* in the 3d conjugation is rare and probably due to analogy; *erīt* and similar futures occasionally occur.

(g) -bus in the dative plural of nouns and adjectives; e.g.
     Merc. 901, *aedibūs; Rud.* 975, *omnibūs.*

(h) es(s), second person singular of *sum* (always long in
     Plautus and Terence); e.g. 333, 412, 427, etc.

(i) fĭ- in *fĭerent* and *fĭeri* for the classical *fīerent, fīeri;*
     e.g. 998, 843.

(j) u- in *fŭi, fŭimus, fŭerim, plŭerat,* etc.; e.g. 262, 555,
     633, etc.

83. Occasionally a syllable which in later poets is regularly long is short in Plautus; e.g. *frustră, neŭtiquam*
(*n(e) utiquam*), *hĭc, illĭc, istĭc* (the last three, as nominative singular masculine, having the *-ic* always short in
Plautus).

It seems probable that *illic* was sometimes pronounced
illc; see note on 751, and Skutsch's *Studien zur Plautin.
Prosodie,* pp. 113 ff.

2. Influence of Verse-Accent and Word-Accent.

84. The most important and far-reaching peculiarity of
prosody to be noted in the dramatic poets is **the frequent
shortening of a long syllable when it is immediately preceded
by a short syllable and immediately preceded, or followed, by
the verse-ictus,**[1] **or the word-accent.** The influence of this
"iambic law" (so called because it concerns the combination ∪ _) may, then, change —

(1) ∪ _ ∠ to ∪ ∪ ∠, e.g. *pŭĕr cáusa* to *pŭĕr cáusa; ĕt ād*
                                   pórtitores to *ĕt ăd pórtitores;*

(2) ∪ _ ⸰ to ∪ ∪ ⸰, e.g. *ŏb hănc ínĭmicitias* to *ŏb hănc ínĭ-*
                                   micitias;

(3) ⸰ _   to ⸰ ∪ , e.g. *ág(e) ērgō* to *ág(e) ĕrgō.*

---

[1] The term ictus is used in this volume in the sense of stress. For
another view regarding the nature of ictus, see Bennett, *Am. Jour.
Phil.,*Vol. XIX, No. 4.

It is important to note, however, that in such cases the long syllable may be shortened only when the short syllable immediately preceeding begins a word. The shortening, furthermore, seems to take place only in the following cases : —

(1) In a dissyllabic iambic word.[1]

(2) In a monosyllabic word (or one that has become such by elision) preceded by a short monosyllable (or a word which has become such by elision).

(3) In the first syllable of a word of two or more syllables preceded by a short monosyllable (or a word that has become such by elision);

(4) In the second syllable of a polysyllabic word beginning with a short syllable.

In the cases under (3) and (4), the rule holds (possibly with rare exceptions) *only for syllables " long by position," but having a short vowel.*

Another effect of the metrical accent is frequently seen in cases where monosyllabic words ending in a long vowel, or in *m*, instead of being elided before a following vowel, or *h*, receive the ictus and are treated as short syllables; see Introd. § 37 (*e*).

3. HIATUS.

85. Hiatus, while comparatively rare in Terence and later writers, is very common in Plautus, as it is in the Saturnian metre and the earliest Latin generally. It is found after both long and short vowels and after *m*; e.g. *Capt.* 196, 476, 534, 862, 950; 24, 31, 372, 373, 395, 665, 709, 1024. It occurs either after the thesis, or within the

---

[1] Here the word-accent on the initial syllable aided in the shortening of the final syllable. Compare the shortening of the originally long final syllable in *mihi, tibi, sibi, ibi, ubi, nisi, quasi, ego, modo,* etc.

thesis, or after the arsis, or between separate feet. The
following occurrences may here be noted:[1] —

(a) In the diaeresis of a tetrameter, e.g.

780, *spērṓquĕ m(e) ōb* | *hŭnc nŭntĭŭm* **āē***térn(um) ădēp*|*tūrŭm cĭbŭm.*
331, *eŭm sĭ rēddīs* | *mĭhĭ prāetĕrĕā* **ū***nŭm nŭmmŭm nē dŭĭs.*

(b) In the caesura of an iambic *senarius*, e.g.

709, *sēd mălĕn(e) ĭd fāc*|*tŭm* ** á***rbĭtrā*|*rĕ ? — Pḗssŭmē.*

(c) At the end of the fourth foot of an iambic *senarius*, e.g.

*sués moriuntur ángin***a** | **a***cérrume.*

(d) In the fifth foot of an iambic *senarius*, e.g.

93, *ĭtă nŭnc bēllĭgĕ*|*rānt Áetŏlī* | *cŭ***m** **Á***lēīs.*

(e) Elsewhere when there is a decided pause in the sense, e.g.

139, *Nē flḗ.* Er. **Ĕ***gŏn(e) ŭl*|*lŭm nŏn fleăm ?* *Ĕgōn* | *nōn dḗfleăm.*

It occurs further, at points in the verse not covered
by the enumeration thus far made.

(f) Before or after interjections (especially monosyllabic
interjections).

(g) After pyrrhic or iambic dissyllables, e.g.

950, *V̆bĭ* **ē***stīs, uōs ?* | *ŭt(e) āctŭtŭm,* | *Tȳndăr(um) hŭc ār*|*cḗssĭtĕ.*

(h) In accented monosyllables, a final *m* was sometimes not
elided before a following vowel, and a final diphthong
or long vowel was merely shortened, instead of being
altogether elided (see under "semi-hiatus," § 37 (e)).
As the syllable involved always has the ictus, it is
probable that the phenomenon is due to this fact.

841, *Iắm ĕg(o) ēx cōrpŏ*|*r(e) éxĭg(am) ōmnīs* | *mắcŭlās māerō*|*rŭm
tĭbĭ.*
705, *Quĭă uĕra ŏbēs*|*sēnt ŭllī quŏ***ĭ** *ŏ*|*pĕrắm dăbăm.*
807, *Tŭm pīstōrēs* | *scrŏfĭpāscī,* | *quĭ* **ắ***lŭnt fŭrfŭrĭ*|*bŭs sŭēs.*

---

[1] Cases formed by initial *h* after a final vowel or *m*, as Birt has shown,
should probably not be regarded as instances of hiatus (see § 74).

VIII.

LANGUAGE.

Peculiarities of usage not mentioned here will be taken up in the notes.

1. PECULIARITIES OF FORM.

In addition to the forms here given, the classical forms are, in many cases, also common. Where only the classical form occurs, no notice is here taken of it. It must not be understood that none of the forms indicated below occur outside of Plautus.

86. General.

(a) *-uos*,[1] *-uom*, *-uont*,[1] *-uontur*, for the later *-uus*, *-uum*, *-uunt*, *-uuntur*, e.g. *seruos*, *tuos*, as forms of the nom. sing., *metuont*, for the later *seruus*, *tuus*, *metuunt*.

-quos, *-quom*, *-quont*, *-quontur*, for the later *-cus*, *-cum*, *-cunt*, *-cuntur* (and, still later, *-quus*, *-quum*, *-quunt*, *-quuntur*), e.g. *equos*, *relinquont*, for the later *ecus*, *relincunt* (and, still later, *equus*, *relinquunt*).[2]

(b) *quoius*, *quoi*, *quor*, *quom* for the later *cuius*, *cui*, *cur*, *cum*.[3]

(c) *ŭ*, for later *ĭ*, in unaccented syllables before labials, e.g. *lubido*, *optumus*, *pessumus*, etc., for *libido*, *optimus*, *pessimus*, etc.,[4] also *lubet* (later *libet*).

(d) *Ei* for later *ī*; e.g. *deico* for *dico*, though this *ei* has been generally changed in our Mss. to conform to the later spelling.

---

[1] It will be noticed that in this edition the same character is used for both vowel and consonantal *u*; *-uos*, *-uom*, etc., will therefore be understood as representing *-vos*, *-vom*, etc., as well as dissyllabic *-ŭŏs*, *-ŭŏm*.

[2] See, for instance, *Appendix to Bennett's Latin Grammar*, § 57, 1.

[3] See *B. App.* 197, 3.   [4] See *B. App.* 6, 2.

(e) The suffix *-clum* for the later *-culum;* e.g. *periclum, saeclum, uinclum,* etc., for *periculum, saeculum,* etc.

(f) *Gnatus* and *gnata,* instead of *natus, nata,* chiefly as substantives.

(g) Probably both *t* and *d* were used at the end of certain pronouns and particles; e.g. *aput, aliut, illut,* etc., as well as *apud, aliud, illud.* The pronunciation in either case was probably the same, viz. that of *t.*

87. Pronouns.

(a) Hic.

	SINGULAR.			PLURAL.		
	Masc.	*Fem.*	*Neut.*	*Masc.*	*Fem.*	*Neut.*
Nom.	hici(ne)[1]	haeci(ne)[1]	hoci(ne)[1]	hisce (heisce)[2]	haec,[3] haeci(ne)[1]	haeci(ne)
Gen.				horunc	harunc	horunc
Dat.				{ hibus hisce[2]		
Acc.	hunci(ne)	hanci(ne)	hoci(ne)	hosce[2]	hasce[2]	
Abl.	hoci(ne)		hoci(ne)	hisce[2]		

(b) Ille.

	SINGULAR.			PLURAL.		
	Masc.	*Fem.*	*Neut.*	*Masc.*	*Fem.*	*Neut.*
Nom.	illic, illici(ne)	illaec	illuc	illisce[4]	illaec	illaec
Gen.						
Dat.	illic	illae				
Acc.	illunc	illanc	illuc			illaec
Abl.	illoc, illoce	illac		illisce[4]	illisce	

---

[1] The forms in *-ne* are of course interrogative forms, the original *-ce* weakening to *-ci* before the enclitic.

[2] The full forms in *-ce* are as a rule used only before vowels and *h.*

[3] *Haec* is the regular plural feminine form in Plautus before vowels and *h.*

[4] The full forms in *-ce* are, as a rule, used only before vowels.

(c) **Iste.**[1]

		SINGULAR.			PLURAL.	
	Masc.	*Fem.*	*Neut.*	*Masc.*	*Fem.*	*Neut.*
Nom.	istic	istaec	istuc, istoc istuci(ne)[2]		istaec	istaec
Gen.	isti (in *isti modi*)					
Dat.	istic	istic, istae				
Acc.	istunc	istanc	istuc	istosci(n)[2]		istaec
Abl.	istoc	istac istaci(ne)[2]	istoc istoci(ne)[2]		istisce	

(d) **Is.**

Eae (?) in the dative singular feminine; *i* in the nominative plural masculine; *ibus* in the dative and ablative plural.

(e) **Ipse.**

Ipsus and *ipsissimus* in the nominative singular masculine.

(f) **Aliquis.**

Aliqui in ablative singular, masculine and neuter.

(g) **Alter.**

		SINGULAR.	
	Masc.	*Fem.*	*Neut.*
Nom.		altra (?)	
Gen.	altrius (?)		
Dat.	altri (?)	alterae	
Acc.			altrum (?)

---

[1] For the declension of this word in Plautus, see Studemund in *Fleckeisen's Jahrbuecher*, 1876, p. 57.

[2] The full forms in *-ce* (with the *e* weakened to *i*) occur in *istucine, istocine, istacine, istoscin.*

(*h*) Qui, Quis.

	SINGULAR.			PLURAL.		
	Masc.	*Fem.*	*Neut.*	*Masc.*	*Fem.*	*Neut.*
Nom.						
Gen.	quoius	quoius	quoius			
Dat.	quoi	quoi	quoi			
Acc.						
Abl.	qui	qui			qui	qui

Quoius (interrogative and relative possessive, *whose*) was sometimes treated as a nominative : —

	SINGULAR.			PLURAL.		
	Masc.	*Fem.*	*Neut.*	*Masc.*	*Fem.*	*Neut.*
Nom.	quoius	quoia			quoiae	
Gen.				quoium(?)		
Dat.						
Acc.		quoiam				
Abl.		quoia				

88. Verbs.

(*a*) *siem, sies, siet, sient,* and *fuam, fuas, fuat, fuant,* instead of *sim, sis, sit, sint; creduam, creduas (creduis), creduat (creduit),* for *credam, credas,* etc.; *duim, duis, duit, duint* (with its compounds *perduim,* etc.), for *dem, des, det, dent* (though from another root); *edim, edis, edit, edimus, editis, edint,* for *edam, edas, edat, edamus, edatis, edant.*

(*b*) *potis* (sometimes *pote*) *sum, potis es, potis est,* for *possum, potes, potest.*

(*c*) *scibam, audibam,* etc., for *sciebam, audiebam,* etc.

(*d*) *scibo, audibo,* etc., for the regular future, *sciam, audiam,* etc.

(*e*) *dice, duce, face,* for *dic, duc, fac.*

(*f*) Passive infinitive in *-arier, -erier, -ier,* etc., for *-ari, -eri, -i,* etc.

(g) *dixti, scripsti, misti,* etc., for *dixisti, scripsisti, misisti;*
     dixe, adduxe, detraxe, etc., for *dixisse, adduxisse, de-*
     traxisse, etc.

(h) *amasso, seruasso, capso,* etc., for *amauero, seruauero,*
     cepero, etc.; *duxim, iussim, locassim,* etc., for *duxerim,*
     iusserim, locauerim, etc.; *faxem* for *fecissem.*

(i) *potior* has forms of the third conjugation; e.g. *potĭtur*
     for *potītur.*

(j) *mauolo, mauolunt, mauolet, mauelim,* etc., for *malo, ma-*
     lunt, malet, malim, etc.; *neuolo, neuis, neuolt,* etc., for
     nolo, non uis, non uolt, etc.

89. Active forms, found in Plautus, of verbs commonly
deponent: *aggredio, amplecto, arbitro, assentio, aucupo, auguro,*
auspico, circumplecto, contemplo, cuncto, faenero, lucto, luⱥifico,
munero, nutrico, opino, secto, tuto, tumultuo, uago, uenero.

2. PECULIARITIES OF SYNTAX.

Substantives.

90. Genitive:—

(a) Is invariably the case used with *similis.*

(b) With *onustus: Aul.* 611, *aulam onustam auri.*

(c) With *exilis: Stich.* 526, *exilem aegritudinum;* with *sanus:*
     Trin. 454, *sanus mentis;* with *falsiloquos: Capt.* 264,
     quarum rerum te falsiloquom mihi esse nolo.

(d) With *saturare: Stich.* 18, *haec res uitae me, soror, saturant.*

(e) With *credere: As.* 459, *quoi omnium rerum credit;* with
     desipio: Epid. 138, *desipiebam mentis;* with *perdere:*
     As. 132, *capitis te perdam;* with *prendere: Bacch.* 696,
     quem mendaci prendit.

(f) With *cupio,* to be desirous of, fond of: *Mil.* 964, *quae*
     cupiunt tui; with *fastidio: Aul.* 245, *fastidit mei.*

(g) Appositional genitive in colloquial uses: *Mil.* 1434,
     scelus uiri (cf. "he's a devil of a fellow").

91. Dative: —

(a) With *studiosus: Mil.* 801, *nisi adulterio studiosus rei nulli aliae.*

(b) With *decet: Amph.* 820, *nostro generi non decet.*

(c) Depending upon a substantive, where one might expect the genitive: *Mil.* 1431, *Philocomasio amator* (cf. "servant to the king").

(d) With *curare: Trin.* 1057, *rebus publicis curare.*

92. Accusative: —

(a) With verbal substantives; e.g. *Aul.* 423, *quid tibi nos tactiost, what right have you to touch us?* literally, *why is there unto you a touching us?* This is found, however, only with *quid?*

(b) With *utor, abutor, fruniscor, fungor, potior* (e.g. *Rud.* 190), instead of the ablative.

(c) With *in* before names of towns, to indicate motion to which: *Trin.* 112; *Pseud.* 1098.

(d) Occasionally with names of countries, without a preposition to indicate motion to: *Capt.* 573.

93. Ablative: —

(a) With *aeque* and *adaeque: Amph.* 293, *hoc metuculosus aeque; Most.* 30.

(b) With *ex* before names of towns, to indicate motion from: *Trin.* 771; *ib.* 845.

(c) Occasionally with names of countries, without a preposition, to indicate place where: *Capt.* 330.

Verbs.

94. Moods: —

(a) Indicative: 1. In indirect questions.

2. In relative clauses of indirect discourse.

3. In a *quom* (*cum*)-clause, even when the clause is causal or adversative.

4. For subjunctive in deliberative questions: *quid ago? what shall I do?* (instead of *quid agam?*) Cf. the English expression, "What do I do now (next)?"

(b) Subjunctive: 1. *Absque* with the ablative and *esset* (*foret*), to represent a condition contrary to fact: *Men.* 1022, *absque te esset, were it not for you.*

2. *Ne* with the perfect subjunctive in prohibitions is common in Plautus, though very rare later (except in Cicero's *Letters*). It is energetic and unceremonious, and therefore colloquial.

95. Tenses:—

(a) *Present:* 1. The present indicative is often loosely used where strict accuracy would require the future or the future perfect: *Stich.* 623, *deos salutabo modo: poste ad te continuo transeo; Pers.* 275, *etiam respicis* (*won't you look around?*); *Capt.* 331, *eum si reddis mihi, praeterea unum nummum ne duis* (for *si reddideris,* etc.).

2. The present subjunctive, instead of the imperfect, is sometimes used in conditional sentences, where the condition is apparently contrary to fact: *As.* 393, *si sit domi, dicam tibi.*

(b) *Future perfect:* The future perfect is frequently used, not as a true future perfect to indicate an act to be finished *prior to* some future time, but as an energetic future to indicate prompt completion of the act *at* a future time: *Bacch.* 211, *abiero, I'll be off; Trin.* 1007, *lubet obseruare quid agat: huc concessero.* Here the force of the tense in *huc concessero* should be brought out in translation by using an expression that connotes the idea of hurried accomplishment, e.g. *I'll step this way, I'll dodge in here,* or the like. The simple future might always be used in such a case, but there is a very distinct difference in tone between the two tenses.

(c) *Pluperfect :* The pluperfect indicative is sometimes used where the perfect would seem more natural to the English idiom, *Capt.* 194, *ad fratrem, quo ire dixeram, mox iuero.* The tense was, however, felt by the Romans as a true pluperfect referring to time prior to a more or less clearly defined point in the past. Similar uses are not wanting in English. One often hears a person say, in reply to a suggestion just made by some one to whom he is talking, "I hadn't thought of that," i.e. "had not a moment ago, before you called my attention to it." It would on such occasions always be equally appropriate to say, "I did not think of that." The choice of tense depends solely upon the point of view.

96. Participles : The perfect passive participle is used in the ablative with *opus est* and *usus est*, e.g. *Cas.* 502, *uicino conventost opus, there is need of meeting the neighbor;* literally, *there is need of the neighbor met.*

3. Miscellaneous Peculiarities.

97. (a) *Ad* in the sense of *apud : Capt.* 699, *ad patrem, at his father's.*

(b) *Prae* used as an adverb : *Am.* 543, *abi prae, go ahead.*

(c) *Clam* used as a preposition : *Merc.* 545, *clam uxorem, without the knowledge of his wife.*

(d) *Quoniam,* meaning *when,* instead of *since : Trin.* 149, *quoniam est profectus peregre Charmides, when Charmides set out for foreign parts.*

(e) *Vt* (instead of *utinam*), introducing a wish : *Poen.* 912, *bene ut tibi sit.*

(f) *Quo,* introducing a purpose clause containing no comparative.

(*g*) Double negative: *Epid.* 664, *neque ille haud obi-
  ciet mihi.

(*h*) *Nec,* used for *non: Bacch.* 119, *tu dis nec recte
  dicis.*

98. *-Ne* introducing a question which expects an affirmative answer. The *-ne* is, however, non-committal in such
cases, and does not in itself suggest the answer. This use
produces a certain rhetorical effect, the implication being
that the answer may safely be left to be inferred. Cf. "Do
I, or do I not, look like an honest man?" The use of *nonne*
in early Latin is at best extremely rare.

4. Order of Words.

99. Generally speaking, the most emphatic points in a
Latin sentence or verse are the beginning (except for the
subject of an independent sentence) and the end (except for
the verb). Emphatic ideas tend to find utterance first,
but special effects are often produced by saving an emphatic
word or phrase till the end of the clause, for the mind to
dwell upon. An unusual arrangement of words (e.g. re-
versed order, wide separation of words belonging together,
juxtaposition of those contrasted, etc.) attracts special attention to such as are out of their normal position, and thus
makes them emphatic. A shifting of words in the middle
of a sentence is less noticeable, and so produces less
emphasis. Freedom of position is limited, for purposes
of emphasis, only by the necessity of avoiding obscurity
or an overburdening of the mind. For the normal order
of words in a Latin sentence, see A. & G. 343; B. 348–
350; G.-L. 674; H. 560 f. In a short sentence, e.g. *Cæsar
interfectus est,* the verb may have to stand first, in order to
make an emphatic place for the subject at the end, in which
case the verb is not necessarily emphatic. Similarly the

subject may come last, in order to make an emphatic place
for the verb at the beginning, in which case the subject is
not necessarily emphatic.   In such sentences the context
commonly shows which part is intended to be emphasized.

IX.

THE PLOT OF THE CAPTIVI.

100. Hegio, a wealthy citizen of Calydon in Aetolia, has
had two sons.   One of these was stolen at the age of four
years, by a faithless slave, and has been given up as irrevo-
cably lost.   The other son, Philopolemus, has, shortly before
the time at which the play is supposed to begin, been taken
captive by the Eleans, who are at war with the Aetolians.
In the hope of recovering this captive son, Hegio has begun
to traffic in Eleans that had been captured by the Aetolians,
with a view to getting some one whom he can exchange for
his son.   Among the captives thus purchased are a noble
Elean by the name of Philocrates and his slave Tyndarus.
These are the two captives referred to in the title of the
play.   They have conceived the plan of exchanging names
and clothing in order to mislead Hegio.   Accordingly Philocrates, in the presence of Hegio, acts the part of the slave,
Tyndarus the part of the master.   It is arranged that Hegio
shall send the supposed slave back to Elis to arrange an
exchange between his master and Philopolemus.   After
Philocrates has thus gained his freedom, the identity of
Tyndarus is betrayed to Hegio by Aristophontes, another
captive, who happened to have known both Philocrates and
Tyndarus in Elis.   Hegio is slow to realize that he has
been made the victim of a trick, but, when it finally dawns
upon him, his indignation knows no bounds.   Tyndarus is
put at hard labor in the stone quarries.   In good time, how-

ever, Philocrates returns, bringing with him not merely Philopolemus but also Stalagmus, the runaway slave that had stolen Hegio's other son. It is now learned that Stalagmus sold the child to the father of this very Philocrates, and that Tyndarus, now in the stone quarries, is none other than Hegio's long-lost son. Hegio is thus reunited to both of his sons, and his happiness is marred only by the regret that he has unwittingly caused one of them so much suffering.

T. MACCI PLAVTI

CAPTIVI

ARGVMENTVM.

Captúst in pugna Hégionis fílius,
Aliúm quadrimum fúgiens seruos uéndidit.
Patér captiuos cómmercatur Áleos
Tantum studens ut natum recuperet,
Et ínibi | emit ólim amissum fílium.   5
Is suó cum domino uéste uersa ac nómine
Vt ámittatur fécit : ipsus pléctitur.
Et ís reduxit cáptum et fugitiuóm simul,
Indício quoius álium agnoscit fílium.

PERSONAE.

ERGASILUS, a parasite ; always hungry.
HEGIO, a rich old gentleman of Aetolia.
LORARII, chastisers, slaves of Hegio.
PHILOCRATES,   prisoners of war captured from the
TYNDARUS, slave of Philocrates,   Eleans by the Aetolians and
ARISTOPHONTES,   afterward purchased by Hegio.
PUER, a slave of Hegio.
PHILOPOLEMUS, son of Hegio, captured by the Eleans.
STALAGMUS, runaway slave of Hegio, who stole the latter's little son
    and sold him in Elis.

2

T. MACCI PLAVTI CAPTIVI.

—∘∘⟩⊚⟨∘∘—

PROLOGVS.

[*Philocrates and Tyndarus, the former dressed as slave, the
latter as master, are seen, heavily chained, in front
of Hegio's house.   The prologue enters to explain to
the audience the general situation and the character of the
play.*]

Hos quós uidetis stáre hic captiuós duos,
Illí qui | astant, — hí stant ambo, nón sedent :
Hoc uós mihi testes éstis me uerúm loqui.
Senéx qui hic habitat, Hégio, est huiús [*pointing to Tyn-
      darus*] pater.

5 Sed ís quo pacto séruiat suo síbi patri,   5
Id ego híc apud uos próloquar, si operám datis.
Seni huíc fuerunt fílii natí duo :
Alt(e)rúm quadrimum púerum seruos súrpuit
Eumque hínc profugiens uéndidīt in Álide
10 Patrí huiusce [*pointing to Philocrates*]. iam hóc tenetis ?
      óptumumst.   10
Negat hércle ille ultumus.†   accedito.

3

Si nón ubi sedeas lócus est, est ubi ámbules,

Quando hístrionem cógis mendicárier.

Ego mé tua causa, ne érres, non ruptúrus sum.

15 Vos quí potestis ópe uostra censérier   15

Accípite relicuom : álieno uti níl moror.

Fugitíuos ille, ut díxeram ante, huiús [*pointing to Philo-
     crates*] patri,

Domŏ quém profugiens dóminum abstulerat, uéndidit.

Is póstquam hunc [*pointing to Tyndarus*] emit, dédit eum

     huic gnató suo [*pointing to Philocrates*]

20 Pecúliarem, quía quasi una aetás erat.   20

Hic [*pointing to Tyndarus*] núnc domĭ seruit suó patri nec

     scít pater :

Enĭm uéro di nos quási pilas hominés habent.

Ratiónem habetis quómodo unum amíserit.

Postquám belligerant Aétoli cum | Áleis,

25 Vt fít in bello, cápitur alter fílius.   25

Medicús Menarchus émit ibidem in Álide.

Coepít captiuos cómmercari hic Áleos,

Si quém reperire pósset, qui mutét suom

(Illúm captiuom : hunc súom ĕsse nescit quí domist) ;

30 Et quóniam heri indaudíuit de summó loco   30

Summóque genere cáptum esse equitem | Áleum,

Nil prétio parsit fílio dum párceret.

Recónciliare ut fácilius possét domum

Emít hosce e praeda ámbos de quaestóribus.

35 Hisce aútem inter sese húnc confinxerúnt dolum,   35

Quo pácto hic seruos súom erum hinc amittát domum :

Itaque ínter se commútant uestem et nómina :

Illíc [*pointing to Tyndarus*] uocatur Phílocrates, hic [*point-
     ing to Philocrates*] Týndarus.

Huius íllic, hic illius hódie fert imáginem.

40 Et hic [*pointing to Tyndarus*] hódie expediet hánc docte
  falláciam
  40

Et súom erum faciet líbertatis cómpotem ;

Eodémque pacto frátrem seruabít suom,

Reducémque faciet líberum in patriam ád patrem .

Inprúdens, itidem ut saépe iam in multís locis

45 Plus ínsciens quis fécit quam prudéns boni.
  45

Sed ínscientes suá sibi fallácia

Ita cómpararunt ét confinxerúnt dolum

Itaque hí commentí dé sua senténtia,

Vt ín séruitute hic [*pointing to Tyndarus*] ád suom ma-
  neát patrem.

50 Ita núnc ignorans suó sibi seruít patri.
  50

Homúnculi quantí sunt, quóm recógito !

Haec rés agetur nóbis, uobis fábula.

Sed étiamst paucis uós quod monitos uóluerim.

Profécto expediet fábulae huic operám dare.

55 Non pértractate fáctast neque item ut céterae,
  55

Neque spúrcidici insunt uórsus, immemorábiles.

Hic néque periurus lénost nec meretríx mala

Neque míles gloriósus.   ne uereámini,

Quia béllum Aetolis ésse dixi cum Áleis :

60 Forís íllic extra scaénam fient proélia.
  60

Nam hoc paéne iniquomst, cómico chorágio

Conári desubito ágere nos tragoédiam.

Proin síquis pugnam exspéctat, litis cóntrahat :

Valéntiorem náctus aduorsárium

65 Si erít, ego faciam ut púgnam inspectet nón bonam,
  65

Adeo út spectare póstea omnis óderit.

Abeó.   ualete, iúdices iustíssumi,

Domí duellique duéllatores óptumi.   [*Exit.*]

ACT I.

SCENE 1.

The parasite introduces himself, commiserates Hegio upon the latter's misfortune in losing his son, and speculates about the effect it will have upon his own prospects. — The whole of the first act is written in iambic *senarii*. For the appropriateness of this verse in introducing the audience to the general situation, see Introd. 42.

ERGASILVS.

[Ergasilus enters from the right, hungry, as usual.]

Er. Iuuéntus nomen índidit Scortó mihi,
       Eo quía ínuocatus sóleo esse in conuíuio.   70
       Scio ăbsúrde dictum hoc dérisores dícere,
       At ego áio recte : nám scortum in conuíuio
5   Sibi amátor talos quóm iacit — scortum ínuocat.
       Estne ínuocatum an nón ? † planissume.
       Verum hércle uero nós parasiti plánius,   75
       Quos númquam quisquam néque uocat neque ínuocat.
       Quasi múres semper édimus alienúm cibum.
10   Vbi rés prolatae súnt, quom rus hominés eunt,
       Simúl prolatae rés sunt nostris déntibus.
       Quasi quóm caletur cócleae in occultó latent,   80
       Suó sibi suco uíuont, roş si nón cadit,
       Itém parasití rébus prolatís latent
15   In ŏccúlto miseri, uíctitant sucó suo,
       Dum rúri rurant hómines quos ligúrriant.
       Prolátis rebus párasiti uenátici   **85**
       Sumús : quando res rédierunt, molóssici

    Odiósicique et múltum incommodéstici.
20   Et híc quidem hercle, nísi qui colaphos pérpeti
    Potést parasitus frángique aulas ín caput,
    Vel íre éxtra portam trígeminam ad saccúm licet.   90
    Quod míhi ne eueniat nón nullum perículumst.
    Nam póstquam meus rex ést potitus hóstium —
25   Ita núnc belligerant Aétoli cum | Áleis :
    Nam Aetólia haec est, íllic [*pointing to the left exit*] est
        captus in Álide
    Philopólemus huius [*pointing to the house in the back-*
        ground] Hégionis fílius,   95
    Senís qui hic habitat, quae aédes lamentáriae
    Mihi súnt, quas quotiensquómque conspició, fleo —,
30   Nunc híc occepit quaéstum hunc fili grátia
    Inhonéstum, maxume álienum ingenió suo :
    Hominés captiuos cómmercatur, sí queat   100
    Aliquem ínuenire suóm qui mutet fílium.
    Quod quídem ego nimís quam cúpio † ut ímpetret :
35   Nam ni íllum recipit, níl est quo me récipiam.
    † Nullast spes iuuĕntútis : sese omnís amant.
    Ille démum antiquis ést adulescens móribus,   105
    Quoius númquam uoltum tránquillaui grátiis.
    Condígne pater est eiús moratus móribus.
40   Nunc ád eum pergam.   séd aperitur óstium,
    Vnde sáturitate saépe ego exii ébrius.

Scene 2.

Hegio, overwhelmed though he is with trouble, still thinks of the com-
    fort of others.   For his own sufferings, he receives an abundance of
    sympathy from Ergasilus, who thus secures an invitation to din-
    ner. — For the metre, see Introd. 42.

Hegio.   Lorarivs.   Ergasilvs.

[*Hegio comes out of his house with an overseer of slaves.
    Ergasilus remains unobserved at first.*]

He. Aduórte animum sis: tu ístos captiuós duos   110
        Herĭ quós emi de praéda de quaestóribus —
        His índito caténas singulárias
        Istás; maiores quíbŭs sunt iuncti démito.
5   Sinito ámbulare, sí foris si intús uolent:
        Sed uti ádseruentur mágna diligéntia.   115
        Libér captiuos áuĭs ferae consímilis est:
        Semél fugiendi sí datast occásio,
        Satis ést — numquam postílla possis préndere.
10 Lo. Omnés profecto líberi lubéntius
        Sumŭs quám seruimus.
    He.   Nón uidere ita tú quidem. 120
    Lo. Si nón est quod dem, méne uis dem ipse — ín pedes?
    He. Si déderis, erit extémplo mihĭ quod dém tibi.
    Lo. Auĭs mé ferae consímilem faciam, ut praédicas.
15 He. Ita ŭt dícis: nam si fáxis, te in caueám dabo.
        Sed sátĭs uerborumst: cúra quae iussi átque abi [*exit
            the lorarius into house*].   125
        Ego íbo ad fratrem ad álios captiuós meos:
        Visám ne nocte hac quíppiam turbáuerint.
        Inde mé continuo [*starts to go*] récipiam rursúm
            domum.

20 *Er.* [*To himself, but purposely loud enough to attract atten-*
　　　　tion] Aegrést mi hunc facere quaéstum carcerá-
　　　　rium

　　　　Proptér sui gnati míseriam miserúm senem.　　　　130
　　　　Sed si úllo pacto ille húc conciliarí potest,
　　　　Vel cárnuficinam hunc fácere possum pérpeti.

He. Quis hĭc lóquitur ?

Er. 　　　　　　　　Ego, qui tuó maerore máceror,
25 Macésco, consenésco et tabescó miser.

　　　　Ossa átque pellis súm misera macritúdine,　　　　135
　　　　Neque úmquam quicquam mé iuuat quod edó —
　　　　　　(*aside*) domi :
　　　　Forís aliquantillum étiam quod gusto íd beat.

He. Ergásile, salue.

Er. 　　　　　　[*Breaking down*] Dí te bene ament, Hégio !

30 *He.* Ne flé.

Er. 　　　　　Egone illum nón fleam ? egon non défleam
　　　　Talem ádulescentem ?

He. 　　　　　　　　　Sémper sensi fílio　　　　140
　　　　Meo te ésse amicum et íllum intellexí tibi.

Er. Tum dénique homines nóstra intellegimús bona,
　　　　Quom quae ín potestate hábuimus ea amísimus.

35 Ego póstquam gnatus tuós potitust hóstium,
　　　　Expértus quanti fúerit, nunc desídero.　　　　145

He. Aliénus quom eius incómmodum tam aegré feras,
　　　　Quid mé patrem par fácerest quoi illest únicus ?

Er. [*With an injured air*] Aliénus ? ego aliénus illi ? aha,
　　　　Hégio,

40 Numquam ístuc dixis néque animum induxís tuom.
　　　　Tibi ílle únicust, mi etiam único magis únicus.　　　　150

He. Laudó, malum quom amíci tuom ducís malum.
　　　　Nunc hábĕ bonum animum. |

Er.   Éheu! huic illúd dolet,
Quia núnc remissus ést edendi exércitus.

45 *He.* Nullúmne interea náctu's, qui possét tibi
Remíssum quem dixti ímperare exércitum ?   155

Er. Quid crédis ? fugitant ómnes hanc prouínciam —
Quod ŏbtígerat postquam cáptust Philopolemús tuos.

He. Non pól mirandumst fúgitare hanc prouínciam.

50   Multís et multigéneribus opus ést tibi
Milítibus.   primumdum ópus est Pistorénsibus :   160
Eorúm sunt aliquot génera Pistorénsium.
Opŭs Pániceis est, ópŭs Placentinís quoque,
Opŭs Túrdetanis, ópŭst Ficedulénsibus.

55   Iam máritumi omnes mílites opŭs súnt tibi.

Er. Vt saépe summa ingénia in occultó latent :   165
Hic quális imperátor nunc priuátus est.

He. Habĕ módo bonum animum.   nam íllum confidó
domum
In hís diebus mé reconciliássere.

60   Nam eccúm hic captiuom ádulescentem | Áleum
Prognátum genere súmmo et summis dítiis :   170
Hoc íllum me mutáre confidó pote.

Er. Ita dí deaeque fáxint. — [*significantly*] sed num quó
foras
Vocátus es ad cénam ?

He.   Nusquam quód sciam.

65   Sed quíd tu id quaeris ?

Er.   Quía mist natalís dies :
Proptérea te uocári — ad te ad cenám uolo.   175

He. Facéte dictum.   séd si pauxilló potes
Conténtus esse, —

Er.   Né perpauxillúm modo :
Nam istóc me adsiduo uíctu delectó domi.

70   Age sís roga emptum : nísi qui meliorem ádferet
      Quae mi átque amicis pláceat condició magis,   180
      Quasi fúndum uendam, meís me addicam légibus.

He.   Profúndum uendis tú quidem, haud fundúm mihi.
      Sed sí uenturu's, témperi.

Er.   Em, uel iam ótiumst.

75 He. I módo, uenare léporem : nunc irím tenes.
      Nam meús scruposam uíctus commetát uiam.   185

Er.   Numquam ístoc uinces me, Hégio : ne póstules :
      Cum cálceatis déntibus ueniám tamen.

He.   Aspér meus uictus sánest.

Er.   Sentisne éssitas ?

80 He. Terréstris cenast.

Er.   [With a wink at the audience] Sús terrestris béstiast.

He.   Multís holeribus.

Er.   [Good-naturedly] Cúrato aegrotós domi. 190
      Numquíd uis ?

He.   Venias témperi.

Er.   Memorém mones [exit on the spectators' right].

He.   Ibo íntro atque intus súbducam ratiúnculam,
      Quantíllum argenti mi ápŭd trapessitám siet.

85   Ad frátrem, quo ire díxeram, mox íuero [goes into
      his house].

ACT II.

Scene 1.

Philocrates and Tyndarus get an opportunity to talk over the respec-
tive parts they are to play in the scheme they have devised for
effecting the former's escape. — The whole of this scene is accompanied by music ; see Introd. 71 and 72. The verse shifts rapidly
from one metre to another to suit the varying moods of the actors.
For the adaptability of the different metres to different moods, see
Introd. 42, 45, 47, 49, 55, etc.

Lorarii.   Captivi [Philocrates, Tyndarvs].

[*Two lorarii come from Hegio's house accompanied by slaves,
and by the captives, who are dressed as in the prologue.*]

Lo. Si di ímmortales íd uoluerunt, uós hanc aerumnam
             éxsequi,   195
    Decet íd pati animo | aéquo: si id faciétis, leuior
      lábos erit.
    Domĭ fuístis credo líberi.
    Nunc séruitus si euénit, ei uos mórigerari mós bonust
5   Eámque et erili império ingeniis uóstris lenem réd-
      dere.
    Indígna digna habénda sunt erŭs quaé facĭt.
Ca.   Oh óh oh !   200
Lo. Éiulatióne haud opus est: múlta oculis multa † mira-
      clitis.
    In ré mala animo sí bono utare, ádiuuat.
Ty. At nós pudet quia cúm catenis súmus.
Lo.   At pigeat póstea

10   Nóstrum erum, sí † uos éximat uínculis

        Aút solutós sinat quós argento émerit.   205

Ty.   Quid ă nóbis metuit? scímus nos   206ª

     Nóstrum officiúm quod est, sí solutós sinat.   206ᵇ

Lo.   Át fugam fíngitis —   207ª

     Séntio quam rem ágitis.   207ᵇ

Ty.   Nós fugiamus? quó fugiamus?

Lo.   Ín patriam.

Ty.   Apage! haud nós id deceat

15   Fúgitiuos imitári.

Lo.   Immo edepol, si érit occasio, haúd dehortor.

Ty. Vnum exoráre uos sínite nos.

Lo.   Quídnam id est?   210

T. Vt sine hisce árbitris [*nodding toward the attendant slaves*] átque uobís nobis

    Detís locum loquéndi.

Lo. Fíat.   [*To the captives*] abscédite hinc: nós concedá-
          mus huc.

20   Séd breuem orátionem íncipisse.   214

Ty. Em, istúc mihi certum erăt.   [*To Philocrates*] cón-
          cede huc.   215ª

Lo. [*To the slaves*] Abíte ab istis.

Ty.   [*To the lorarii*] Obnóxii ambo 215ᵇ

    Vóbis sumŭs própter hanc rém, quom, quae uólu-
        mus nos,

    Cópia est — † ea fácitis nos cómpotes.

Ph. [*To Tyndarus*] Sécede huc núnciam, sí uidetúr,
      procul,

25   Ne árbitri dícta nostra árbitrarí queant

    Neú permanét palam haec nóstra fallácia.   220

    Nám doli nón doli súnt, nisi astú colas:

    Séd malum máxumum, si íd palam próuenit.

Nam sí | erus mihi ĕs tu | átque ego me tuom ésse
     seruom assímulo,

30   Tamĕn uíso opust, cautóst opus, ut hoc sóbrie sineque
           árbitris   225

    Accúrate agátur, docte ét diligénter.

    Tanta íncepta rés est: haud sómniculóse hoc
    Agéndumst.

Ty.   Ero út me uolés esse.

Ph.   Spéro.

Ty.   Nám tú nunc uidés pro tuó caro cápite

35   Carum ófferre mé meum capút uilitáti.   230

Ph. Sció. |

Ty.   At scire meménto quando id quód uoles habébis.

    Nám fere maxima párs morem hunc hominés ha-
          bent: quod síbi uolunt,

    Dum id ímpetrant, boní sunt:

    Sed íd ubi iam penĕs sése habent,

40   Éx bonis péssumi et fraúdulentíssumi   235
    Fíunt.   nunc út mihi té uolo esse aútumo.

Ph.   Quód tibi suádeam, suádeam meó patri.

    Pól ego, si te aúdeam, meúm patrem nóminem:

    Nám secundúm patrem tu és pater próxumus.

45 *Ty.* Aúdio.

Ph.   Et proptérea saepiús te uti memíneris moneo: 240
    Nón ego erus tibí, sed seruos súm.   nunc obsecró te
          hoc unum —

    Quóniam nobis di ímmortales ánimum ostenderúnt
          suom,

    Út qui erum me tíbi fuisse atque ésse nunc conser-
          uóm uelint —

    Quom ántehac pro iure ímperitabam meó, nunc te oro
          pér precem,

50   Pér fortunam incértam et per mei te érga bonitatém
           patris   245

      Pérque conseruitiúm commune quód hŏstica euenít
           manu,

      Né me secus honóre honestes quám quom seruibás
           mihi

      Átque ut qui fuerís et qui nunc sís meminisse ut mé-
           mineris.

Ty. Scío quidem me te ésse nunc et te ésse me.

Ph.   Em, istuc sí potes
55   Mémoriter meminísse, inest spes nóbis in hăc astútia.

Scene 2.

Hegio has a private interview with Philocrates (as he thinks) and pro-
cures what seems to be interesting and important information. He
realizes that this is a deceitful world, but he feels great confidence
in his ability to look after his own interests. However, he is per-
suaded to release temporarily one of his captives. — The music still
continues throughout the scene. For the movement of trochaic
septenarii, and for the manner of rendering them, see Introd. 57
and 70.

           Hegio.   Philocrates.   Tyndarvs.

[Hegio comes out of his house, addressing some one within.]

He. Iam égo reuortar íntro, si ex his quaé uolo ex-
            quisíuero. *[Looking this way and that]*   251
       Vbi sunt isti quós ante aedis iússi huc producí foras ?

Ph. Édepol tibi ne in quaéstione essémus cautum intél-
            lego :

       Íta uinclis custódiisque círcummoenití sumus.

5 *He.* Quí cauet ne décipiatur, uíx cauet quom etiám cauet. 255
       Étiam quom cauísse ratus est, saépe is cautor cáptus
            est.

Án uero non iústa causast út uos seruem sédulo,
Quós tam grandi sím mercatus praésenti pecúnia?

Ph. Néque pol tibi nos, quía nos seruas, aéquomst uitio
     uórtere

10 Néque te nobis, sí | abeamus hínc, si fuat occásio. 260

He. Vt uos hic, itidem íllic apŭd uos meús seruatur fílius.

Ph. Cáptus est?

He.   Ita.

Ph.   Nón igitur nos sóli ignaui fúimus.

He. Sécede huc: nam súnt quae | ex te sólo scitarí uolo,
    Quárum rerum té falsiloquom mi ésse nolo.

Ph.   Nón ero,

15 Quód sciam: siquíd nescibo, id néscium tradám tibi
     [*they go aside*].   265

Ty. [*To the audience*] Núnc senex est ín tostrina — núnc
     iam cultros ádtinet.

Ne íd quidem, inuolúcrum inicere, uóluit, uestem ut
     ne ínquinet.

Séd utrum strictimne ádtonsurum dícam esse an per
     péctinem,

Néscio: uerúm si frugist, úsque admutilabít probe.

20 *He.* Quíd tu? seruosne ésse an liber máuelis, memorá
     mihi.   270

Ph. Próxumum quod sít bono quodque á malo longíssume,
    Íd uolo: quamquám non multum fuít molesta séruitus
    Néc mihi secus erát quam si essem fámiliaris fílius.

Ty. [*Aside*] Eúgepae! Thalém talento nón emam Milé-
     sium.

25 † Nam ad sapientiam huius nímius nugatór fuit. 275
    Vt facete orátionem ad séruitutem cóntulit!

He. Quó de genere nátust illic Phílocrates?

Ph.   Polyplúsio:

Quód genus illi est únum pollens átque honoratíssu-
    mum.

He. Quíd ĭpsus hic? quo honórest illic?

Ph.   Súmmo atque ab summis uiris.

30 *He.* Tum ígitur, ei quom in Áleis tanta grátiast ut praé-
        dicas,   280

Quíd diuitiae? súntne opimae?

Ph.   Vnde éxcoquat sebúm senex.

He. Quíd pater? uiuítne?

Ph.   Viuom quom índe abimus líquimus.

    Núnc uiuatne nécne, id Orcum scíre oportet scílicet.

Ty. [*Aside*] Sálua res est: phílosophatur quóque iam,
        non mendáx modost.

35 *He.* Quíd erat ei nomén?

Ph.   Thensaurochrýsonicochrýsides. 285

He. Vídĕlicet proptér diuitias índitum id nomén quasist?

Ph. Ímmo edepol proptér auaritiam ipsíus atque audá-
        ciam.

    Nam ílle quidem Theodóromedes fuít germano
        nómine.

He. Quíd tu ais? tenáxne pater est eiús?

Ph.   Immo edepol pértinax.

40 Quín etiam ut magĭs nóscas, genio súo ubi quando
        sácruficat,   290

    Ád rem diuinám quibus est opŭs Sámiis uasis útitur,

    Ne ípse Genius súrripiat.   proinde áliis ut credát uide.

He. Séquere hac me igitur.   eádem ego ex hoc quaé uolo
        exquaesíuero [*approaches Tyndarus*].

    Phílocrates, hic fécit hominem frúgi ut facere opór-
        tuit.

45 Nám | ego ex hoc quo génere gnatus sís scio; hic
        fassúst mihi.   295

c

Haéc tu eadem si cónfiteri uís, tua ex re féceris,

Quaé tamen scio scíre me ex hoc.

Ty.   Fécit officium híc suom,

Quóm tibist conféssus uerum : quámquam uolui
    sédulo

Meám nobilitatem óccultare et génus et diuitiás
    meas,

50 Hégio: nunc quándo patriam et líbertatem pérdidi, 300

Nón ego ístunc me pótius quam te métuere aequom
    cénseo.

Vís hostilis cum ístoc fecit meás opes aequábiles.

Mémini quom dicto haúd audebat, fácto nunc laedát
    licet.

Séd uiden? fortúna humana fíngit artatque út lubet.

55 Mé qui liber fúeram seruom fécit, e summo ínfumum.

Qui ímperare insuéram nunc alt(e)ríus imperio óbse-
    quor.   306

Ét quidem si, proínde ut ipse fui ímperator fámiliae,

Hábeam dominum, nón uerear ne iniúste aut grauiter
    mi ímperet.

Hégio, hoc te mónitum, nisi forte ípse non uis, uólu-
    eram.

60 *He.* Lóquere audacter.

Ty.   Tam égo fui ante líber quam gnatús tuos.   310

Tám mihi quam illi líbertatem hostílis eripuít manus.

Tam ílle apud nos séruit quam | ego núnc hic apŭd
    te séruio.

Ést profecto déŭs qui quae nos gérimus auditque ét
    uidet.

Ís uti tu me hic hábueris proinde íllum illic curáuerit.

65 Béne merenti béne profuerit, mále merenti pár erit. 315

Quám tu filiúm tuom, tam páter me meus desíderat.

He. Mémini ego istoc: séd faterin éadem quae hic fas-
    súst mihi?

Ty. Égo patri meo ésse fateor súmmas diuitiás domi
    Méque summo génere gnatum.   séd te optestor,
    Hégio,

70   Né tuom animum auáriorem fáxint diuitiaé meae, 320
    Né patri, tam etsi únicŭs sum, decére uideatúr magis
    Mé saturum seruíre apud te súmptu et uestitú tuo
    Pótius quam illi ubi mínume honestumst méndican-
    tem uíuere.

He. Égo uirtute deum ét maiorum nóstrum diues súm
    satis.

75   Nón ego omninó lucrum omne esse útile homini ex-
    ístumo: 325
    Scío ego, multos iám lucrum lutuléntos homines
    réddidit.
    Ést etiam ubi profécto damnum praéstet facere
    quám lucrum.
    Ódi ego aurum: múlta multis saépe suasit pérperam.
    Núnc hoc animum aduórte, ut ea quae séntio paritér
    scias.

80   Fílius meus íllic apŭd uos séruit captus Álide.   330
    Eúm si reddis míhi, praeterea | únum nummum né
    duis;
    Ét te et hunc amíttam hinc — alio pácto abire nón
    potes.

Ty. Óptumum atque aequíssumum oras óptumusque
    hominum és homo.
    Séd ĭs priuatam séruitutem séruit illi an públicam?
85 *He.* Príuatam — medicí Menarchi.

Ty.   [*Aside*] Pól ĭs quidem huius [*pointing to
    Philocrates*] ést cluens!   335

       [*To Hegio*] Tam hóc quidem tibi ín procliui quam
         ímber est quandó pluit.

He.   Fác is homo ut redimátur.

Ty.   Faciam.   séd te id oro, Hégio —

He.   Quíduis, dum ab re néquid ores, fáciam.

Ty.   Ausculta, túm scies.
       Égo me amitti dónicum ille huc rédierit non póstulo :

90   Vérum, te quaeso, aéstumatum hunc míhi des quem
         mittam ád patrem,   340
       V́t is homo redimátur illi.

He.   Immo álium potius mísero
       Hínc, ubi erunt indútiae, illuc, tuóm qui conueniát
         patrem,
       Quí tua quae tu iússeris mandáta ita ut uelís pérferat.

Ty.   Át nil est ignótum ad illum míttere : operam lúseris.

95   Húnc mitte, hic † omne transactum réddet, si illuc
         uénerit.   345
       Néc quemquam fidéliorem néque quoi plus credát
         potes
       Míttere ad eum néc qui magís sit séruos ex senténtia
       Néque adeo quoi tuóm concredat fílium hodie audá-
         cius.
       Né uereare : meó periclo huiús ego | experiár fidem

100   Frétus ingenio eiús, quod me esse scít sese erga
         béniuolum.   350

He.   Míttam equidem istunc aéstumatum tuá fide, si uís.

Ty.   Volo.
       Quám citissumé potest, tam hoc cédere ad factúm
         uolo.

He.   Núm quae causast quín, si ille huc non rédeat,
         uigintí minas
       Míhi des pro illo ? |

Ty.   Óptuma immo.

He.   [*To the lorarii*] Sóluite istum núnciam,
105   Átque utrumque.

Ty.   Dí tibi omnes ómnia optata ófferant, 355

Quóm me tanto honóre honestas quómque ex uinclis
    éximis.

Hóc quidem haud moléstumst, iam quod cóllus col-
    larí caret.

He. Quód bonis benefít beneficium / grátia ea grauidást
    bonis.

Núnc tu illum si illo és missurus, díce, demonstra,
    praécipe,

110   Quae ád patrem uis núntiari.   uín uocem huc ad té ?

Ty.   Voca. 360

SCENE 3.

Hegio, having heard from Philocrates (whom he supposes to be Tyn-
    darus) the plausible story about the high standing and importance
    at home of the latter's pretended master, now puts into execution the
    proposed plan for securing the return of his captured son. He sends
    the supposed Tyndarus back home to effect an exchange.   The
    parting, in the presence of Hegio, between the pretended slave and
    the pretended master gives an opportunity for a clever bit of acting.
    — The scene opens with a matter-of-fact dialogue in iambic *senarii*.
    As the interest quickens, and as the time comes to formulate the
    message to be carried to the prisoner's father (385, *cf.* 384) and to
    say the parting words, the verse changes to trochaic *septenarii*; the
    music again strikes up and continues to the end of the scene.   See
    Introd. 57 and 70.

HEGIO.   PHILOCRATES.   TYNDARVS.

[*Hegio, after his interview with Tyndarus, crosses over to
                Philocrates.*]

He. Quae rés bene uortat míhi meoque fílio

Vobísque : uolt te nóuos erus operám dare

Tuo uéteri domino, quód is uelit, fidéliter.

Nam ego te aéstumatum huíc dedí uigintí minis.

5   Hic aútem te ait míttere hinc uelle ád patrem,   365

Meum ut íllic redimat fílium : mutátio

Intér me atque illum ut nóstris fiat fíliis.

Ph. Vtróque uorsum réctumst ingeniúm meum,

Ad te átque ad illum : pró rota me utí licet.

10   Vel ego húc uel illuc uórtar quo imperábitis.   370

He. Tuté tibi tuopte ingénio prodes plúrumum,

Quom séruitutem | íta fers ut ferrí decet.

Sequere : [*going back with Philocrates, to Tyndarus*]

ém tibi hominem.

Ty.   Grátiam habeó tibi,

Quom cópiam istam mi ét potestatém facis,

15   Vt ego ád parentes húnc remittam núntium,   375

Qui mé quid rerum hic ágitem et quid fierí uelim

Patrí meo ordine ómnem rem illuc pérferat.

Nunc íta conuenit ínter me atque hunc, Týn-

dare,

Vt te aéstumatum in Álidem mittam ád patrem;

20   Si nón rebitas húc, ut uigintí minas   380

Dem pró te.

Ph.   Recte cónuenisse séntio.

Nam páter exspectat aút me aut aliquem núntium,

Qui hinc ád se ueniat.

Ty.   Érgo animum aduortás uolo,

Quae núntiare hinc té uolo in patriam ád patrem.

25 *Ph.* [*Feelingly*] Phílocrates, ut adhúc locorum féci, faciam

sédulo,   385

Vt potissumúm quod in rem récte conducát tuam

Íd petam † id persequarque córde et animo atque

aúribus.

Ty. Fácis ita ut te fácere oportet : núnc animum aduortás
uolo.

Ómnium primúm salutem dícito matri ét patri

30 Ét cognátis ét siquem alium béneuolentem uíderis : 390
Me híc ualere et séruitutem séruire huic homini óp-
tumo,

Quí me honore honéstiorem sémper fecit ét facit.

Ph. Ístuc ne praecípias : facile mémoria meminí tamen.

Ty. Nám quidĕm nisi quod cústodem habeo líberum me
esse árbitror.

35 Dícito patrí quo pacto míhi cum hoc conuénerit 395
De húius filió.

Ph.   Quae memini móra merast monérier.

Ty. Vt eum redimat ét remittat nóstrum huc amborúm
uicem.

Ph. Méminero.

He.   At quam prímum poteris : ístuc in rem † utri-
quest maxume.

Ph. Nón tuom tu mágĭs uidere quam ílle suom gnatúm
cupit.

40 *He.* Méŭs mihi, suos quoíquest carus.

Ph.   [*To Tyndarus*] Núm quid aliud uís patri 400
Núntiari ?

Ty.   Me híc ualere et — [*aside, to himself*] túte
audacter dícito,

Týndare — inter nós fuisse ingénio haud discordábili,

Néque te commeruísse culpam néque me aduorsatúm
tibi

Béneque ero gessísse morem in tántis aerumnís
tamen,

45 Néque med umquam déseruisse té neque factis néque
fide   405

Rébus in dubiís, egenis.   haéc pater quandó sciet,

Týndare, ut fuerís animatus érga suom gnatum
átque se,

Númquam erit tam auárus, quín te gratus emittát
manu.

Ét mea opera, si hínc rebito, fáciam ut faciat fácilius.

50   Nám tua opera et cómitate et uírtute et sapiéntia 410

Fécisti, ut redíre liceat ád parentis dénuo,

Quóm | apud hunc conféssus es et génus et diuitiás
meas:

Quó pacto emisísti e uinclis túom erum tua sapiéntia.

Ph.   Féci ego ïsta ut commémoras et te méminisse id
gratúmst mihi.

55   Mérito tibi | ea éuenerunt á me: nam nunc, Phílo-
crates,   415

Sí | ego item memorém quae me erga múlta fecistí bene,

Nóx diem adimat: nám quasi seruos meús (e)sses,
nihilo sétius,

Míhi | obsequiosús semper fuísti.

He.   [*Aside*] Di uostrám fidem,

Hóminum ingenium líberale! ut lácrumas excutiúnt
mihi!

60   Vídeas corde amáre inter se: quántis † laudauit 420

Súom erum seruos cónlaudauit.

Ph.   Pól ïstic me haud centésumam

Pártem laudat quam ípse meritust út laudetur
laúdibus.

He.   Érgo quom optumé fecisti, núnc adest occásio

Bénefacta cumuláre, ut erga hunc rém geras fidéliter.

65 *Ph.*   Mágïs non factum póssum uelle quam ópera experiar
pérsequi.   425

Íd ǔt scias, Iouém supremum téstem laudo, Hégio,

Me ínfidelem nón futurum Phílocrati.

He.   Probus és homo.

Ph. Néc me secus umquam eí facturum quícquam quam
     memét mihi.

Ty. Ístaec dicta: te éxperiri | ét opera et factís uolo,

70   Ét quo minŭs dixí quam uolui dé te animum aduortás
     uolo.   430

Átque horunc uerbórum causa cáuěto mi iratús fuas.

Séd, te quaeso, cógitato hinc té mea fidě mittí domum,

Te aéstumatum et méam ěsse uitam hic pró te posi-
     tam pígnori,

Né tu me ignorés, quom extemplo meo é conspectu
     abscésseris,

75   Quóm me seruom in séruitute pró te hic relíqueris 435

Túque te pro líbero esse dúcas, pignus déseras,

Néque des operam pró me ut huius réducem facias
     fílium.

Scíto te hinc minís uiginti | aéstumatum míttier.

Fác fidelis sís fideli, cáuě fidem fluxám geras.

80   Nám pater, scio, fáciet quae illum fácere oportet
     ómnia.   440

Sérua tibi ín perpétuom amicum me átque hunc
     inuentum ínueni.

Haéc per dexterám tuam [*taking Philocrates' hand*]
     te déxtera retinéns manu

Ópsecro, infidélior mihi né fuas quam ego súm tibi.

Tú hoc age: tu míhi erus nunc es, tú patronus, tú
     pater:

85   Tíbi commendo spés opesque meás.

Ph.   Mandauistí satis. 445

Sátin habes mandáta quae sunt fácta si referó?

Ty.   Satis.

Ph. Ét tua [*bowing to Hegio*] et tua [*bowing to Tyndarus*]
    húc ornatus réueniam ex senténtia.

    Númquid aliud?

Ty.   V́t quam primum póssis redeas.

Ph.   Rés monet.

He. Séquere me, uiáticum ut dem | á trapessitá tibi.

90   Eádem opera a praetóre sumam sýngraphum.

Ty.   Quem sýngraphum? 450

He. Quem híc ferat secum ád legionem, hinc íre huic ut
    liceát domum.

    [*To Tyndarus*] Tu íntro abi.

Ty. [*As he goes into the house*] Bene ámbulato.

Ph.   Béne uale.

He. [*Soliloquizing*]   Edepol rém meam
    Cónstabiliui, quom íllos emi dé praeda a quaestóribus:
    Éxpediui ex séruitute fílium, si dís placet.

95   Át etiam dubitáui hos homines émerem an non
    emerém diu.   455

    [*To the lorarii, who go at once inside*] Séruate istum
    súltis intus, sérui, ne quoquám pedem

    Écferat sine cústode:† ego apparebó domi.

    Ád fratrem modó captiuos álios inuisó meos.

    Eádem percontábor, ecquis hŭnc ádulescentem nó-
    uerit.

100 [*To Philocrates*] Séquere tu, te ut ámittam: ei rei
    prímum praeuortí uolo. [*They leave the stage by
    the right-hand exit.*]   460

ACT III.

Scene 1.

Ergasilus is still on the hunt for a dinner.   He thinks times are not what
they used to be. — Appropriate music accompanies his soliloquy.

Ergasilvs.

[*He enters at the right of the stage, looking quite discouraged.*]

Er. Míser homost, qui ipsús sibi quod edit quaérit et id
aegre ínuenit.

Séd íllest miseriór, qui et aegre quaérit et nil ínuenit.

Ílle miserrumúst, qui, quom esse † cupit, quod edit
nón habet.

Nam hércle ego huic dieí, si liceat, óculos effodiám
lubens :

5   Íta malignitáte onerauit ómnis mortalís mihi.   465

Néque ieiuniósiorem néque magis ecfertúm fame

Vídi nec quoi mínŭs procedat quícquid facere occé-
perit:

Íta uenter guttúrque resident ésurialis férias.

Ílicet parasíticae arti máxumam malám crucem !

10   Íta iuuentus iám ridiculos ínopesque ab se ségregat.

Níl morantur iám Lacones únisubsellí uiros,   471

Plágipatidas, quíbŭs sunt uerba síne penu et pecúnia.

Eós requirunt, quí lubenter quom éderint reddánt
domi.

Ípsi obsonant, quaé parasitorum ánte erat prouíncia.

15   Ípsi de foró tam aperto cápite ad lenonés eunt   475

Quam ín tribu | apérto capite sóntes condemnánt
  reos.

Néque ridiculos iám terrunci fáciunt: sese omnés
  amant.

Nam út dudum hinc ábii, accessi ad ádulescentes ín
  foro.

'Sáluete' inquam. 'quo ímus una' inquam 'ad
  prándium?' atque illí tacent.

20 'Quís ait: hoc? aut quís profitetur?' ínquam: quasi
  mutí silent,   480

Néque me rident. 'úbi cenamus?' inquam: | atque
  illi ábnuont.

Díco unum ridículum dictum dé dictis melióribus,
Quíbŭs solebam ménstrualis épulas ante adipíscier:
Némo ridet. scíui extemplo rém de compectó geri.

25 Né canem quidem írritatam uóluit quisquam imi-
  tárier,   485

Sáltem, si non árriderent, déntes ut restríngerent.
Ábeo ab illis, póstquam uideo mé sic ludifícárier:
Pérgo ad alios, uénio ad alios, deínde ad alios — úna
  res.

Ómnes compectó rem agunt quasi | ín Velabro
  oleárii.

30 Núnc redeo inde, quóniam me | ibi uídeo ludificá-
  rier.   490

Ítem alii parasíti frustra obámbulabant ín foro.
Núnc barbarica lége certumst iús meum omne pérsequi:

Quí concilium iniére, quo nos uíctu et uita próhibe-
  ant,

Ís diem dicam, írrogabo múltam, ut mihi cenás decem
35 Meo árbitratu dént, quom cara annóna sit. sic égero!

Núnc ibo ad portum hínc. est illic mi úna spes
    cenática:
                                                               496
Si éa decolabít, redibo huc ád senem ad cenam áspe-
    ram [*leaves the stage by the left-hand exit*].

SCENE 2.

Hegio is highly elated over the prospects of securing the return of his
son and congratulates himself upon his clever management of
affairs. — His soliloquy forms another *canticum* (see Introd. 71 and
72), but the exact metrical structure of each verse is so uncertain
that no attempt is here made to indicate the scansion.

HEGIO.

[*Hegio and Aristophontes enter from the right.*]

He. Quid est suauius quam bene rem gerere bono publico,
    sicut ego feci heri,   498, 499, 500
    Quom emi hosce homines? ubi quisque uident, eunt
      obuiam
5   Gratulanturque eam rem. ita me miserum restitando
    Retinendoque lassum reddiderunt:
    Vix ex gratulando miser iam eminebam.
    Tandem abii ad praetorem. ibi uix requieui,   505
10   Rogo syngraphum: datur mihi ilico: dedi Tyndaro:
    ille abiit domum.   506, 507
    Inde ilico reuortor domum, postquam id ac-
    tumst.   508, 509
    Eo protinus ad fratrem inde abii, mei ubi sunt alii
    captiui: 510
    Rogo Philocratem ex Alide ecquis omnium
15   Nouerit. tandem hic [*pointing to Aristophontes*] ex-
    clamat eum sibi esse sodalem.

Dico eum esse apud me : hic extemplo orat obse-
 cratque,
Eum sibi ut liceat uidere. iussi ilico hunc exsolui.
 nunc [*turning to Aristophontes*] tu sequere me,
Vt quod me orauisti impetres, eum hominem ut
 conuenias. [*They go inside.*]   515

SCENE 3.

Tyndarus finds himself in trouble. The arrival of an old acquaintance
on the scene upsets his plans. — The music still continues.

TYNDARVS.

[*Tyndarus comes rushing out of Hegio's house.*]

Ty. Nunc íllud est, quom mé fuisse quam ésse nimio
 máuelim :
Nunc spés opes auxíliaque a me ségregant spernúnt-
 que se.
Hic íllest dies, quom núlla uitae meaé salus sperá-
 bilist :
Neque exítium exitiost néque adeo spes, quaé mi
 hunc aspellát metum :
5 Nec súbdolis mendáciis mihi úsquam mantellúmst
 meis.   520
(Nec sýcophantiís nec fucis úllum mantellum óbui-
 amst.)
Neque déprecatió perfidiis meís nec malefactís fugast,
Nec cónfidentiae úsquam hospitiumst néc deuorti-
 culúm dolis.
Opérta quae fuére aperta súnt, patent praestígiae.
10 Omnís res palam | est : néque de hac re negótiumst,

Quín male occidam óppetamque péstem eri uicem
meamque.   526

Pérdidit me Arístophontes híc, qui uenit módo | intro.

Ís me nouit: ís sodalis Phílocrati et cognátus est.

Néque iam Salŭs seruáre, si uolt, mé potest: nec
cópiast,

15   Nisi si áliquam corde máchinōr astútiam.   530

Quám, malum? quid máchiner? quid cómminiscar?
máxumas

Nugás, ineptias íncipisse: haéreo.

Scene 4.

Tyndarus is brought to bay, as it were, before Aristophontes. He
tries to brazen it out by a clever fiction invented on the spur of the
moment, but the case against him is too clear. Hegio finally
awakens to the fact that a trick has been played upon him. —
Music continues throughout the scene.

HEGIO. ARISTOPHONTES. TYNDARVS.

[*Hegio and Aristophontes come out of the former's house.*]

He. [*Looking this way and that*] Quo illúm nunc hominem
próripuisse fórăs se dicam ex aédibus?

Ty. [*Aside*] Núnc enĭm uero ego óccidi: | eúnt ad te
hostes, Týndare.

Quíd loquar? quid fábulabor? quíd negabo aut quíd
fatebor?   535

Mihi rés ŏmnis in ĭncertó sitast: quid rébus confi-
dám meis?

5   Vtinám te di priŭs pérderent quam périisti e patriá
tua,

Arístophontes, qui éx parata re ímparatam omném
facis.

Occísast haec res, nísi reperio atrócem mi aliquam
astútiam.

He. [*To Aristophontes*] Sequere: ém tibi hominem, adi
átque adloquere.

Ty.   [*Aside*] Quís homost me hominum míserior?

Ar. Quíd ĭstuc est, quod meós te dicam fúgitare oculos,
Týndare,   541

10   Próque ignoto me áspernari, quási me numquam nó-
ueris?

Équidem tam sum séruos quam tu, etsi égo domi
libér fui,

Tu úsque a puero séruitutem séruiuisti in Álide.

He. Édepol minume míror, si te fúgitat aut oculós tuos
Aút si te odit, qui ístum appelles Týndarum pro
Phílocrate.   546

15 *Ty.* Hégio, hic homó rabiosus hábitus est in Álide:
Né tu quod ĭstic fábuletur aúris immittás tuas.
Nam ístic hastis ínsectatus ést domi matrem ét
patrem,
Ét ĭllic isti quí sputatur mórbus interdúm uenit. 550
Proín tu ab istoc prócŭl recedas.

He.   Vltro istum a me.

Ar.   Ain, uérbero?

20   Mé rabiosum atque ínsectatum esse hástis meum me-
morás patrem?

Ét eum morbum mi ésse, ut qui me | ópŭs sit inspu-
tárier?

He. [*Sympathetically*] Né uerere: múltos iste mórbus
homines mácerat,

Quíbus insputarí saluti fŭit atque is prófuit.   555

Ar. Quíd tu autem? etiam huic crédis?

He.   Quid ego crédam huic?

Ar.   Insanum ésse me.

25 *Ty.* [*Pulling Hegio away*] Vídĕn tu hunc, quam inimíco
       uoltu intúitur ? concedi óptumumst,
       Hégio: fit quod tíbi ego dixi, glíscit rabies : cáuĕ tibi.

He. Crédidi esse insánum extemplo, ubi te áppellauit
       Týndarum.

Ty. Quín suom ipse intérdum ignorat nómen neque scit
       quí siet.   560

He. Át etiam te suóm sodalem esse aíbat.

Ty.   Haud uidí magis :

30   Ét quidem Ălcumeus átque Orestes ét Lycurgus póstea
       V̄na opera mihi súnt sodales qua íste.

Ar.   At etiam, fúrcifer,
       Mále loqui mi audés ? non ego te nóui ?

He.   Pol planum íd quidemst
       Nón nouisse, qui ístum appelles Týndarum pro Phí-
                       locrate.   565
       Quém uides, eum ignóras : illum nóminas, quem nón
                       uides.

35 *Ar.* Ímmo iste eum sese aít qui non est ésse et qui uero
       ést negat.

Ty. Tu énĭm repertu's, Phílocratem qui súperes ueriuér-
       bio.

Ar. Pól ego ut rem uideó, tu inuentu's, uéra uanitúdine
       Quí conuincas.   séd quaeso hercle agedum áspice ad
       me.

Ty.   Em.

Ar.   Díc modo :   570
       † Te negas Tyndarum esse ?

Ty.   Négo ĭnquam.

Ar.   Tun te Phílocratem

40   Ésse ais ?

       D

Ty.   Ego inquam.

Ar.   [*To Hegio*] Túne huic credis?

He.   Plús quidĕm quam tibi aút mihi:

Nam ílle quidem, quem tu húnc memoras esse, hódie
    hinc abiit Álidem

Ád patrem huius.

Ar.   Quém patrem, qui séruos est?

Ty.   Et tú quidem

Séruos es, libér fuisti: et égo me confidó fore,   575
Si húius huc recónciliasso in líbertatem fílium.

45 *Ar.* Quíd ais, furcifér? tun te gnatúm memoras † líbe-
    rum?

Ty. Nón equidem me Líberum, sed Phílocratem esse aió.

Ar.   Quid est?

Vt scelestus, Hégio, nunc íste te ludós facit.

Nám | is est seruos ípse neque praetér se umquam
    ei seruós fuit.   580

Ty. Quía tute ipse egés in patria néc tibi qui uiuás
    domist,

50 Ómnis inueníri similis tuí uis.   non mirúm facis:

Ést miserorum, ut máleuolentes sínt atque inuideánt
    bonis.

Ar. Hégio, uidĕ sís, nequid tu huic témere insistas cré-
    dere:

Átque ut perspició, profecto iám | aliquid pugnae
    édidit.   585

Fílium tuom quód redimere se aít, id ne utiquam
    míhi placet.

55 *Ty.* Scío te id nolle fíeri: efficiam támen ego id, si di
    ádiuuant.

Íllum restituam huíc, hic autem in Álidem me meó
    patri:

Própterea ad patrem hínc amisi Týndarum.

Ar. Quin túte is es:

Néque praeter te in Álide ullus séruos istoc nómi-
    nest. 590

Ty. Pérgin seruom me éxprobrare esse, íd quod ui hostili
    óptigit?

60 *Ar.* Énĭm uero† iam nequeo cóntineri.

Ty. [*To Hegio*] Heus aúdin quid ait? quín fugis?
    Iam íllic hic nos ínsectabit lápidibus, nisi íllúnc iubes
    Cónprehendi.

Ar. Crúcior.

Ty. Ardent óculi: fit opus, Hégio. 594
    Vídĕn tu illi maculári corpus tótum maculis lúridis?
    Átra bilis ágitat hominem.

Ar. At pól te, si hic sapiát senex,

65 Píx atra agitet ápŭd carnuficem tuóque capiti in-
    lúceat.

Ty. Iám deliraménta loquitur: láruae stimulánt uirum.

He. Hércle quid si hunc cónprehendi iússerim?

Ty. Sapiás magis.

Ar. Crúcior lapidem nón habere mĕ́, ut illi mastígiae 600
    Cérebrum excutiam, quí me insanum uérbis concin-
    nát suis.

70 *Ty.* Aúdin lapidem quaéritare?

Ar. Sólus te solúm uolo,
    Hégio.

He. Istinc lóquere, siquid uís: procul tamen aúdiam.

Ty. Námque edepol si adbítes propius, ós denasabít tibi
    Mórdicus.

Ar. Neque pól me insanum, Hégio, esse créduis
    Néque fuisse umquám neque esse mórbum quem istic
    aútumat. 606

75 Vérum siquid métuis a me, iúbĕ me uincirí: <u>uolo</u>,
    Dum ístic itidem uínciatur.

Ty.   Ímmo enim uero, Hégio,
    Ístic qui uolt uínciatur.

Ar.   Tácĕ modo: ego te, Phílocrates,
    Fálse, faciam ut uérus hodie réperiare Týndarus. 610
    [*Tyndarus makes signs to him*] Quíd mi abnutas?

Ty.   Tíbi ego ăbnuto?

Ar.   [*To Hegio*] Quíd agat, si absis lóngius?

80 He. Quíd ais? quid si adeam húnc insanum?

Ty.   Núgas: ludificábitur,
    Gárriet quoi néque pes umquam néque caput com-
        páreat.
    Órnamenta absúnt: Aiacem, hunc quóm uides, ipsúm
        uides.   615

He. Níhili facio, támen adibo.

Ty.   [*Aside*] Núnc ego omnino óccidi,
    Núnc ego ĭnter sacrúm saxumque stó nec quid faciám
        scio.

85 He. Dó tibi operam, Arístophontes, síquid est quod mé
    uelis.

Ar. Éx me audibis uéra quae nunc fálsa opinare, Hégio.
    Séd hŏc primum me expúrigare tíbi uolo, me insá-
        niam   620
    Néque tĕnere néque mi esse ullum mórbum nisi quod
        séruio.
    Át ita me rex deórum atque hominum fáxit patriae
        cómpotem,
90 Vt ĭstic Philocratés non magis est quam aút ego aut
        tu.

He.   Eho, díc mihi,
    Quís ĭllic igitur ést?

Ar.   Quem dudum díxi a principió tibi.
Hóc si secŭs repéries, nullam caúsam dico, quín mihi
Ét parentum et líbertatis ápŭd te deliquió siet. | 626

He. [*To Tyndarus*] Quíd tu ais ?

Ty.   Me túom ĕsse seruom et té meum erum.

He.   Haud istúc rogo.
95   Fuístin liber ?

Ty.   Fúi.

Ar.   Enĭm uero nón fuit, nugás agit.

Ty. Quí tu scis ? an tú fortasse fuísti meae matri óbstitrix,
Qui íd tam audacter dícere audes ?

Ar.   Púerum te uidí puer.

Ty. Át ego te uideó maior maiórem : | em rursúm tibi!
Meám rem non curés, si recte fácias : num ego curó
tuam ?
                                          632
100 *He.* Fúitne huic patér Thensaurochrýsonicochrýsides ?

Ar. Nón fuit, neque égo ĭstuc nomen úmquam audiui
ante húnc diem.
Phílocrati Theodóromedes fuít pater.

Ty.   [*Aside*] Pereó probe.
[*Pressing his hand to his heart*] Quín quiescis ? í die-
rectum, cór meum, ac suspénde te :   636
Tú sussultas, égo miser uix ásto prae formídine.

105 *He.* Sátin istuc mihi éxquisitumst, fuísse hunc seruom
in Álide
Néque ĕsse hunc Philocratém ?

Ar.   Tam satĭs quam númquam hoc inueniés secus.   639
Séd ubi is nunc est ?

He.   Vbi ego minume atque ípsus se uolt máxume.
Tum ígitur ego derúncinatus, deártuatus súm miser
Huiús scelesti téchinis, qui me ut lúbitumst ductauít
dolis.

110   Séd uidě sis.

Ar.   Quin éxploratum díco et prouisum hóc tibi.

He. Cérton ?

Ar.   Quin nil, ínquam, inuenies mágis hoc certo cértius:

Phílocrates iam inde úsque amicus fuít mihi a pueró

      puer.   645

He. Séd qua faciest tuós sodalis Phílocrates ?

Ar.   Dicám tibi :

Mácilento ore, náso acuto, córpore albo, oculís nigris,

115   Súbrufus aliquántum, crispus, cíncinnatus.

He.   Cónuenit.

Ty.   [*Aside*] V́t quidem hercle in médium ego hodie pés-

      sume procésserim !

Vae íllis uirgis míseris, quae hodie in térgo morien-

      túr meo !   650

He. Vérba mihi data ésse uideo.

Ty.   [*Aside*] Quíd cessatis, cómpedes,

Cúrrere ad me méaque amplecti crúra, ut uos custó-

      diam ?

120 *He.* Sátĭn me illi hodié scelesti cápti ceperúnt dolo.

Íllic seruom se ássimulabat, híc sese autem líberum.

Núculeum amisí, reliqui pígnori putámina.   655

Íta mi stolido súrsum uorsum os súbleuere offúciis.

Hícquiděm me numquam írridebit.   [*Calling inside*

      to his lorarii] Cólaphe, Cordalió, Corax,

125   Íte istinc, ecférte lora.   [*Lorarii enter, with thongs in*

      their hands.]

Colaphus.   Núm lignatum míttimur ?

Scene 5.

Tyndarus suffers the consequences of his trickery. — The music has ceased, and the dialogue is carried on throughout the scene in iambic *senarii*. See Introd. 40 and 70.

Hegio. Lorarii. Tyndarvs. Aristophontes.

[*Hegio addresses the lorarii who have just entered.*]

He. Inícite huic manicas † mastígiae.

Ty. Quid hoc ést negoti ? quíd ego deliquí ?

He.   Rogas ? 660
     Satór sartorque scélerum et messor máxume.

Ty. Non óccatorem dícere audebás prius ?

5   Nam sémper occant priŭs quam sariunt rústici.

He. At út confidentér mihi contra ástitit.

Ty. Decet ínnocentem séruom | atque innóxium   665
     Confídentem esse, suom ápud erum potíssumum.

He. Adstríngite isti súltis uehementér manus.

10 *Ty.* Tuós sum : tu has quidém [*holding out his hands*] uel
     praecidí iube.
     Sed quíd negotist ? quam ób rem suscensés mihi ?

He. Quia mé meamque rém, quod in te unó fuit,   670
     Tuís scelestis fálsidicis falláciis
     Delácerauisti deártuauistíque opes,

15   Confécisti omnis rés ac rationés meas.
     Ita mi éxemisti Phílocratem falláciis.
     Illum ésse seruom crédidi, te líberum :   675
     Ita uósmet aiebátis itaque nómina
     Intér uos permutástis.

Ty.   Fateor ómnia
20   Facta ésse ita ut tu dícis et falláciis
     Abísse eum abs te méa opera atque astútia :
     An, óbsecro hercle te, íd nunc suscensés mihi ? 680

He.   At cúm cruciatu máxumo id factúmst tuo.

Ty.   Dum ne ób malefacta péream, parui | aéstumo.

25   Si ego híc peribo, ast ílle ut dixit nón redit,

      At erít mi hoc factum mórtuo memorábile,

      Me méum erum captum ex séruitute atque hóstibus

      Reducém fecisse líberum in patriam ád patrem,   686

      Meúmque potius mé caput perículo

30   Praeóptauisse quam ís periret pónere.

He.   Facito érgo ut Ācherúnti clueas glória.

Ty.   Qui pér uirtutem, périit, at non ínterit.   690

He.   Quando égo te exemplis péssumis cruciáuero

      Atque ób sutelas tuás te Morti mísero,

35   Vel te ínteriisse uél periisse praédicent:

      Dum péreas, nil † interdico dicant uíuere.

Ty.   Pol si ístuc faxis, haúd sine poena féceris,   695

      Si ille húc rebitet, sícut confido áffore.

Ar.   [*Aside*] Pro di ínmortales! núnc ego teneo, núnc scio

40   Quid hŏc sít negoti: méŭs sodalis Phílocrates

      In líbertatest ád patrem in patriá. bene est: 699

      Nec quísquam | est mihi aéque melius quoí uelim.

      Sed hóc mihi aegrest me huíc dedisse operám malam,

      Qui núnc propter me méaque uerba uínctus est.

45 *He.*   Votuín te quicquam mi hódie falsum próloqui?

Ty.   Votuísti.

He.   Cur es aúsus mentirí mihi?

Ty.   Quia uéra obessent ílli quoi | operám dabam: 705

      Nunc fálsa prosunt.

He.   Át tibi oberunt.

Ty.   Óptumest:

      At erúm seruaui, quém seruatum gaúdeo,

50   Quoi mé custodem addíderat erŭs maiór meus.

      Sed málene id factum | árbitrare?

He.   Péssume.

Ty. At ego áio recte, qui ábs te sorsum séntio :   710
Nam cógitato, síquis hoc gnató tuo
Tuos séruos faxit, quálem haberes grátiam ?

55   Emítteresne nécne eum seruóm manu ?
Essétne apud te is séruos acceptíssumus ?
Respónde.

He.   Opinor.

Ty.   Cúr ergo iratûs mihi es ?   715

He. Quia illí fuisti quám mihi fidélior.

Ty. Quid tu ? úna nocte póstulauisti ét die
60   Recéns captum hominem, núperum et nouícium,
Te pérdocere, ut mélius consulerém tibi
Quam illí quicum una a púero aetatem exégeram ?   720

He. Ergo áb eo petito grátiam istam.   [*To the lorarii*]
dúcite,
Vbi pónderosas cróssas capiat cómpedes :

65   [*To Tyndarus*] Inde íbis porro in látomias lapidárias.
Ibi quom álii octonos lápides effodiúnt, nisi
Cottídiano sésquiopus conféceris,   725
Sescéntoplago nómen indetúr tibi.

Ar. Per deós atque homines égo te obtestor, Hégio,
70   Ne tu ístunc hominem pérduis.

He.   Curábitur :
Nam nóctu neruo uínctus custodíbitur,
Intérdius sub térra lapides éximet.   730
Diu ego húnc cruciabo, nón uno absoluám die.

Ar. Certúmnest tibi ístuc ?

He.   Nón moriri cértius.

75   [*To the lorarii*] Abdúcite istum actútum ad Hippo-
lytúm fabrum,
Iubéte huic crassas cómpedes inpíngier :

Inde éxtra portam ad meúm libertum Córdalum   735
In lápicidinas fácite deductús siet.
Atque húnc me uelle dícite ita curárier,
80   Nequí deterius huíc sit quam quoi péssumest.
Ty. Cur égo te inuito me ésse saluom póstulem?
Períclum uitae meaé tuo stat perículo.   740
Post mórtem in morte níl est quod metuám mali.
Et sí peruiuo usque ád summam aetatém, tamen
85   Breue spátiumst perferúndi quae minitás mihi.
Vale átque salue, etsi áliter ut dicám meres.
Tu, Arístophontes, dé me ut meruisti, íta uale: 745
Nam míhi propter te hoc óptigit.
He.   Abdúcite.
Ty. At únum hoc quaeso, si húc rebitet Phílocrates,
90   Vt mi éius facias cónueniundi cópiam.
He. Perístis, nisi hunc iam é conspectu abdúcitis.   [*The
            lorarii push and drag him toward the right-hand
            exit.*]
Ty. [*Struggling*] Vis haéc quidem herclest, ét trahi et
            trudí simul [*exit*].   750
He. Illic ést abductus récta in phylacam, ut dígnus est.
Ego íllís captiuis áliis documentúm dabo,
95   Ne tále quisquam fácinus incipere aúdeat.
Quod ábsque hoc esset, quí mihi hoc fecít palam,
Vsque óffrenatum suís me ductarént dolis.   755
Nunc cértumst nulli pósthac quicquam crédere:
Satís súm semel decéptus. sperauí miser
100   Ex séruitute me éxemisse fílium,
Ea spés elapsast. pérdidi unum fílium,
Puerúm quadrimum quém mihi seruos súrpuit,   760
Neque eúm seruom umquam répperi neque fílium:
Maiór potitus hóstiumst. quod hŏc ést scelus?

105   Quasi in órbitatem líberos prodúxerim.

[*To Aristophontes*] Sequere hác : reducam te úbi
        fuisti.   néminis

Miserére certumst, quía mei miseret néminem.   765

Ar. Exaúspicaui ex uínclis : nunc intéllego

Redaúspicandum esse ín catenas dénuo.   [*They leave
        the stage by the right-hand exit.*]

ACT IV.

SCENE 1.

Ergasilus feels assured of feasting without end, in consequence of a
    good piece of news he has for Hegio. — His soliloquy, uttered now
    in trochaic *septenarii*, now in iambic *octonarii*, is accompanied
    by appropriate music. See Introd. 56, 57, 43, 45, 70.

ERGASILVS.

[Ergasilus enters from the left, in high glee.]

Er. Iúppiter supréme, seruas mé measque augés opes :
      Máxumas opímitates ópiparasque offérs mihi :
      Laudém lucrum ludúm iocum festíuitatem férias 770
      Pompám penum potátiones sáturitatem gaúdium.
5   Néc quoiquam homini súpplicare núnc certumst †
          mihi :
      Nam uél prodesse amíco possum uél inimicum pér-
          dere.
      Íta hÍc me amoenitáte amoena amoénus onerauít dies :
      Síne sacris heréditatem sum áptus effertíssumam. 775
      Nunc ád senem cursúm capessam hunc Hégionem,
          quoí boni
10   Tantum áffero, quantum ípse a diuis óptat, atque
          etiam ámplius.
      Nunc cérta res est, eódem pacto ut cómici seruí solent,
      Coníciam in collum pállium, primo éx me hanc rem
          ut aúdiat :
      Speróque me ob hunc núntium | aetérnum adeptu-
          rúm cibum.   780

Scene 2.

Ergasilus breaks the good news to Hegio. — Verses 781 to 790 form the third *canticum;* the music continues throughout the scene. See Introd. 71 and 72.

HEGIO.   ERGASILVS.

[Hegio enters from the right.   He and Ergasilus do not see each other at first.]

He. [*To himself*] Quanto ín pectore háng rem meó magis
           uolúto,

    Tantó mi aegritúdo auctiór est in ánimo.

    Ad íllum modúm sublitum ós esse mi hódie!

        Neque íd perspicere quíui.

5   Quod quóm scibitúr, tum per úrbem inridébor.   785

    Quom extémplo ad forum áduenero, ómnes loquéntur

    'Hic íllest senéx doctus, quoí uerba dáta sunt.'

    Sed Érgasilus éstne hic, procúl quem † uideo?

    Conlécto quidémst pallió: quidnam actúrust?

10 Er. [*To himself*] Moue áps te moram atque,† Ergasile,
           age hánc rem.   790

    Éminōr intérminorque, nequis † mihi obstiterit ób-
           uiam,

    Nísi qui satĭs diú uixisse sése homo arbitrábitur:

    Nám qui obstiterit óre sistet.

He.   [*Aside*] Híc homo pugilatum incipit.

Er. Fácere certumst.   proínde ut omnes ítinera insistánt
           sua,   794

15   Né quis in hanc plateám negoti cónferat quicquám
           sui:

    Nám meus est ballísta pugnus, cúbitus catapultást
           mihi,

Vmerus aries : túm genu ăd quemque iécero, ad ter-
rám dabo.

Déntilegos omnés mortales fáciam, quemque offén-
dero.

He. [*Aside*] Quae íllaec eminátiost nam ? néqueo mirarí
satis.

20 *Er.* Fáciam, ut huius dieí locique meíque semper mémi-
nerit :   800

Quí mihi ĭn cursu, opstíterit faxo uítae is extempló
suae.

He. [*Aside*] Quíd hic homo tantum íncipissit fácere cum
tantís minis ?

Er. Príus edico, néquis propter cúlpam capiatúr suam,
Cóntinete uós domi, prohibéte a uobis uím meam.

25 *He.* [*Aside*] Míra edepol sunt ni hic ĭn uentrem súmpsit
confidéntiam.   805

Vaé misero illi, quoíus cibo iste fáctust imperiósior !

Er. Túm pistores scrófipasci quí alunt furfuribús sues,
Quárum odore praéterire némo pistrinúm potest :
Eórum si quoiúsquam scrofam in público conspéxero,

30 Éx ipsis dominís meis pugnis éxculcabo fúrfures. 810

He. [*Aside*] Básilicas edíctiones átque imperiosás habet.
Sátur homost, habét profecto in uéntre confidentiam.

Er. Túm piscatorés qui praebent pópulo pisces foétidos,
Qui áduehuntur quádrupedanti crúcianti canthério,

35 Quórum odos subbásilicanos ómnes abigit ín forum :
Eís ego ora uérberabo súrpiculis piscáriis,   816
Vt sciant aliéno naso quam éxhibeant moléstiam.
Túm lanii autem quí concinnant líberis orbás oues,
Quí locant caedúndos agnos ét duplam agninám
danunt,

40　　　Quí petroni nómen indunt uérueci sectário:　　820
　　　　Éum ego si in uiá petronem pública conspéxero,
　　　　Ét petronem et dóminum reddam mórtales misér-
　　　　　rumos.

　He. [*Aside*] Eúgepae : | edíctiones aédilicias hícquidem
　　　　habet,
　　　　Mírumque adeost ni húnc fecere síbi | Aetoli agorá-
　　　　　nomum.

45 Er. Nón ego nunc parasítus sum, sed régum rex regá-
　　　　lior :　　825
　　　　Tántus uentri cómmeatus méo adest in portú cibus.
　　　　Séd ego cesso hunc Hégionem oneráre laetitiá senem ?
　　　　Quí hominē | adaéque nemo uíuit fortunátior.

　He. [*Aside*] Quae íllaec est laetítia quam illic laétus
　　　　largitúr mihi ?

50 Er. [*Knocking at Hegio's door*] Heús ! ubi estis ? écquis †
　　　　hoc aperit óstium?　　830

　He. [*Aside*] Híc homo ad cenam récipit se ad me. |

　Er.　　　　　　　　　　Áperite hasce ambás fores
　　　　Príŭs quam pultando ássulatim fóribus exitium
　　　　ádfero.

　He. [*Aside*] Perlúbet hunc hominem cónloqui. | [*Aloud*]
　　　　Ergásile !

　Er.　　　[*Without turning*] Ergasilum quí uocat ?

　He. Respíce.

　Er.　　　　Fortuna quód tibi nec fácĭt nec faciet, mé
　　　　iubes.

55　　　Séd quis est ?

　He.　　　　Réspice ad me : Hégio sum.

　Er.　　　　　　　　　[*Turning around*] Óh mihi, 835
　　　　†Quantumst hominum optumorum optume, in tem-
　　　　pore aduenis.

He. Nescíŏquem ad portum náctus es ubi cénes: eo
      fastídis.

Er. Cédo manum.

He.   Manúm ?

Er.   Manum, inquam, cédo tuam actutúm.

He.   [*Holding out his hand*] Tene.

Er. [*Shaking it heartily*] Gaúde.

He.   Quid ego gaúdeam ?

Er.   Quia ego ímpero: age [*shaking it with
              both of his own*] gaudé modo.

60 *He.* Pól maerores míhi ănteuortunt gaúdiis.

Er.   840

      Iám | ego ex corpore éxigam omnis máculas mae-
         rorúm tibi:

      Gaúde [*still shaking Hegio's hand*] audacter.

He.   Gaúdeo, etsi níl scio quod gaúdeam.

Er. Béne facis: iubé —

He.   Quid iubeam ? |

Er.   Ígnem ingentem fíeri.

He. Ígnem ingentem ?

Er.   Ita díco, magnus út sit.

He.   Quid ? me, uólturi,

65   Tuán causa aedis íncensurum cénses ?

Er.   Noli iráscier. 845

      Iúbĕn an non iubés astitui | aúlas, patinas élui,
      Láridum atque epulás foueri fóculis feruéntibus,
      Álium pisces praéstinatum abíre ?

He.   [*Aside*] Hic uigilans sómniat.

Er. Álium porcinam átque agninam et púllos galliná-
      ceos ?

70 *He.* Scís bene esse, sí sit unde.

Er.   Pérnam | atque ophthálmiam, 850

Hóraeum scombrum ét trugonum et cétum et mollem
    cáseum ?

He. Nóminandi istórum tibi erit mágis quam edundi·cópia
    Híc apud me, Ergásile.

Er.   Mean me caúsa hoc censes dícere ?

He. Néc nil hodie néc multo plus tu híc edes, ne frústra sis:
75   Proín tu tui cottídiani uícti uentrem ad me ádferas.

Er. Quín ita faciam, | út te cupias fácere sumptum, etsi
      égo uetem.   856

He. Égone ?

Er.   Tune.

He.   Túm tu mi igitur érus es.

Er.   Immo béneuolens.
    Vín te faciam fórtunatum ?

He.   Málim quam miserúm quidem.

Er. Cédo manum.

He.   [*Extending it*] Em manúm.

Er.   Di te omnes ádiuuant.

He.   Nil séntio.

80 *Er.* Nón enim es in sénticeto, eó non sentis.   séd iube
    Vása tibi pura ápparari | ád rem diuinám cito   861
    Átque | agnum afférri proprium pínguem.

He.   Cur ?

Er.   Vt sácrufices.

He. Quoí deorum ?

Er.   Mihi hércle : nam ego nunc tíbi sum summus
              Iúppiter,

    Ídem ego sum Salús Fortuna Lúx Laetitia Gaúdium :
85   Proín tu deum hunc sáturitate fácias tranquillúm
      tibi.   865

He. Ésurire míhi uidere.

Er.   Míquidem esurio, nón tibi.

E

He. Tuo árbitratu: fácile patior.

Er.   Crédo: consuetú's puer.

He. Iúppiter te díque perdant.

Er.   Te hércle — mi aequomst grátias

    Ágere ob nuntiúm: tantum ego nunc pórto a portu
       tíbi boni.

90   Núnc tu mihi placés.

He.   Abĭ, stultu's: séro post tempús uenis.   870

Er. Ígitur olim si áduenissem, mágĭs tu tum istuc
       díceres.

    Núnc hanc laetitiam áccipe a me quám fero: nam
       fílium

    Tuóm modo in portú Philopolemum uíuom, saluom
       et sóspitem

    Vídi in publicá celoce ibidémque illum adulescéntu-
       lum

95   Áleum una et tuóm Stalagmum séruom qui aufugít
       domo,   875

    Quí tibi surripuít quadrimum púerum filiolúm tuom.

He. Ábi ĭn malam rem, lúdis me.

Er.   Ita me amábit sancta Sáturitas,

    Hégio, itaque suó me semper cóndecoret cognómine,

    V́t ego uidi.

He.   Meúm gnatum?

Er.   Tuóm gnatum et geniúm meum.

100 *He.* Ét captiuom illum Álidensem?

Er.   Μὰ τὸν Ἀπόλλω.

He.   Et séruolum 880

    Meúm Stalagmum, meúm qui gnatum súrripuit?

Er.   Ναὶ τὰν Κόραν.

He. Iám diu?

Er.   Ναὶ τὰν Πραινέστην.

He.   Vénit?

Er.
                                        Ναὶ τὰν Σιγνίαν.

He. Cérton?

Er.   Ναὶ τὰν Φρουσινῶνα.

He.   Vídĕ sis!

Er.
                                        Ναὶ τὰν 'Αλάτριον.

He. Quíd tu per barbáricas urbes iúras?

Er.   Quia enim item ásperae
105   Súnt ut tuom uictum aútumabas ésse.

He.   Vae aetatí tuae! 885

Er. Quíppe quando míhi nil credis, quód ego dico sédulo.
       Séd Stalagmus quoiús erat tunc nátionis, quom hínc
                abit?

He. Sículus.

Er.   At nunc Sículus non est: Bóius est, boiám
                terit:
       Líberorum quaérundorum caúsa ei credo uxór datast.

110 *He.* Díc, bonan fidé tu mi istaec uérba dixistí?

Er.   Bona. 890

He. Di ínmortales, íterum gnatus uídeor, si uera aútu-
                mas.

Er. Aín tu? dubium habébis, etiam sáncte quom ego
                iurém tibi?
       Póstremo, Hegió, si parua iúri iurandóst fides,
       Víse ad portum.

He.   Fácere certumst: tu íntus cura quód opus est.
115   Súme, posce, próme quiduis: té facio cellárium.   895

Er. Nam hércle nisi mantíscinatus próbe ero, fusti péc-
                tito.

He. Aéternum tibí dapinabo uíctum, si uera aútumas.

Er. Vnde id?

He.   A me meóque gnato.

Er.   Spónden tu istud ?

He.   Spóndeo.

Er. Át ego tuom tibi áduenisse fílium respóndeo.

120 *He.* Cúra quam optumé potes.

Er.   Bene ámbula et redámbula.   [*Hegio leaves the
                          stage by the left-hand exit.*]   900

Scene 3 (?)

Ergasilus thinks his turn has come at last. — Music continues.

Ergasilvs.

Er. Íllic hinc abiit : míhi rem summam crédidit cibáriam.
      Di ímmortales, iam út ego collos praétruncabo tégo-
              ribus !
      Quánta pernis péstis ueniet, quánta labes lárido,
      Quánta sumini ábsumedo, quánta callo cálamitas,
5   Quánta laniis lássitudo, quánta porcináriis.   905
      Nám si alia memorém quae ad uentris uíctum con-
              ducúnt morast.
      Núnc ibo, ut pro praéfectura meá ius dicam lárido,
      Ét quae pendent índemnatae pérnis auxilium út
              feram [*goes into Hegio's house*].

Scene 4 (?).

The stage remains unoccupied for some time after Ergasilus has gone
   inside.   Then a slave rushes out, in headlong haste, to tell of the
   havoc that is being made. — The music still continues.

Pver.

Pu. Diéspiter te deíque, Ergasile, pérdant et uentrém
      tuom

Parasítosque omnis ét qui posthac cénam parasitís
　dabit.　　　　　　　　　　　　　　　　910
Cladés calamitasque íntemperies módo ín nostram
　aduenít domum.
Quasi lúpus esuriens tímui ne in me fáceret ímpe-
　tum † :
5　Vbi uoltus ... sur .. ntis ... ímpetum　　　912ᵇ
Nimísque hércle ego illum mále formidaui : íta fren-
　debat déntibus.
Aduéniens totum déturbauit cúm carnē carnárium,
Arrípuit gladium, praétruncauit tríbŭs tegoribus
　glándia,　　　　　　　　　　　　　　915
Aulás calicesque omnís confregit nísi quae modialés
　erant :
10　Coquŏm pércontabatúr, possentne sériae feruéscere :
　Cellás refregit ómnis intus réclusitque armárium.
Adséruate istunc, súltis, serui : ego íbo, ut conueniám
　senem.
Dicam, út sibi penum álibi adornet, síquidem sese
　utí uolet :　　　　　　　　　　　　920
Nam híc quidem | ut adórnat aut iam níl est aut iam
　níl erit [*rushes back into the house*].

ACT V.

Scene 1.

The lost is found, and general good feeling prevails. The future of
Tyndarus looks brighter. — From this point on, the music is continuous throughout the play until 1029.

Hegio. Philopolemvs. Philocrates. Stalagmvs.

[*Hegio, accompanied by his elder son, Philocrates and the runaway slave, enter from the left of the stage.*]

He. [*To his son*] Iouí deisque agó gratiás merito mágnas,
  Quom te† reducem tuo patrí reddidérunt
  Quomque éx miseriís plurumís me exemérunt,
  Quae adhúc te caréns dum hic fuí sustentábam,   925
5   Quomque húnc [*pointing to Stalagmus*] conspicór in
    potéstate nóstra
  Quomque haéc . . . repértast fidés firma nóbis.
Philop. Sátis iam dolui ex ánimo et cura, sátis me lacru-
    mis máceraui,
  Sátis iam audiui tuás aerumnas ád portum mihi quás
    memorasti:
  Hóc agamus.
Philoc.   [*To Hegio*] Quíd nunc, quoniam técum
    seruauí fidem   930
10 Tíbique hunc reducem in líbertatem féci?
He.   Fecisti út tibi,
  Phílocrates, numquám referre grátiam possím satis,
  Proínde ut tu proméritu's de me et fílio. |

Philop.   Immó potes,

    Páter, et poteris ét ego potero et dí eam potĕstatém
      dabunt,
                                     934

    V́t beneficium béne merenti nóstro merito múneres :

15   Sícut tu huic [*nodding toward Stalagmus*] potés,
      pater mi, fácere merito máxume.

He. Quíd opust uerbis ? [*to Philocrates*] língua nullast
    quá negem quidquíd roges.

Philoc. Póstulo abs te, ut mi íllum reddas séruom quem
    hic relíqueram

      Pígnus pro me, quí mihi melior quám sibi sempér
        fuit,

      Pró benefactis éius ut ei prétium possim réddere.

20 *He.* Quód bene fecistí, referetur grátia. id quod pó-
    stulas,
                                       941

    Ét id et aliud quód me orabis ímpetrabis : átque te
    Nólim suscensére, quod ego irátus ei fecí male.

Philoc. Quíd fecisti ?

He.   In lápicidinas cónpeditum cóndidi,
    V́bi resciui míhi data esse uérba.

Philoc.   Vae miseró mihi ! 945

25   Própter meum capút labores hómini euenisse óp-
      tumo !

He. Át ob eam rem míhi libellam pró eo ărgenti né
    duis :

    Grátiis a me út sit liber dúcito.

Philoc.   Edepol, Hégio,
    Fácĭs benigne.   séd quaeso hominem ut iúbeas
    arcessí.

He.   Licet.
    [*Calling inside to his slaves*] V́bi | estis, uos ? íte
    actutum, Týndarum huc arcéssite.
                                       950

30   [*To Philocrates and Philopolemus*] Vós ite intro :
            intéribi ego ex hac státua [*looking sternly at
            Stalagmus*] uerbereá uolo
       Érogitare, meó minore quíd sit factum fílio.
       Vós lauate intéribi.

Philop.   Sequere hac, Phílocrates, me intró.

Philoc.   Sequor. [*Philopolemus and Philocrates go
                    inside.*]

SCENE 2.

Hegio questions Stalagmus, with rather startling results.

HEGIO. STALAGMVS.

[*Hegio turns and addresses Stalagmus, who has hitherto been
            standing at the back of the stage.*]

He. [*With a sneer*] Áge tu illuc procéde, bone uir, lépi-
            dum mancupiúm meum.

St. Quíd me oportet fácere, ubi tu tális uir falsum
            aútumas ?   955
       Fúi ego bellus, lépidus : bonus uir númquam neque
            frugí bonae
       Néque ero | umquam ; né spem ponas mé bonae frugí
            fore.

5 *He.* Própemodum ubi locí fortunae tuaé sint facile intél-
            legis :
       Sí eris uerax, tua éx re : facies éx mala meliúsculam.
       Récte et uera lóquere : sed neque uére neque recté |
            adhuc   960
       Fécisti umquam.

St.   Quód ego fatear, crédin, pudeat quom aútumes ?

He. Át ego faciam ut púdeat: nam in rubórem te totúm
  dabo.

10 *St.* Éia, credo ego, ímperito plágas minitarís mihi:

  Tándem | ista aufér, dic quid fers, út feras hinc
   quód petis.

He. Sátis facundu's: séd iam fieri dícta compendí uolo. 965

St. Vt uis fiat.

He.   [*Aside*] Béne morigerus fuít puer: nunc nón
   decet.

  Hóc agamus. iam ánimum aduorte ac míhi quae
   dicam edíssere.

15 Sí eris uerax, éx tuis rebus féceris meliúsculas.

St. Núgae istaec sunt: nón me censes scíre quid dignús
   siem?

He. Át ea subterfúgere potis es paúca, si non ómnia. 970

St. Paúca effugiam, scío: nam multa euénient, et meritó
  meo,

  Quía et fugi et tibí surripui fílium et eum uéndidi.

20 *He.* Quoí homini?

St.   Theodóromedi in Álide Polyplúsio
  Séx minis.

He.   Pro di ínmortales! ís quidem huius ést pater
  Phílocrati.

St.   Quin méliŭs noui quám tu et uidi saépius. 975

He. Sérua, Iuppitér supreme, et me ét meum gnatúm
  mihi!

  [*Calling excitedly into the house*] Phílocrates, per
  tuóm te genium | óbsecro, exi: té uolo.

Scene 3.

The prospects of Tyndarus look still brighter. Hegio's cup of
happiness is finally filled to overflowing. Still, there is some
bitter along with the sweet.

PHILOCRATES. HEGIO. STALAGMVS.

[*Philocrates hurries out of the house at the urgent call.*]

Ph. Hégio, assum: síquid me uis, ímpera.

He.   Hic gnatúm meum
Tuó patri ait se uéndidisse séx minis in Álide.

Ph. [*To Stalagmus*] Quám diu id factúmst?

St.   Hic annus íncipit uicénsumus. 980

Ph. [*To Hegio*] Fálsa memorat.

St.   Aút ego aut tu: nám tibi quadrímulum
5 Tuós pater pecúliarem páruolo pueró dedit.

Ph. [*To Stalagmus*] Quíd erat ei nomén? si uera dícis,
memoradúm mihi.

St. Paégnium uocitátust: post uos índidistis Týndaro.

Ph. Cúr ego te non nóui?

St.   Quia mos ést obliuisci hóminibus 985
Néque nouisse quóius nili sít faciunda grátia.

10 *Ph.* Díc mihi, isne istíc fuit quem uéndidisti meó patri,
Quí mihi pecúliaris dátus est?

St.   [*Nodding assent and with a gesture toward
Hegio*] Huius fílius.

He. Víuitne is homo?

St.   Argéntum accepi, níl curaui céterum.

He. [*To Philocrates*] Quíd tu ais?

Ph.   Quin ístic ipsust Týndarus tuos fílius, 990
Vt quidem hic arguménta loquitur: nam ís mecum a
pueró puer

15 Béne pudiceque éducatust úsque ad adulescéntiam.

Hẹ. Ét miser sum | ét fortunatús, si uera dícitis.

Eó miser sum, quía male illi féci, si gnatúst meus.

Éheu, quom | ego plús minusue féci quam me aequóm
fuit. 995

Quód male feci, crúcior: modo si inféctum fieri pós-
siet!

20 Séd ẽccum incedit húc ornatus haúd ex suis uirtúti-
bus.

Scene 4.

An affecting meeting takes place between Hegio and Tyndarus. Stalagmus comes to grief.

Tyndarvs. Hegio. Philocrates. Stalagmvs.

[*Tyndarus enters from the right, loaded down with chains and
carrying a heavy pick-axe.*]

Ty. Vídi ego multa saépe picta quae Ácherunti fíerent

Crúciamenta: uérum enĩm uero núlla adaequest
Ácheruns

Átque ubi ego fui in lápicidinis: íllic ibi demúmst
locus, 1000

Vbi labore lássitudost éxigunda ex córpore.

5 Nam úbi illo adueni, quási patriciis púeris aut moné-
rulae

Aút anites aut cóturnices dántur quicum lúsitent,

Ítidem mi haec aduénienti upupa quí me delectém
datast.

[*Noticing the others*] Séd erus eccum ante óstium: et
erus álter eccum ex Álide 1005

Rédiit.

He. Salue, | éxoptate gnáte mi.

Ty.   Hem, quid 'gnáte mi'?

10 Áttat, scio quor té patrem adsimulés esse et me
    fílium :

  Quía mi item ut paréntes lucis dás tuendi cópiam.

Ph. Sálue, Tyndare.

Ty.   Ét tu quoius caúsa hanc aerumnam éxigo

Ph. Át nunc liber ín diuitias fáxo uenies : nám tibi
   Páter hic est : hic séruos, qui te huic hínc quadri-
    mum súrpuit,   1011

15 Véndidit patrí meo te séx minis. is té mihi
   Páruolum pecúliarem páruolo pueró dedit.
   Íllic indicium fécit : nam hunc ex Álide huc redúci-
    mus.

Ty. Quíd huius filium ?

Ph.   Íntus eccum frátrem germanúm tuom. 1015

Ty. Quíd tu aīs ? addúxtin illum huius † filium captiuom ?

20 *Ph.* Quín, inquam, intus híc est.

Ty.   Fecisti édepol et recte ét bene.

Ph. Núnc tibi pater [*pointing to Hegio*] hic ést. hic
   [*pointing to Stalagmus*] fur est tuós qui paruom
   hinc te ábstulit.

Ty. Át ego hunc grandis grándem natu ob fúrtum ad car-
   nuficém dabo.

Ph. Méritus est.

Ty.   † Ergo edepol méritam mercedém dabo. 1020
   Séd dic, oro, pátĕr meus tun és ?

He.   Ego sum, gnáte mi.

25 *Ty.* Núnc demum in memóriam redeo — quóm mecum
    recógito —
   Núnc edepol demum ín memoriam régrediŏr audísse
    me,
   Quási per nebulam, Hégionem meúm patrem uocárier.

He. Ís ego sum.

Ph.   Compédibus quaeso ut tíbi sit leuior fílius   1025
Átque hic grauior séruos.

He.   Certumst príncipio id praeuórtier.
30   Eámus intro, ut árcessatur fáber, ut istas cómpedis
Tíbi adimam, huic dem.

St.   Quoí peculi nil est, recte féceris.

[*All the actors come forward.*]

CATERVA.

Spéctatores, ád pudicos móres facta haec fábulast,
Néque in hac subigitátiones súnt neque ulla amátio
Néc pueri suppósitio nec ărgénti circumdúctio,   1031
35   Néque ubi amans aduléscens scortum líberet clam
suóm patrem.
Huiús modi paucás poetae réperiunt comoédias,
Vbi boni melióres fiant.   núnc uos, si uobís placet,
Ét si placuimús neque odio fúimus, signum hoc mít-
tite,   1035
Quí pudicitiae ésse uoltis praémium: plausúm date.

ABBREVIATIONS.

A. & G., Allen and Greenough's Latin Grammar.

B., Bennett's Latin Grammar.

G.-L., The Gildersleeve-Lodge Latin Grammar.

H., The latest edition of Harkness's Latin Grammar.

NOTES.

PERSONAE.

THE early Greek comedy seldom employed more than three actors, but after the chorus was abolished this number was often exceeded. With the exception of the *Cistellaria* and the *Stichus*, the plays of Plautus always require at least four; those of Terence require at least five. In the *Captives* four actors are necessary; among these the parts might be distributed as follows : —

(1) Hegio.
(2) Philocrates, Aristophontes, puer.
(3) Tyndarus, Philopolemus, the *lorarius* who speaks in Act I. Scene 2.
(4) Ergasilus, Stalagmus, the *lorarius* who speaks in Act II. Scene 1, and Act III. Scene 5.

Besides these, supernumeraries would be necessary, e.g. in Act II. Scene 1.

The names in *fabulae palliatae* are commonly Greek names with Latin forms. Such names are usually chosen as will in themselves convey some idea of the characters to whom they belong. For instance, in the present play : —

Ergasilus indicates "the worker" (ἐργάζομαι), who "means business" and is not to be trifled with. The reader should picture him in the ordinary dress of a parasite, i.e. in black or gray garments of outlandish style, and whatever "extras" might add to his ridiculous appearance.

Hegio, "the prominent citizen," "the leading man" of the place (cf. ἡγέομαι). This actor accordingly wears, with befitting dignity, the usual dress of a well-to-do Greek.

Philocrates, "fond of ruling." Plautus himself probably spelled this name Pilocrates; see note on *Talem* in 274.

Aristophontes, "killer of chiefs." For the Plautine spelling, see note on 274.

Philopolemus, "the lover of war" (φίλος, πόλεμος). For the Plautine spelling, see note on 274.

Stalagmus, "the dropper."

63

ARGUMENTUM.

The *argumenta* prefixed to the plays of Plautus are not the productions of that poet, but were written in a later age, during a revival of interest in archaic Latin. See Introd. § 21. Such brief summaries were also written for other authors (e.g. for the different books of Vergil's *Aeneid* and for the plays of Terence, by Sulpicius Apollinaris in the second century A.D.), the prosody and the language of the author in hand being in each case carefully imitated.

1. captust: i.e. *captus est;* final *s* after a short vowel was very faintly pronounced in early Latin. *Captus est* would therefore easily become *captu' est* and then (by prodelision) *captust*. With this disappearance of the initial *e*, compare, e.g. *optumumst*, for *optumum est*, in 10 ; *domist* for *domi est*, in 29 ; the English *it's* for *it is*, etc. On the position of *captust*, see Introd. § 99. Here *captust* sounds the keynote of the entire play, and accordingly takes the most prominent place for the verb. **pugna Hegionis** : probably not a case of hiatus. *H* seems to have been capable of preventing elision and of "making position" after a final consonant. See Introd. § 74.

2. seruos : for the form, see Introd. § 86 (*a*).

4. A word has apparently fallen out of this verse. See App. **studens ut** : one of the few instances in which *studeo* is followed by an *ut*-clause.

5. If the reading is correct, there is hiatus after *inibi.* **filium** : i.e. Tyndarus.

6. is : i.e. Tyndarus. **suo** : with synizesis, *suȏ ;* see Introd. § 78. **uersa** : i.e. *mutata.*

7. amittatur : here equivalent to *dimittatur.* See note on 36. The subject is *dominus*, i.e. Philocrates in the disguise of a slave. **ipsus** : for the classical *ipse.*

8. is : i.e. Philocrates. **fugitiuom** : see Introd. § 86 (*a*).

9. quoius : for the classical *cuius ;* Introd. § 86 (*b*). **alium** : i.e. Tyndarum ; *alium* is here equivalent to *alterum.*

PROLOGVS.

On the prologues to the plays of Plautus, see Introd. § 19.

The *rôle* of prologue seems to have been usually taken by one of the younger actors or by the manager of the company, who was attired for the occasion in a particular costume. While the whole burden of the prologues of Terence consists of answers to the unkind criticisms he received from his enemies, those to the plays of Plautus show a great variety of subject matter and commonly explain the plot of the play.

1. hos: this leads one to expect a verb to follow, of which it is to be the object or the subject-accusative, but the anacoluthon in the next verse leaves this pronoun without government. The accusative might however be explained by supposing it to be attracted to agree with *quos*.

2. Illi qui astant, — hi stant ambo, etc.: similar humor might be brought out in English : "Those bystanders there — they are standing, both of them — the 'standers' aren't seated." This good-natured attempt to cheat the spectators out of the interesting information the prologue had led them to believe was coming would in itself tend to put them in good humor. One might have expected *i*, instead of *hi*. See App. If the text is correct, there is hiatus after *qui*.

3. testes estis: equivalent to *testamini;* hence the infinitive *loqui*.

4. hic: with a gesture toward Hegio's house.   **huius**: with a gesture toward Tyndarus.

5. suŏ sibi: the *sibi* intensifies the idea of *suo*, but at the same time lays stress upon the interests involved in the possession and in the general situation ; *ipsius* might have taken the place of *suo sibi*, but that would have concerned itself only with the idea of possession.

6. operam datis: starts with the idea, *put forth an effort ;* according to the application of this idea to various situations, it may be translated *render service*, *take pains*, or (as here) *give attention*.

8. alterum: to be pronounced *altrúm*; cf. such phenomena in English as "ev'ry," "quiv'ring," etc., for "every," "quivering," etc.: cf. also note on 306. The "iambic law" does not apply to such cases (see Introd. § 84), and the scansion *āltĕrŭm quod* is not permissible.   **seruos**: nominative. The nominative and accusative singular of the second declension end in the earliest times in *-os* and *-om*. These endings became *-us* and *-um* toward the close of the third century B.C., except in words in which they were preceded by *u* (either vowel or consonant). See Introd. § 86 (*a*); cf. note on *uiuont*, 81.   **surpuit**: by syncope, for *surripuit*.

9. eum: to be pronounced *eŭm*.   **profugiens**: the present participle here refers to an act prior to that of the principal verb ; strictly, it should refer to an act going on at the time of the selling, but even Latin, and especially colloquial Latin, is sometimes inaccurate in its use of tenses. The lack of a perfect active participle is often responsible for such a use as this ; accuracy is sacrificed in the interest of brevity.   **uendidīt**: for the long final syllable, see Introd. § 82 (*e*).

F

Alide: *Alis* is Doric for *Elis*. As Doric was the dialect of the Greeks in southern Italy, it is not strange that Doric forms were adopted into Latin.

10. patrí huiusce: the *h* apparently prevents elision here, as often. See Introd. § 74, and App. **iam hoc tenetis**: *have you caught the idea?* literally, *have you already hold of this?* (cf. the English slang, "catch on?"). The prologue takes an affirmative answer, on the part of the spectators, for granted, and expresses his satisfaction with their attention and interest by saying *optumumst*. At this point, however, for the purpose of stirring up his audience, he pretends to see some one at a distance from the stage waggishly shaking his head, or giving some other indication of dissent. What is said in lines 11–16 must not be taken too seriously; the prologue is too good-natured, and too desirous of putting his hearers in good humor, to lose his temper easily. **optumumst**: *very well*. For the loss of initial *e* in *est*, see note on *captust* in verse 1 of the Argumentum. But see App. The forms *optimus*, *maximus*, etc., began to replace the early forms *optumus*, *maxumus*, etc., toward the end of the Republic.

11. This verse can be read metrically only by admitting hiatus between *hercle* and *ille*, and again between *ille* and *ultumus*, and by treating the final syllable of *ultumus* as long. The first hiatus might be obviated by treating the final syllable of *negat* as long. The verse is probably corrupt. **hercle**: *confound him!* **ultumus**: some one in the edge of the crowd. For the form, see note on *optumum* in 10. **accedito**: the future imperative is commonly used only when a distinct interval is supposed to elapse before the command is to take effect or to be obeyed; hence its use in laws, maxims, recipes, etc. Sometimes (and apparently in the present passage) it is used in a command that is intended to be obeyed as soon as uttered. *Abscedito* would seem to make better sense, and is actually adopted by some editors.

12. si non ubi, etc.: as no one makes a move in obedience to his *accedito*, the prologue changes his tone somewhat; if the fellow cannot find a seat and behave himself, he may "take a walk" (outside, of course). **ubi sedeas, ubi ambules**: *to sit, to walk;* literally, *where you may sit, where you may walk* — volitive characterizing clauses. The following sorts of characterizing clauses should be noted: —

1. Predicating a hypothetical case: *is est qui mentiatur, he is a man who would cheat.* In a clause of this type, the subjunctive has the same force as in an independent paratactical clause; e.g. *is mentiatur, he would cheat.*

2. Predicating an act actually performed, or a state actually existing (a type developed from 1):[1] *is est qui mentiatur, he is a man who cheats.* Sometimes such a clause is used of the future; e.g. 613, *garriet quoi neque pes neque caput compareat, he will rattle off something, to which there will appear neither head nor tail.*

3. Predicating obligation or propriety (a type probably also developed from 1): *nihil ego uideo quod gaudeas, I see nothing that you should (ought to) rejoice over.*

4. Volitive. The relative clause, besides characterizing the antecedent, may at the same time express the purpose of the act of the principal clause, as in the English sentence, "Men are trying to make machines that shall[2] fly"; here the flying of the machines is the act which the men purpose to bring about, and at the same time the flying is to characterize the machines — they are to be flying machines. Cf. Tac. *Dial,* 28. 6, *cuius . . . committeretur.*

Another type of volitive characterizing clause is represented by *hic est locus ubi sedeas,* which may have originated in some such paratactic use as *hic est locus; hic sedeas (here is a place; sit here, if you like),* where *sedeas* would be a weak jussive subjunctive, expressing mere permission.

13. mendicarier: *play the beggar,* i.e. by asking favors of you, by making personal entreaties, which the actor regards as beneath his dignity. The passive infinitive in -*ier,* for the classical -*i,* is very common in early Latin, especially at the end of a verse.

14. ego me tua: the juxtaposition of these pronouns heightens the emphasis (see Introd. § 99) and the swaggering tone: *I am not going to burst myself for you — don't fool yourself.*   **tua**: to be read *tǔa* or *tǔǎ;* see Introd. §§ 78 and 84.   **ne erres**: see translation in the preceding note. Perhaps, however, this clause denotes negative purpose.   **rupturus**: for *rumpo* and *dirumpo* in this sense, cf. Plaut. *Cas.* 809; *Poen.* 540; *Merc.* 138; Ter. *Hec.* 435; Cic. *ad fam.* VII. 1. 4; Hor. *Ep.* I. 19. 5.

15. qui potestis ope uostra censerier: *who can claim a place among men of means ;* literally, *who can be rated by your wealth.*

---

[1] This is the type of clause commonly designated as the "Clause of Characteristic."

[2] "Shall" is used here to indicate the determination of the men; "will" would indicate mere futurity without connoting any other idea.

The reference is to the list of citizens prepared by the censor. Opposite the name of each citizen information was given regarding his wealth. Those who were here recorded as having property were said to be *opibus censi, rated according to wealth;* those who had no property were merely *capite censi.* In 194 B.C. the part of the auditorium near the stage was reserved for the senators; later, places behind the senators were similarly reserved for the *equites.* Even before 194, however, it is probable that the wealthier class, as a rule, found places near the stage. The words here quoted imply a slur, that the fellow does not belong to the same class as "the rest of you, gentlemen." **ope**: rare for *opibus;* cf. Ennius, quoted in Cic. *Tusc. Disp.* III. 19. 44, *ope barbarica;* Verg. *Aen.* VIII. 685.

16. accipite relicuom: *receive the balance due,* a phrase taken from the language of accounts, here of course referring to the rest of the argument.   **relicuom**: quadrisyllabic in early Latin. See note on *seruos,* 8.   **alieno uti nil moror**: *I don't care about being in debt; alieno* (sc. *aere*) *uti* literally means *to be using another's money. Nihil morari* starts with the idea *to make no delay about;* according to the application of this idea, it may mean (1) *to have no liking for, to dislike, to be averse to,* as here and Plaut. *Most.* 830; *Cas.* 748, etc.; (2) *to feel indifferent about, not to object to,* as in Verg. *Aen.* II. 365; *et esse nil moror, I do not care if I am;* Liv. III. 54, *nihil . . . moror quominus abeam, I do not object to leaving.*   **nil**: accusative of the "result produced" (the "inner object"). A. 238; B. 176. 2; G.-L. 333 and 329 note; H. 409. 1.   See note on *quippiam,* 127.

17. dixeram: *had said,* i.e. prior to the interruption; *dixi* might seem to us more natural, but the pluperfect in such cases is never equivalent to the perfect; see Introd. § 95 (*c*).

18. dominum: i.e. the son of his master.

19. is: i.e. Theodoromedes, to whom he sold him.   **gnato**: in the majority of cases, *gnatus* seems to be the form of the substantive in early Latin, *natus* that of the participle; but see 891.

20. quasi una: *about the same;* for *quasi* in this sense, cf. Plaut. *Most.* 617; Ter. *Heaut.* 145; Cic. *Verr.* I. 8.

21. suo: *suŏ;* see Introd. § 78.

22. enim uero: in early Latin the use of *enim* differs in two respects from its use in classical times, viz.: (1) it is not necessarily post-positive; *enim uero* came later to be fused into a single word *enimuero,* which, standing as it commonly does at the beginning of its sentence, forms a reminiscence in classical times of this earlier use; (2) *enim* is commonly used, as here, in the sense of *indeed;* this use is not uncommon even in the best classical prose.   **pilas** : *playthings ;* literally, *balls.*   **habent** : *use, treat.*

23. quomodo . . . amiserit : instead of this, we might have had *qua amisit.*

24. Postquam belligerant : A. and G. 324 ; B. 287. *a* ; G.-L. 561; H. 602.   **cum | Aleis** : for the hiatus, see Introd. § 85.

25. fīt : the original length of the vowel was frequently preserved in early Latin ; in the classical period we should expect *fĭt ;* see Introd. § 82 (*e*).

27. coepit : *he began to ;* the position of the verb (see Introd. § 99) seems to indicate that the necessity for continuing the traffic was of short duration.   **hic** : i.e. Hegio.

28. si quem . . . posset : (*to see*) *if* or *whether ; si,* like the English " if," frequently introduces an indirect question ; cf. Verg. *Aen.* I. 181 ; Dryden, "uncertain *if* by augury or chance."   **qui** : a form (especially common in early Latin) of the ablative or instrumental, used of *any gender or number.* It may be used : —

(1) for the usual ablative *quo* (as here) or *qua ;* cf. verse 101 ;
(2) as an interrogative adverb, *how ? why ? ;*
(3) as an indefinite particle, *anyhow ;*
(4) to introduce a curse (with this use, cf. *ut* (*utinam*), which, from an adverb of manner, came to introduce a wish) ;
(5) as an intensive particle (see notes on 243 and 553), *surely.*

qui : though this here refers to a person, the same construction is allowed as when the reference is to an inanimate thing.   **qui mutet suom** : *to exchange for his son ;* literally, *through whom he might receive his son in exchange. Mutare* may take either (1) the accusative of the thing received in exchange and the ablative of the thing given, or (2) the accusative of the thing given in exchange and the ablative of the thing received.   **mutet** : we should expect *mutaret* after the imperfect *posset.*

29. domist : for the loss of the *e,* see note on *captust* in line 1 of the *argumentum.*

30. indaudiuit : *got an inkling ;* for the old forms (*ind* and *indu*) of the preposition *in,* cf. *ind-ipiscor, ind-uo, indu-perator* (= *imperator*), *ind-igeo, indi-genus, ind-oles, indu-gredior* (Lucretius).   **de summo loco,** etc.: the prepositional phrases that are most frequently used to modify substantives are those formed by *de* and *ex.*   **loco** : *station.*

31. genere : *birth.*   **equitem | Aleum** : for the hiatus, see Introd. § 85.

32. nil: see references in note on *nil* in 16, and *quippiam* in 127.
nil . . . parsit . . . dum parceret: *he was not saving of his money,
if only he might save his son* (Sonnenschein), i.e. he spent money
freely in the hope of recovering his son; B. 310. I.   **parsit**:
regularly in Plautus, and often in Terence, for *pepercit*.

33. reconciliare: originally meant *to bring together again;* then
it came to be used, as in the present passage, of only one of the
parties to be brought together, in the sense of *to bring back*. This
latter meaning, however, is confined to early Latin.

34. emīt: the length of the final syllable may be due to the
following *h*, but not necessarily, as the vowel was originally long and
this quantity is occasionally retained; see Introd. § 74.   **de quaestoribus**: although *fabulae palliatae* are, generally speaking, distinctly Greek in coloring, allusions to Roman life are frequent in
Plautus, and are found occasionally in Terence. Here (though it
must be remembered that the prologue may not have been written
by Plautus) there is a distinct allusion to the Roman *quaestores*, the
officers who had charge of the financial affairs of Rome and accordingly of the disposition of the booty and the prisoners taken in war.

35. hisce: an old form of the nominative plural (see Introd.
§ 87 (*a*)). In early inscriptions the nominative plural of *o*-stems
frequently ends in *-eis* (*-is*), e.g. *heis, magistreis, publiceis, uireis.
Hisce* shows this early *-s*, the *-ce* being merely the strengthening
demonstrative particle seen in *hic* (for *hice*), *illic*, etc. Cf. *illisce*
in *Most.* 499.   **hunc . . . dolum**: i.e. the one already made clear
to the audience by the appearance of the captives and what has been
said of them.

36. quo pacto . . . amittat: a purpose clause (not an indirect
question).   **amittat**: very frequent in early Latin in its etymological sense, *to send away* (*a, mitto*). This original meaning weakened
to *let get away* (unintentionally), i.e. *to lose*, its regular meaning in
classical Latin and one not unusual even in Plautus, e.g. lines 23,
143, etc.

38. illic: for *ille*, see Introd. § 87 (*b*). For the *c*, compare the
c in *hic* and see note on *hisce*, 35.

39. huius: *huĭus*; see Introd. § 79.   **illic**: this is probably to
be pronounced here as a monosyllable *illc;* see Introd. § 83, and App.
illius: *illĭus*.   **fert imaginem**: *is disguised as;* literally, *bears the
likeness*.

40. hic: regularly short in early Latin.   **expediet**: *will set on
foot, work out; expedire* literally meaning *to get the feet out* (*ex, pes*).

42. eodem : with synizesis, *ēŏdem*.   **pacto** : *stroke*.   **suom** : emphasized by its position (see Introd. § 99) to indicate the unexpected result of their scheme.

43. reducem . . . faciet : *will restore;* the expression differs from *reducere* in bringing into greater prominence the resulting state.

44. inprudens : *unawares*, i.e. without realizing that he was doing so; *inprudens* (*inprovidens*) literally means *unforeseeing*.

45. insciens : for the classical *inscius*.   **quis** : *a person, many a one*.   **prudens** : *intentionally*, though *prudens* was felt by the Romans as an adjective, attributing a characteristic.

46. sua sibi : the juxtaposition produces emphasis ; see Introd. § 99.

48. de sua sententia : *by their own wits*, a special application of the general idea in *sententia*, viz. *way of thinking*.

49. ad : for the usual *apud;* cf. 699 ; *Cas.* 192, *ad mulieres; Stich.* 439, *ad Sagarinum; Poen.* 726, *ad praetorem;* Ter. *Heaut.* 979, *ad sororem; Andr.* 728, *ad erum;* Cic. *ad Att.* X. 16. 1, *ad me; pro Lig.* 10. 30, *ad parentem;* Liv. VII. 7, *ad bellum*.

51. homunculi quanti sunt : *poor weak mortals — what insignificant things they are!* Notice the force of the position of *homunculi* (see Introd. § 99), and the force of the diminutive form.   **quanti** : though *quantus* is commonly translated by *how great*, it strictly refers merely to size in general.   Its meaning therefore covers the whole range of ideas between *how very small* and *how very great*, including both of these extremes.   **quom** : always thus spelled till after Plautus and Terence.   The form *cum* began to be used toward the end of the republican period, but *quum* is not found till five and a half centuries later.   **recogito** : the *re-* seems to imply a return to previous thoughts.

52. res : *plot*, but with a play on the other meaning of *res*, viz. *reality* as contrasted with fiction.   **res . . . nobis, uobis fabula** : i.e. this *res* (*plot*) will now be acted by us — *res* (*reality*), did I say ? Yes, a *res* (*reality*) indeed for us actors, but for you a *fabula* (*a mere play, an entertaining fiction*).   **nobis** : felt as a dative of agent with *agetur* and at the same time a dative of interest (reference) corresponding to the following *uobis*.   The " dative of agent " is only a dative of interest specialized in its application.   In *agetur nobis*, the only idea, strictly speaking, expressed by the dative is that of interest in the act of *agetur*.   When the context, as here, shows that the particular interest felt by the persons referred to in *nobis* is that of the performers of the act, then *nobis* may be translated *by us*.   **fabula** : (from *fari*) first meant *talk* about something, *a story;* then a special kind of story, viz. *a drama;* sometimes *mere talk, fiction.* Here two meanings are in mind : (1) *a drama* with reference to *agetur nobis;* (2) *a fiction* in contrast with *res (reality).*

53. uos quod monitos uoluerim : *which I have wanted you advised of.* The subjunctive *uoluerim* is due to the fact that it stands in a clause of characteristic. It is not a subjunctive of "contingent futurity," meaning *I should like.* See App. **uos quod** : A. & G. 238. *b* ; B. 178. 1. *d* ; G.-L. 333. 1 ; H. 412. **monitos** : *monere* starts with the idea *to bring to the mind;* according to the character of what is thus brought to the mind, the verb may be translated by *inform, advise, warn.* For a transition from the idea of "advise" to that of "inform," cf. "advise of" (in the sense of "inform"), where the idea of giving advice is no longer present.

54. operam dare : see note on 6.

55. pertractate : *in the ordinary hackneyed manner, pertractus* meaning literally *much (thoroughly) handled. Pertractate* is elsewhere used only in a good sense, *elaborately,* etc. See App.

56. uorsus : frequent in early Latin for *uersus;* cf. *uoster* for *uester, uortex* for *uertex,* etc. **immemorabiles** : *not to be repeated.* Adjectives in *-bilis* commonly denote capacity or ability in a passive sense, but "can not be" easily merges into "ought not to be," and this latter idea is the predominant one here in *immemorabiles.* Cf. our phrase "not to be avoided," which may mean : (1) "cannot be avoided"; (2) "ought not to be avoided."

57-58. leno, meretrix, miles gloriosus : stock characters in the plays of Plautus.

58. ne uereamini : Sonnenschein compares the words of Bottom (*Midsummer Night's Dream,* Act III. Scene 1) : —

"Fair ladies, I would entreat you not to fear . . . if you think I come hither as a lion, it were pity of my life," etc.

60. fŏrĭs fĭllic : for the shortening of the *-ĭs,* see Introd. § 84.

61. paene iniquomst : *(that we should all of a sudden attempt to act a tragedy,* etc.) *is hardly a fair thing to ask* (and therefore of course you will not expect it). Cf. *longum est, it's a long story* (and so I will not trouble you with it). In English one would be more likely to say "it would be hardly fair," "it would be a long story," but one must not suppose that the Romans felt *iniquomst* and *longum est* as equivalent to *iniquom sit* and *longum sit.* The indicative *est* in such phrases was felt to have the ordinary meaning of that mood. In the few cases like *si alia memorem . . . , morast* (906), i.e. *forthwith time is lost,* the indicative is purely rhetorical, and may be compared with such English uses as "If you *should do* that, I *am forthwith ruined*" (instead of "I *should be ruined*").   **comico choragio**: *with an equipment intended only for comedy.*

62. desubito: similar in make-up to the English "of a sudden." Cf. *derepente* for the classical *repente.*   **tragoediam**: another Roman allusion (see note on 34), viz. to the *fabula praetexta*, a type of tragedy that was purely Roman in character.   No other type of tragedy, either Greek or Roman, ever represented battles upon the stage.   See Hor. *Ep.* II. 1. 189 ff., and Cic. *ad fam.* VII. 1. 2.

63. litis contrahat: *let him get up a quarrel*, i.e. with me, by disturbing the performance.

64. ualentiorem nactus aduorsarium: these words are the all-important ones (hence the position before *si;* see Introd. § 99), containing the point of the good-natured threat.   The *aduorsarium* is the speaker himself, and the meaning is: *If the fellow finds me too much for him, I'll show him a fight that will not be good for him.* **aduorsarium**: for this spelling, see note on 56.

65. inspectet: this word is commonly used of a passive observer, and so here adds to the humor of the picture: the speaker proposes to "do him up" so promptly that the other will have no chance to take part in the fight further than to see how it is done.   All this is of course good-natured raillery, calculated to put the spectators in good spirits.

66. I.e. he will never want to see another.

67. iudices iustissumi: *kind critics* (Lindsay).   For the spelling in *iustissumi*, see note on *optumum* in 10.

67-68. Notice the effective chiasmus in these two verses.

68. duelli... duellatores: for the later *belli, bellatores; duonorum* is found in early Latin for *bonorum, Duellona* for *Bellona, duis* for *bis*, etc.; *bellum (duellum)* comes from *duo*, and indicates a state of "twoness," i.e. lack of unity; cf. German *Zwist* from *zwei*.   **optumi**: for the spelling, see note on 10.

ACT I.   SCENE 1.

69. Scorto: for the construction, see A. and G. 231. *b;* B. 190. 1; G.-L. 349. Rem. 5; H. 430. 1.

70. eo: *for the following reason; eo* here is to be pronounced $\widehat{eo}$. **inuocatus**: a play is intended upon the two meanings of this word, which is to be understood in the sense of *uninvited* (*in + uocatus*), with reference to the parasite, and in that of *called upon, implored* (participle of *inuocare*), with reference to the *scortum*.

71. absurde dictum: i.e. that it is a poor attempt at jesting, without any point.   **derisores**: *my brother jesters*, i.e. those who, like himself, got a living by their jesting.

72. recte (sc. *dictum*): *right to the point.*   **scortum**: notice the position of this word (see Introd. § 99): *it is his scortum that the lover calls upon — his scortum, I repeat.* See App.

73. talos quom iacit: playing with dice was a favorite pastime among both Greeks and Romans. The lover is here represented as calling upon his mistress instead of upon a deity to bring him a lucky throw. For the two kinds of dice, see dictionaries under *tali* (ἀστράγαλοι) and *tesserae* (κύβοι).   **scortum**: an effective repetition; see the note on 72 ; see also App.

74. inuocatum: still playing upon the two meanings of the word. This verse is incomplete. See App.

75. planius: sc. *inuocati sumus.*

76. Parasites are constantly complaining of the " cold, cold world," where invitations to dinner are so very few.

77 ff. See App.

78. ubi res prolatae sunt: *when business is suspended* (*carried forward*). Public business was suspended during the public games, during the heat of summer and on certain other special occasions.

80. quasi: in the sense of *sicut*.   **caletur**: for the classical *calet*.

81. suo sibi: see note on 5.   **uiuont**: for the later *uiuunt;* see Introd. § 86 (*a*). The third person plural in early times had *-ont* for the later *-unt*, e.g. *cosentiont* (*C.I.L.* I. 32), *sont* (*C.I.L.* I. 1166). Wherever this early *-ont* followed *u* (either vowel or consonantal) the original *o* was retained till Augustan times and in many cases till even later. Thus, long after such forms as *consentiont* and *sont* became *consentiunt* and *sunt*, such forms as *relinquont, sequontur* continued to be used.   **ros si non cadit**: on the place best adapted to snails, Varro (*de re rust.* III. 17) says: *locus est melior quem et non coquit sol et tangit ros*, etc.

83. in ŏccúlto: for the shortening, see Introd. § 84.   **miseri**: *poor fellows.* The force of the position of this word should be brought out in translating ; see Introd. § 99.   **uictitant**: the force of the frequentative seems to be *keep living along.*

84. rurant: specially coined, apparently, to gain assonance with *ruri;* the usual word would be *rusticantur.*   **homines quos ligur-**

riant : *men for them to feed upon*, not the *men whom they feed upon*, an idea which would call for the indicative.

85. uenatici (sc. *canes*): i.e., because they are always lean and hungry. See App.

86. redierunt: sc. *res*.   **molossici**: a choice breed of hounds from Epirus, greatly prized as watch and shepherd dogs and as household pets, corresponding in some respects to our Newfoundlands or St. Bernards ; they were large and proverbially ravenous.   **molossici, odiosici, . . . incommodestici**: humorously formed from *molossus*, *odiosus*, and *incommodus*, to correspond with *uenatici*, as if indicating other breeds. Lindsay brings out the coloring by translating the last two words by *dear-hounds* and *bore-hounds*, though the clever pun is a touch not found in the Latin.

87. multum: *very;* such adverbs formed in their origin an accusative construction, perhaps akin to the accusative of extent, and meaning *to a high degree, to a great extent;* cf. the similar English use of "much" in "much amused," etc.

88. hic: i.e. at Calydon.   **nisi qui**: *unless any*.   **colaphos**: *cuffs*. Plautus himself wrote *colapos*. There were originally no aspirates in Latin, the Greek φ, χ, and θ being represented in transcriptions from that language by *p, c*, and *t ; ph, th*, and *ch* did not begin to be used till about 100 B.C. This is clearly shown in early Latin inscriptions. See the pun *Thalem . . . talento* in 274 and note thereon. **perpeti**: the *per* seems to add the idea of *to the end*, implying that the "cuffs" might always be expected.

89. aulas: the early form of *olla ;* cf. *plaustrum, Claudius* for *plostrum, Clodius*.

90. uel: *even*, to be understood not merely with *extra portam*, but with all that follows ; he may even have to work for a living (for aught anybody cares).   **ïre** : see Introd. § 84. See App. **portam trigeminam** : another purely Roman allusion ; see note on *quaestoribus*, 34, which contrasts strangely with *Aetolia haec est* in 94. The *porta trigemina* (so called from its three archways) was a gate situated between the Tiber and the Aventine Hill and opening into the road to Ostia. The point of the present passage is probably that day-laborers here found plenty of work in handling grain and other imports.   **ad saccum** : *saccus* is a general word for bag, and here probably refers to the bags of grain, the carrying of which would form one of the principal occupations of the laborers engaged *extra portam trigeminam*. One is tempted to understand it as referring to a beggar's wallet (cf. *Trin.* 423), but there is no parallel for *saccus* in this sense; when *saccus* means *money-bag*, it stands for wealth instead of beggary. **licet**: i.e. he may take to day-labor.

91. mihi ne: note the emphatic position of *mihi* (see Introd. § 99).

92. meus: *meûs*. **rex**: *patron*, as often; cf. 825; *Asin.* 919; *Stich.* 454; Ter. *Phorm.* 338, etc.; βασιλεύς is similarly used in Greek comedy. **est potitus hostium**: *fell into the hands of the enemy;* literally, *was brought into the power of the enemy*, the genitive depending upon the idea of *potestas* (or some similar substantive) implied in the verb. *Est potitus hostium* is merely the passive form of the construction seen in *Amph.* 178, *eum potiuit pater Seruitutis, the father brought him into the power of Seruitus* (i.e. reduced him to slavery), which would in the passive have been *is potitus est a patre Seruitutis;* cf. *Capt.* 144, 762; *Epid.* 562, *hostium est potita;* Lucr. IV. 766.

93. ita: i.e. with such deplorable results. See App.

94. illic: probably this should be pronounced *illc;* see note on 39. **capt(us)**: the final syllable should probably be elided before the following vowel, as Plautus does not commonly allow either short syllable of a resolved long to end a word of more than one syllable. See App.; also notes on 466, 532, and App. thereon. **in Alide**: an explanation of *illic*.

96. quae aedes: the antecedent *aedes*, which would be in apposition with the substantive implied in *hic*, is here (as often) drawn into the relative clause, *which house* for *a house which*. **lamentariae**: occurs only here.

98. nunc: the sentence begun in 92 (*postquam meus rex*, etc.) is left unfinished. This is probably not due so much to the poet's carelessness as to an attempt to imitate the style of daily conversation. **hīc**: apparently an early instance of long *i* in this word; it is regularly short in Plautus. See App. **occepit**: an early compound replaced in classical times by *incipio*.

99. inhonestum: slave dealers were, as a class, despised. Very respectable Romans, however (e.g. Cato the Elder), seem sometimes to have speculated in slaves; see Plut. *Cato Maior*, 21.

100. si queat: see note on 28.

101. qui mutet: see note on 28.

102-107. See App.

102. quod quidem ego nimis quam cupio: notice the emphatic touches at every point, the *quidem* (underscoring the *quod*), the *ego*, the *nimis quam* (indicating excess), *cupio* (of passionate longing): *and this is what I at any rate am mighty anxious to have him accom-*

plish.   **nimis quam cupio** : seems to be a fusion of two expressions,
nimis cupio and *quam cupio* (*how I long*).   Perhaps, however, *quam*
is to be regarded as modifying *nimis*, in which case *nimis quam* would
mean *how exceedingly;* cf. *Truc.* 469, *nimis quam paucae; Most.* 1123,
nimis quam catus. This verse is incomplete metrically ; see App.

103. recipit : *get back ;* in colloquial language, the present is
sometimes loosely used where strict accuracy would require the future
or future-perfect.   **nil est quo me recipiam** : *there's no way for me
to get back,* literally, *there is nothing to which* (*whither*) *I may betake
myself. Quo me recipiam* is a volitive characterizing clause. See
note on 12.

104. This verse can not be read metrically and is probably corrupt.
iuuentutis : *from the young men.*   **sese** (emphatic for *se*): *no
one but themselves.*   **omnis** : in early Latin the nominative plural
of *i*-stems often ends, as the accusative regularly does, in *-īs.* Later,
-es is the only form of the nominative ; even in the accusative, the *-es*
of consonant stems gradually encroaches upon the original *-is,* and by
the close of the Augustan period has driven it out almost entirely,
the principal exception after that time being *omnīs.*

105. ill(e) demum : *but there's a young man who ;* literally, *he at
length,* etc. *Demum* is often best translated by laying emphasis upon
the word it immediately follows, which is commonly a pronoun or an
adverb. The *e* of *ille* was probably silent in such cases ; see Introd.
§ 77.   **antiquis** : *good old ; antiquis* commonly refers to something that has long since passed away.

106. quoĭus : *quoius* became *cuius* about the beginning of the
Ciceronian period. *Quoi* seems to have been retained till much later,
to avoid confusion between *cui* and *qui* (see Quintil. I. 7. 27). See
Introd. § 86 (*b*).   **uoltum** : see note on 8.   **gratiis** : *for nothing,
unrewarded; gratiis* was originally an ablative of cause, meaning *out
of kindness or favor,* i.e. *without reward,* in which sense it came to be
felt as an adverb (sometimes, though not in Plautus or Terence, contracted to *gratis;* cf. *dis* for *diis*).

107. condigne . . . eius moratus moribus : *endowed with the
same worthy character as he,* literally, *very* (*con-*) *worthily characterized by his* (i.e. the young man's) *character; eius* is probably felt as
modifying both *pater* and *moribus;* when a word is thus used to
modify two words, its normal position is, as here, between the two
words.

109. und(e): for the silent *e,* see Introd. § 77.   **saturitate**:
with gorging.   **saepe ego** : *many a time I* (*too*), the emphatic *ego*

implying vain regret for the "good old days."   **ebrius**: the
saturitate (from *satur, sated with food*), occupying the first place in
the clause (see Introd. § 99), has already done justice to the memories
of the good things he had to eat ; at an equally emphatic place in the
sentence, *ebrius* lingers over memories of the all-too-tempting drinks.
The dependence of *saturitate* upon *ebrius* is incongruous, and for that
reason humorous ; his condition at such times was the result of both
food and drink, and he wished to give full credit to the merits of each.

ACT I.   SCENE 2.

For the general make-up of Hegio and Ergasilus, see p. 63.

110. Notice the anapaestic word in the second foot — a comparatively rare phenomenon in the second foot of an iambic senarius ; cf.
Pers. III. 1; *Pseud.* III. 2. 19 ; *Merc.* IV. 3. 29 ; etc.   **sis**: *si uis;*
cf. *sultis* for *si uoltis* (*uultis*) in 456.   **tu**: emphatic: *you, I mean,*
riveting the attention of the person addressed and fixing the responsi-
bility.   **istos**: *those in your charge;* the accusative by attraction
(cf. *hos* in 1).

111. de quaestoribus: see note on 34.   See App.

112. his: see App.   **indito**: see note on 11.   **singularias**:
the use of *iuncti* instead of *uincti*, in 113, shows that the two captives
were bound together, and makes it probable that *singularias* means
separate, i.e. *one for each*, instead of the heavier (*maiores*) chains
which were used for the two together.   This would allow the captives
greater freedom of movement, and the order would be in harmony with
that in the next line.   This word seems extremely rare in any sense.

113. For the punctuation, see App.   **sunt iuncti**: *sunt* alone is
the verb, *iuncti* expressing the state in which they are.

114. si . . . si: for the later *siue . . . siue;* cf. *si . . . siue* in *Trin.*
183.   **foris**: *outside;* originally an ablative of place where, to which
corresponded *foras* (*forth out of doors*), as an accusative of end of
motion.

115. uti: for the later *ut;* a reminiscence of the earlier form is
found in *utinam.*   **uti adseruentur**: *ut* seems sometimes to introduce a jussive subjunctive, just as it often does an optative; cf. 794 ;
Trin. 349; *Curc.* 257 ; *operam ut det.*   Such subjunctives are commonly
explained by assuming the ellipsis of *uide*, or some similar expression,
but such an assumption often seems unnatural.

116. liber captiuos auis ferae consimilis: (chiasmus) *a captive
free is,* etc., i.e. he is away in a twinkling and you can never catch

him again.   **consimilis**: *similis* takes the genitive in early Latin, the dative (commonly) in post-Augustan Latin. The intervening period is one of transition, in which both the genitive and the dative are frequent.

117. **semel**: emphatic position.

118. postilla: *after that*, formed like *postea*, and differing from it in meaning, as *ille* differs from *is*.   **possis**: *you would never be able*, i.e. no matter how much you should try; "you can" would be *potes*.

120. uidere: i.e. *uideris*.   **ita**: equivalent to *liber lubentius esse quam seruire*, depending upon *uidere*, referring to the preceding verbs in 118–119.   **non uidere ita tu quidem**: the position of *tu* with its intensifying *quidem* indicates an impatient, spiteful tone. Hegio says that the *lorarius* does not act as though *he* cared about being free; if he did, he would try to be a better slave. Slaves were sometimes manumitted from motives of kindness or gratitude; sometimes they purchased their freedom from what they had saved (*peculium*) out of their allowance.

120–121. See App.

121. quod dem: (*anything*) *for me to give*, literally, (*anything*) *which I may give*, a volitive characterizing clause (see note on 12). **mene**: *-ne* in early, as in classical, Latin is non-committal. Sometimes the answer "yes" is expected, sometimes, as here and in 121, the answer "no," but in neither case is the answer suggested by the form of the question, but rather by external circumstances. In such cases the use of *-ne*, instead of *nonne* or *num*, produces a certain rhetorical effect, the implication being that the answer may safely be left to be inferred. Cf. "Do I, or do I not, look like an honest man?" Sometimes *necne* is actually added, as in 713, *emitteresne necne?* See App.   **uis dem**: the subjunctive in such cases probably originated in a deliberative question; *uis? dem?* In the course of time *dem* came to be looked upon as depending upon *uis*. The next step would be the insertion of a word that would show this dependence, e.g. *uis ut dem?* but this use of *ut* always remained rare.   The play of words in this line should be noticed: *if I have nothing (else) to give (for my freedom), do you want me to give you — the slip myself?* With the expression *me dem in pedes*, cf. *me contuli in pedes* (*Bacch.* 374), *se in pedes conicere* (Ter. *Phorm.* 190), *in uiam se dare* (Cic. *ad fam.* XIV. 12), and the English expression "take to one's heels."

122. erit extemplo: the emphatic position chosen for *erit* heightens the contrast with the *non est* of the preceding verse and intensifies the threatening tone: *there soon will be something that I'll give to you.*

quod dem tibi: a predicating characterizing clause referring to the future (see note on 12); notice the emphatic position of *tibi* (see the translation given above, and Introd. § 99).

123. me: the position of *me*, coming between *auis* and *ferae*, attracts attention (see Introd. § 99), (*instead of one of these captives*) I'*ll be the one to make myself like the wild bird you talk about* (viz. in 116).

124. ita ut dicis: i.e. very well, then — I'll treat you accordingly; I'll cage you.   **faxis**: archaic for *feceris*.   **dabo**: *will put;* there were apparently two distinct verbs with the form *do* (infinitive, *dare*), one cognate with δίδωμι and meaning *to give*, the other cognate with τίθημι and meaning *to put*. The two verbs seem to have been sometimes confused even by the Romans, but instances of the latter verb seem to occur, especially in compounds: e.g. here; *Capt.* 797, *ad terram dabo;* Ter. *And.* 1. 3. 9, *praecipitem me in pistrinum dabit;* such expressions as *in fugam dare, aliquem in uincula dare*, etc., and in the compounds *abdo, to put away; condo, to put together.*

125. cura atque abi: *hysteron proteron;* we should expect *abi atque cura, go and attend to*, instead of *cura atque abi.*

127. uisam ne: I'*ll go see, lest*, the *ne*-clause depending upon the implied idea of fear; cf. *Aul.* 39, *aurum inspicere uolt ne subreptum siet; Pers.* 77, *uisam nequis obreptauerit.*   **quippiam turbauerint**: *have made any disturbance*, the *quippiam* to be taken as the inner object. Cf. notes on *nil* in 16 and 32.

128. īnd(e) mḕ: for the pronunciation and scansion of *inde* and certain other particles in such cases, see Introd. § 77.

129. aegrest: *it pains me;* literally, *it is with annoyance; male* and *bene* are other adverbs frequently used as modifiers of *esse;* cf. 273, 639, 701, 706, 754, and such English expressions as "it is *well*" (though "well" is here sometimes regarded as an adjective), "it is *with difficulty*."   **facere quaestum carcerarium**: *is following the jailer's trade; facere* is frequently used of following a profession; e.g. *carnuficinam facere* (132), *facere piraticam* (Cic. *post red. in sen.* 5), *facere mercaturas* (Cic. *ad Quint. fr.* III. 1. 2), etc.

130. gnati miseriam: *sorrow for his son*, the genitive being objective; for the form of *gnati*, see note on 19.   **miserum senem**: in an emphatic position (see Introd. § 99), taking up again, as a sort of afterthought, the preceding *hunc: poor old fellow*, though this translation misses the echo of *miseriam* still sounding in *miserum.*

131. huc conciliari: *conciliare*, originally meaning *to bring together* two or more things, came to be used, as here, in the sense *to bring* (*one thing*) *to* (*another*, *or to a place*). See note on *reconciliare* in 33.

132. uel: *even.*

133. quĭs hĭc lóquitur: for the shortening, see Introd. § 84.

**133-134. tuo maerore maceror, macesco, consenesco et ta-
besco**: notice the alliteration and assonance, producing somewhat the
same effect as: *it is I, who, at thy sorrow, suffer, sadden, decline, and
pine.*

134. et: here adding the last of a series, a rare use of *et*, but one
found in *Pseud.* 44; *Curc.* 37; 283; *Trin.* 273, and elsewhere.

135. ossa atque pellis: where we say *skin and bones.*

136-137. See App.

137. foris: *away from home*, has an emphatic position (see Introd.
§ 99) contrasting strongly with the *domi;* what he gets at home doesn't
go far, and it costs something, but the little bit that he sponges from
others — that's the taste that does him good.   See note on 114.

138. salue: *greetings to you;* the expression is, like our "good
morning" and "good afternoon," used either at meeting or at parting.

139. ego illum: i.e. *I* of all men, *him* my best friend.   **egone**:
for the non-committal force of *-ne* see note on 121.   **non fleam**: a
rhetorical question of obligation or propriety, *should I not weep for?*
equivalent to the statement *surely I ought to weep for* (see note on 208).
There is no such thing in Latin as a negative question of deliberation,
corresponding to μή with the subjunctive in Greek, though such a use
is commonly recognized in Latin grammars. See App.   **defleam**:
weep my eyes out for.

140. semper sensi: in an emphatic position, *always did feel.*

142. tum denique : *then and not till then.*   **intellegimus** :
understand, i.e. *appreciate.*

144. tuos: *tŭōs.*   **potitust**: see note on *captust* in Argumentum, 1.   **hostium**: see note on 92.

145. expertus quanti fuerit : serves the purpose of an adverb
modifying *desidero: with a full sense of what I have lost;* literally, *it
is after finding out how much he was to me (that I am now missing
him).*   **quanti**: A. & G. 252. *a*; B. 203. 3; G.-L. 380; H. 448. 1.
desidero : commonly used of a desire for something once possessed,
but possessed no longer, *miss.*

146. alienus: in emphatic position, *mere stranger (outsider) as
you are.*   **quom eius**: to be read *qu(om) eius.*   **quom . . . feras**:
a rare construction in Plautus, who, even in causal and adversative
clauses, regularly uses the indicative with *quom.* The subjunctive
constructions with *quom* (*cum*) represent a comparatively late growth
(the indicative being the rule even in Terence), due to the influence of

G

the subjunctive *qui*-clauses, *quom* itself being a relative (from the same root as *qui*) with some form of *tempus* understood as its antecedent. For *quom* with the indicative, see *Cist.* 115, *sine trahi, quom egomet trahor; Amph.* 753, *tu quoque etiam insanis, quom id me interrogas;* 1134, *quom sum Iuppiter; Capt.* 216, 280, 423, etc. Even *praesertim quom* takes the indicative, e.g. *Asin.* 80. The subjunctive in the present passage may be due to the dependence of the *quom*-clause upon an infinitive.

147. par : originally *equal*, then *equal to the requirements of the case*, i.e. *suitable, proper, natural* (as here).   **quoi** : see note on 106.

148. aha, Hegio : for the non-elision, see Introd. § 74, and cf. 85 f. See App.

149. dixis . . . induxis : for the more common *dixeris, induxeris* (see note on 124). Such archaic subjunctive forms are used only with future meanings ; they never refer to the past as forms like *dixeris, induxeris*, etc., frequently do (e.g. in result clauses). **animum induxis** : the two words are felt as constituting a single verbal conception (*bring the mind to*, i.e. *resolve upon, or think*) and as such may take a direct object ; here *istuc* is the object of *animum induxis*, as well as of *dixis*. Cf. *animum aduertere* and *animum attendere*, expressions which were similarly used with a direct object and the former of which was ultimately fused into a single word, *animaduertere*.   **tuom** : see note on *seruos* in 8.

151. malum : in an emphatic position ; one might be expected to interest himself in a friend's prosperity, but his *misfortune* — you stand by him *even in that*.   **quom** : commonly interpreted as causal, in which use it regularly takes the indicative in Plautus (see note on 146). It is possible, however, that *quom* is here equivalent to an explicative *quod, that, the fact that*. This use was entirely distinct, in both origin and development, from the temporal or causal *quom* (*cum*) and was always associated with the indicative. It is very common in early Latin and is not infrequent in classical times, especially after such expressions as *gratulor, gratias ago*, etc. See App. If the *quom* in this passage is explicative, the *quom*-clause will here be the direct object of *laudo* : *I commend your making your friend's misfortune your own*. The common interpretation makes it necessary to supply an object for *laudo*.

152–167. See App.

152. nunc : i.e. his present plans for recovering his son promise success.   **eheu** : for the hiatus, see Introd. § 85 f. Here, again, *h* prevents elision.   **huic** : referring to himself, just as a Southern

negress frequently refers to herself as "dis po' chile."   **dolet** :
is the trouble with.

153. quia : explicative, *the fact that*, the clause being in apposition with *illud ;* this use of *quia* is common in Plautus, though in
classical times it gave place to *quod* and *cum* (see latter part of note
on *quom* in 151); cf. 203, *nos pudet quia . . .* ; *Epid.* 107, *idne pudet
te quia . . .* ; *Cas.* 378, *iniquomst quia . . .* ; *Mil.* 1210, *istuc acer-
bumst quia . . .* ; etc., etc.   In their origin, *quod* and *quia* alike
probably represent some accusative construction, *quod* being the
accusative neuter singular of a relative *o*-stem, and *quia* the accusative neuter plural of a relative *i*-stem ; cf. the ablative *qui* and the
dative and ablative *quibus* from the same stem, by the side of the
ablative *quo* and the dative and ablative *quīs* from the *o*-stem.   **remissus est edendi exercitus** : the assembly of the Roman people
known as the *comitia centuriata*, though it early acquired political
power, was originally a military organization ; the expression for
assembling this organization was *exercitum imperare*, and that for
dismissing it was *exercitum remittere*.   The expression is here trans-
ferred to companies of banqueters.   So long as Philopolemus was
present, there was some one to muster the troops, i.e. some one
to give dinner parties ; in his absence, the banqueting army has
disbanded.

154. nullum : rarely used as a substantive in good classical prose,
except in the genitive and ablative, where it regularly supplants
neminis and *nemine.*

155. dixti : for *dixisti ;* cf. *dixem* (*dixissem*), *dixe* (*dixisse*), *uixe*
(*uixisse*), *uixem* (*uixissem*), *misti* (*misisti*), *scripsti* (*scripsisti*),
sumpsti (*sumpsisti*), *duxti* (*duxisti*), *duxe* (*duxisse*), *traxe* (*traxisse*),
etc.   Such shorter forms are very common in the early dramatists
and are not uncommon in later poets.   There is a tendency among
recent authorities to regard them as having a different origin from the
full forms, but it may be that they are merely the result of syncope
(see Lindsay, *The Latin Language*, p. 464).

156. fugitant : this frequentative form is almost entirely confined
to comedy ; it here indicates eagerness and unceremonious haste
(*hurry away from*), and its emphatic position adds to the humor.
They all know too well what it meant to give Ergasilus his dinner.
prouinciam : *office, duty.*

157. quod obtigerat, etc. : *whatever of it* (i.e. of the *prouincia*)
had fallen to their lot after the capture of your Philopolemus.   With
this use of *quod*, cf. such passages as Liv. 31. 4. 2, *agro Samniti*

Apuloque, quod eius publicum populi Romani esset; 38. 23. 10 ; 38.
54. 3, and often ; cf. also *quantum* in *Phorm.* 854, *O omnium, quantumst qui uiuont, homo hominum ornatissume.* See App. Notice the
proceleusmatic in this verse.

160. Ergasilus, still keeping up the figure of soldiers preparing
for battle, proceeds to enumerate the different classes of troops.
Pistorensibus : *the Mill-villers,* playing upon the words *pistor*
(*miller,* in the time of Plautus) and *Pistoriensis* (an inhabitant of
Pistorium, a town in Etruria).

162. Paniceis : *the Bread-villers,* playing upon *panis* (*bread*)
and perhaps *Panna* (a town in Samnium, mentioned by Strabo).
Placentinis : *the Cake-villers,* playing upon *placenta* (*cake*) and
Placentia (a town in Gallia Cispadana).

163. Turdetanis : *the Thrush-villers,* playing upon *turdus* (*thrush*)
and *Turdetani* (a people of Spain). For allusions to the thrush as a
great delicacy, see Mart. XIII. 5 ; Hor. *Ep.* I. 15. 40.   **Ficedulen-
sibus** : *the Little Fig-eat-onians,* playing upon *ficedula* (literally, *the
little fig-eater* [from *ficus, fig, edo, to eat,* and the diminutive suffix
-ula], the name of another bird that was considered a great delicacy
for the table; cf. Juv. XIV. 9 ; Mart. XIII. 5 ; Gell. XV. 8) and probably some town of which the identity is uncertain.

164. iam : originally used, in the sense of *already,* to contrast a
time, whether past, present, or future, with a preceding time ; from
indicating transition in point of time, it came to be used, as here,
in making a transition from one subject to another : *then again.*
maritumi omnes milites : *all the marines,* i.e. the fishmongers. For
maritumi instead of *maritimi,* see note on *optumi* in 68.   **opus
sunt** : notice the change in construction, *opus* here being a predicate
nominative : they *are a necessity.*

165. ut saepe . . . latent : not *how often they lie hidden !* which
would be *quam saepe,* etc., but *how they often lie hidden, ut* being an
adverb of manner rather than degree.   **saepe** : note the emphatic
position.

166. hic . . . priuatus : notice the force of position : *this man
here (for instance) — what a general he is, though in citizen's dress.*

167. modo, *only,* colloquially used to strengthen imperatives.
illum : emphatic position, *as regards that boy of mine, I'm sure
I,* etc.

168. in his diebus : *within the next few days; hic* is used of
what is near the speaker in thought, locality, etc. ; in such an expression as this, therefore, it may refer either to the immediate past (e.g.

nocte hac in 127), or, as here, to the immediate future.   **recon-ciliassere**: a form of the future infinitive found in a few verbs of the first conjugation (cf. *aueruncassere, impetrassere, oppugnassere*). The origin of this form is problematical. See note on 33.

169. eccum: i.e. *ecce eum; eam, eos, eas, ea, illum,* etc., are similarly combined into *eccam, eccos,* etc. The accusative seems to be due to the general objective feeling involved in *ecce*, which, with its accusative, is often used without reference to the construction of the rest of the sentence, e.g. Ter. *Phorm.* 484, *eccum ab sua palaestra exit foras;* Plaut. *Mil.* 1281, *nescio quis eccum incedit. Eccum* is commonly used of a person already in sight, but see, in addition to the present passage, 1015; *Am.* 120; *Aul.* 781; *Bacch.* 568.   **eccúm hic**: the initial *h*, as frequently in Plautus, prevents elision, and makes the preceding syllable long. See Introd. § 74, and App.

171. hoc: ablative; see note on *qui* in 28.   **pote**: (sc. *esse*) used here for *posse*. Either *potis* or *pote* may be used in early Latin as nominative or accusative, and as singular or plural.

172. faxint: i.e. *fecerint*; such archaic forms long continued to be used as favorite forms in prayers, just as early forms of expression have preserved themselves in English; e.g. "*Thy* kingdom *come*," "*Thy* will *be done*," etc. The perfect tense in its future uses disregards the progress of the act, and conceives of it as one that is to be promptly and energetically performed and finished (cf. the English "be gone!" instead of "go!"). This tense is accordingly used in prayers only where the speaker is, or pretends to be, stirred with such emotion at the thought of the possible occurrence of the act that he cannot think of the progress of it, but only the prompt accomplishment of it. Formal or indifferent prayers take the present tense. See App.   **quo**: *anywhither*, though the English now uses *anywhere* in this sense.   **foras**: see note on 114.

173. nusquam: sometimes, as here, used in early Latin in the sense of *no whither*, where we should expect *non quoquam;* it is commonly used of rest in, instead of motion toward, a place. Such confusion of meanings is common enough in colloquial language, cf. *intus* usually *within*, but used also in the sense of *from within* (e.g. *Most.* 675); *peregre* may indicate, in Plautus, rest in, motion to, or motion from.   **quod sciam**: *that I know of (so far as I know); sciam* is the subjunctive used in a restrictive clause which itself represents a development from a clause of characteristic.

174. tu: used for emphasis, and to contrast with *id*: *why do you ask that?*   **mist**: i.e. *mi est (mi* for *mihi*).

175. te uocari — ad te: the wit of Ergasilus's words (cf. *facete dictum* in 176) is commonly removed by emendations; see App.

176. sed si . . . potes contentus esse: Hegio is at this point interrupted by Ergasilus, who takes it for granted that the former was about to finish the sentence by inviting him to dinner. Such an invitation is, of course, what Ergasilus has been hinting at.

177. ne . . . modo: *only let it not be.*

178. adsiduo: probably an adverb.　　**delecto:** *regale,* humorous, in connection with the *perpauxillo.*

179-181. See App.

179. age sis: *come now, if you please;* see note on *sis* in 110. **roga emptum:** *propose the terms of the bargain;* literally, *ask* (*me*) *about the bargain;* with this use of *rogare,* cf. the expression *legem rogare, to ask* (*the people*) *about a law,* i.e. *to propose a law for them to vote on.* Ergasilus feels that he is taking an important step — his dinner is at stake; and he wants the contract made with due formality. He is about to give Hegio his company (jests and all), but he proposes to have it understood what he is to get in return. **nisi qui,** etc.: *unless any one shall,* etc. This use of *qui* as an indefinite pronoun occurs only after *si, sin, nisi, siue, ne,* and *num.*　　**meliorem:** modifying *condicionem* (*terms*), which is here drawn into the *quae-* clause.

180. quae . . . placeat: a predicating, characterizing clause referring to the future; see note on 12.　　**mi atque amicis:** it is not a mark of rudeness or impropriety in a Roman to refer to himself first. Persons are regularly mentioned in Latin in their grammatical order, viz. first, second, third, *ego, tu, is* (*ille*).

181. quasi . . . uendam: *as if I were selling;* the " as if " conjunctions in Latin commonly take the construction of contingent-future ("less vivid future," "ideal") protases.　　**fundum:** *an acre of ground* (literally, *a farm*), a translation which makes it possible to preserve the pun in the following verse, *profundum, an acher for grub.*　　**meis:** *meîs.*　　**meis . . . legibus:** emphasized by position and separation (see Introd. § 99), *on conditions to be dictated by myself.*　　**me addicam:** *addicere* is an auctioneer's term for "knocking down" to the highest bidder.

182. profundum: literally, *an abyss;* but see note on 181.

183. si uenturu's: *if you are bound to come,* differing from *uenies* (the future act) in calling attention rather to the present state of mind or the present purpose.　　**temperi:** the locative case of *tempus;* cf. our " in time."　　**em:** *look! see here!* etc., while *hem*

is an expression of surprise, joy, grief, etc., *well! what!* See note on
373.   **iam**: *right away.*

184. **uenare leporem**: Hegio pretends not to understand the
bearing of Ergasilus's words; if the latter has plenty of leisure, he
had better continue his hunt till he finds a dinner worth having.
irim: a word of uncertain meaning; perhaps it is equivalent to *erem*
(from *er*), *a hedgehog: at present (in me) you've got hold of a
hedgehog.*

185. **meus . . . uiam**: *my living travels a rough road.* Ergasilus
replies that he will come *calceatis dentibus,* i.e. *with teeth well-shod
for the journey* (187).

186. **ne postules**: the distinction that has been commonly made
between the perfect and the present tenses in prohibitions — viz. that
the perfect is used when the prohibition is addressed to a definite
person, the present when it is addressed to an indefinite person —
will not hold for any period of the language. The only distinction to
be made is that the perfect is emotional and unceremonious, and indicates that the speaker is (or pretends to be) aroused at thought of the
possible occurrence of the prohibited act; the present is almost exclusively confined to prohibitions of commonplace and unimportant acts.
But in dignified styles, *noli* with the infinitive almost entirely supplants both forms of expression.

187. **tamen**: i.e. though the fare is rough, and I must come with
well-shod teeth, I'll come *in spite of it all;* notice the emphatic position of *tamen* (see Introd. § 99).

188. **sane**: *it is indeed* (i.e. you had better change your mind
before you go too far).   **essitas**: (frequentative of *edo) are you
wont to eat.*

189. **terrestris cenast**: *my dinner consists of the roots of the
earth* (i.e. a humble meal of vegetables, etc.), a translation which
makes it possible to preserve the pun that follows.   **sus terrestris
bestiast**: *a pig is an animal that "roots in the earth."* A pig was
considered a great delicacy. Ergasilus says, in effect, "You can't
fool me by such talk — you refer now to a pig — I'll be on hand."

190. **multis holeribus**: (*no, no! I mean) of many vegetables;*
an ablative of quality, to be understood with *cena.*   **curato aegro-
tos**: *feed sick folks then.* All of this has of course been good-natured
raillery.

191. **numquid uis**: a common formula of leave-taking, *that's all,
is it?* literally, *do you want anything (else)?* Sometimes (e.g. Ter.
Phorm. 151) the fuller formula, *num quid aliud me uis?* is found.

192-193. ratiunculam, quantillum : there is a humorous touch
here that has commonly passed unnoticed. Just before meeting
Ergasilus, Hegio was on the point of going at once to his brother's.
But as soon as he finds that he will have to entertain Ergasilus, he
changes his mind and goes to his bank instead. The diminutives show
how little the balance seems to him, when he reflects upon the appetite of his coming guest.

193. apŭd trapessitam : see Introd. § 84. Perhaps, however,
the *d* was silent (see App.). **trapessitam** : commonly written
trapezitam, but it is probable that the character *z* was not used by
Plautus. This character was perhaps occasionally used at a very
early period (cf. *C. I. L.* I. 14, Cozano, where the letter should, according to Lindsay (see App.), have the ordinary *z*-form ; also Velius
Longus [7, 51 K]) ; but *ss* (medial) and *s* (initial) were commonly
used in its stead. In the time of Cicero, *z* was revived for the more
accurate transliteration of Greek words.

194. ire : where we should expect the future, but a loose use of
tenses is common in colloquial Latin ; cf. the English " said he was
going the next day," instead of " said he would go," etc. **dixeram** : i.e. had said prior to my meeting with Ergasilus ; see Introd.
§ 95. **iuero** : *I'll be off;* the future perfect, instead of the future,
emphasizes the promptness with which the act will be completed ; see
Introd. § 95. This rhetorical use of the tense commonly indicates
emotional or energetic utterance. The more energetic form of expression is sometimes chosen, apparently for metrical convenience, in
cases where the energetic tone will not be inappropriate. See App.

ACT II. SCENE 1.

195. id : anticipating *uos . . . exsequi*, which is in apposition with it.

196. id : we should expect *eam*, but the speaker has in mind the
general conception, rather than the particular word *aerumnam*. **an-
imo | aequo** : for the hiatus, see Introd. § 85. **leui|ōr lăbŏs |** :
for the shortening of the final syllable of *lăbōs*, see Introd. § 84.

197. domĭ : for the shortened -*ĭ*, see Introd. § 84. **fuistis** :
synizesis ; see Introd. § 78.

198. ei . . . morigerari : *to make the best of it;* literally, *to humor
it, to give in to it.*

199. This line is commonly considered corrupt (see App.) As it
stands, it may mean *and by your good behavior to make it easy for
your master also to control you (as well as easier and pleasanter for*

yourselves); literally, *and by your dispositions to make it easy for* (or *in respect to*) *the master's control also.*

201. oculis multa miraclitis: unintelligible; possibly Plautus wrote *multam iram editis, you are manifesting plenty of anger by your eyes.* See App.

202. si ... utare, adiuuat: for some reason not yet understood, a condition in which the subject of the verb is an indefinite *second* person takes the subjunctive, though the apodosis takes the indicative. When the subject is an indefinite *third* person (e.g. *quis*), on the other hand, the protasis takes the indicative.

203. This line offers a good illustration of the two common uses of *at:* (1) to introduce an objection to some one's statement, (2) to introduce the reply to such an objection.   **nos pudet quia:** such passages as *idne pudet te quia* (*Epid.* 107) make it probable that the *quia*-clause is a substantive clause and that *quia* here means *the fact that.* See note on 153.   **cum catenis:** where we should say *in chains;* the Latin expression treats the chains as forming an accompaniment.

204. pigeat. . . nostrum erum: A. & G. 221. *b, c*; B. 209; G.-L. 377; H. 409, III.; 457.

205. solutos sinat: an expression exactly parallel in form to our "let loose," though *esse* is probably to be understood with the Latin; it differs from *solui sinat* in calling attention to the state resulting from the act, rather than to the act itself.   **emerit:** the mood may be due to attraction, or it may be due to the causal-adversative idea involved; the *quos . . . emerit* gives the reason for saying *pigeat* (*it would be vexatious,* etc., <u>*since he has paid money for them*</u>), but it has at the same time an adversative relation to *si solutos sinat* (*if he should let them loose and incur the risk of losing them,* <u>*in spite of the fact that*</u> *they have cost money*). Causal and adversative *qui*-clauses probably originated in the clause of characteristic.

206a. ă: see Introd. § 84.   **scimu(s) nos:** as the last foot must be a pure iambus (Introd. § 39), it is clear that the *s* of *scimus* was slighted in pronunciation.   **nos:** emphatic *we.*

206b. quod est: *what it is;* in Cicero we should expect *quid sit.* The indicative is very frequently found in indirect questions in early Latin. The reason for this may be that they are not as yet far removed from parataxis, — a theory that is supported by the fact that, with comparatively rare exceptions, these indicative indirect questions are such as might actually be interpreted as independent. E.g. Ter. *Phorm.* 358, *uide, auaritia quid facit,* which might be punctuated *uide!* *aua-*

ritia quid facit ! The substantive use of *qui* for *quis* is common in
early Latin and in poetry (cf. 833). *Quod* here is probably a similar
use of the neuter.   **si . . . sinat:** the apodosis to this protasis might
at first thought seem to be *quod est*, in which case the difference of
mood would seem strange. The real apodosis to *si . . . sinat* is, however, merely implied in *quod est* (*what it is our duty that we should do
in case he should*, etc.).

207ᵃ. at: see note on *at* in 203.   **fingitis:** *concoct.*

207ᵇ. quam rem agitis : *what you are driving at.* For the mood,
see note on 206ᵇ.

208. nos fugiamus: *we take to flight ?* The subjunctive is frequently used, as here, merely to echo, as it were, in interrogative form,
a word or a thought that has just been uttered or suggested. *Fugiamus*
is here a sort of indirect quotation of the thought suggested in *fugam*
(207ᵃ). This use is distinct from that in a deliberative question.
quo fugiamus : a rhetorical deliberative question, *whither shall we
flee ?* It is here intended to imply *there is no place to flee to.* The
following varieties of questions should be noted : —

Indicative :

(1) Question of fact, asking about *what is, was, or will be ;* e.g.
quid fecit ? what did he do ?

(2) Question of deliberation, asking about *what course shall be
willed or determined upon ;* e.g. *quid ago ? what shall I do ?* The
indicative in such questions is colloquial, like our "what do I do
next ? " See (5) below.

Subjunctive :

(3) Question of contingent futurity, asking about *what would be ;*
e.g. *quis dubitet ? who would doubt ?*

(4) Question of obligation or propriety, asking about *what ought
to be ;* e.g. *cur gaudeam ? why should I (ought I to) rejoice ?*

(5) Question of deliberation, asking about *what course shall be
willed or determined upon ;* e.g. *quid faciam ? quid fiat ? what shall
I do ? what shall be done ?* One must guard against designating
questions of this type as "dubitative" or "indignant" questions,
as doubt and indignation are quite as characteristic of the other
types above mentioned as they are of this.

Any one of these types may be used as a merely rhetorical question.   **in patriam :** instead of understanding *quo fugiamus ?* in a
rhetorical sense, as it was intended, the *lorarius* treats it as a real

deliberative question, and answers it.   **apage**: indicates indignation, impatience, or the like.   **id**: anticipating *nos imitari*.

209. immo: is always corrective. It sometimes objects to something as altogether wrong, when it may be translated by *not at all*, *on the contrary;* sometimes, while admitting that an assertion is true, it objects to it as not being strong enough and adds something to make it more forcible, when it may mean *yes, but one would rather say*, or the like. This explains the apparently contradictory definitions of dictionaries: *no indeed; yes indeed*. Both definitions represent the same idea differently applied.   **erīt**: notice the long quantity of the *ī*; see Introd. § 82 (*e*).   **dehortor**: this word is commonly dissyllabic (*dehŏrtor*), but it is here trisyllabic, as in *Poen.* 674 (677).

210. exorare: *ex* in composition frequently adds the idea of *successfully;* e.g. *orare*, to implore, *exorare*, to implore successfully, to get by imploring; *pugnare*, to fight, *expugnare*, to fight successfully, to take by fighting; etc.   **quidnam**: differs from *quid*, as *what in the world?* differs from *what?*

211. arbitris: *witnesses;* refers apparently to other slaves that had come out with the *lorarii* from motives of curiosity. *Arbiter* comes from *ad* and *bito* (*beto*), *to go*, and originally meant *one who goes to* a place, i.e. *a by-stander, a witness;* later it became specialized. But see App.

214. breuem orationem, etc.: with emphasis upon *breuem, short be the talk you begin*.   **incipisse**: from *incipisso*, a word used only by Plautus.

215ᵃ. em: *mind you!*   **istuc mihi certum erat**: *that is just what I intended;* literally, *that had been decided by me*. In this expression, *certum* is the perfect passive participle of *cerno;* see note on 492.   **mihi**: the dative here indicates interest, or concern, in the idea *certum erat*, the implication being that in this particular case the interest was manifested *by actually performing the act*. See note on 52.

215ᵇ. istis: *those you see*.   **ambo**: denotes concerted action or feeling, while *uterque* brings into prominence the individual.

216. quom: *that*, introducing a clause in apposition with *hanc rem;* see note on *quom* in 151. The expression *propter hanc rem quom* is then exactly parallel in make-up with the common *propterea quod*.   **quae**: with *eorum* understood as its antecedent.

216–217. quae uolumus nos, copia est — ea facitis nos compotes: *whatever we want, plenty of it is on hand — you let us profit by it;* literally, *you make us partakers of it*. The antecedent of *quae* is *eorum* understood. *Ea* is apparently an early instance of the rare use of the ablative with *compos;* but the line is corrupt. See App.

218. nunciam: probably composed of *nunc* and *iam;* it is, however, trisyllabic, the *i* becoming vocalic as in *quoniam, etiam.* Another view regards *nunciam, etiam,* etc., as made up of *nunce,* *eti (cf. ἔτι), etc., and an adverbial termination -*am.* **si uidetur:** *if you please;* literally, *if it seems (good to you).*

219. arbitri, arbitrari: for the original meaning, here preserved, of *arbiter,* see note on 210; *arbitrari* originally meant *to be an arbiter,* i.e. a witness; then as a witness of a thing would have an opinion regarding the thing, it came to mean *to judge, to think.* The present passage preserves one of the few instances of the original use of this verb.

220. permanet: *leak out;* literally, *trickle through.* Notice the emphatic position.

221. astu: ablative of *astus.* **colas:** *manage.*

222. id: referring to the general idea, without reference to the particular word (*doli*) already used.

225. tamen: i.e. even though the present prospects are good for our successfully carrying out our scheme. **uiso opust:** *there is need of* (our looking out, i.e.) *foresight;* literally, *there is need of it having been looked out (by us),* where *uiso* is of course to be understood as impersonal and as used in the sense of *prouiso.* The neuter of the perfect passive participle is often thus used in the comic poets with *opus est* and *usus est.* It may be translated as though it were a gerund, though it differs from the gerund in substantivizing the conception of the verb in a *perfected passive* form, rather than in a progressing, active form. Cf. the English expression, "There is no need of its being known," where the use of "its" shows that "being known" is practically felt as a substantive, expressing a state resulting from an act of *becoming known.*

227. haud somniculose: cf. our expression, "wide-awake," used in similar connections.

229. nam: (*and you may well hope*) *for.* **tu:** i.e. *I* do not need to tell you.

230. offerre ... uilitati: i.e. am counting my own safety of but little consequence in comparison with yours; literally, *am offering my own head to cheapness.* **meum:** *meūm.*

232. maxima pars ... homines: a sudden change in the form of the sentence. Such changes are common in daily conversation such as this is supposed to be. If the reading here were *homines ... maxima* *pars, maxima pars* might be explained as in partitive apposition with *homines,* but with the reverse order this seems impossible.

233. impetrant: attempted action, *are trying to obtain.*

234. penes sese: *in their own hands.*

236. ut mihi te uolo esse: *how I want you to be to me,* just as I promised you (228) how *I* would be to *you.* For the mood of *uolo,* see note on *quod est* in 206ᵇ.

237. meo patri: emphatic position, *my own father,* i.e. so you must not feel offended that I do so to *you* — my anxiety must be my excuse.

238. ego: *on my part.*   **si te audeam** (sc. *nominare*) : *if I chose (should choose).*   *Audere* is connected with *auidus* and originally referred to *wishing, desiring,* etc.   Cf. *sodes,* i.e. *si audes, if you please.* The transition from the idea of *desiring* to that of *daring* may be easily traced.

239. secundum: *after,* a preposition derived from *sequor.*   **patrem:** *real father.*

240. audio: often thus used to denote impatience, real or pretended, at another's remarks, implying that they are unnecessary. Lindsay translates, *I know, I know.*   **propterea:** anticipating the *ut*-clause.   **te uti:** perhaps, however, Plautus wrote *ut ted,* instead of *uti. Ted* would then be an accusative formed after the analogy of the ablative, which originally ended in *d.* This *d* was dropped at an early date, but perhaps Plautus still retained it in *med, ted, sed.*   **memineris:** viz. that we have exchanged characters.   *Memini* and *odi* were originally true perfects, meaning *I have kept in mind* and *I have conceived hatred for,* ideas which at an early date came to be felt merely as equivalent to *I remember* and *I hate.*   Exactly the same thing has happened in the English use of "I have got," which originally meant "I have obtained" ("have got" being felt as the perfect tense of "get"), but which is now frequently used with exactly the same sense as "I have," "I possess," the notion of the perfect tense having entirely disappeared.

241. obsecro te hoc unum: this use of two accusatives with *obsecro* is rare.

242. animum: *will.*

243. ut qui . . . uelint: in apposition with *animum, that they wish.* The *qui* is merely an intensive particle (originally an ablative or instrumental form), adding here the same force that it adds to *at* in *atqui ;* cf. *Capt.* 553, *et eum morbum mı esse ut qui me opus sit insputarier;* *Men.* 1092 ; *Am.* 705, 776 ; *As.* 930 ; *Aul.* 348 ; and often elsewhere. It seems to have meant, originally, *anyhow*, then, *at any rate*, *at least*, *surely*. See note on 28. **fuisse** : *to be no longer;* literally, *to have been* (as a thing of the past); cf. Verg. *Aen.* II. 325, *fuit Ilium*, *Ilium is no more; Capt.* 516, *fuisse mauelim*, *I should prefer to be dead;* etc. **ess**(e) **nunc** : the final *e* of *esse* was probably silent sometimes, like the final *e* of *nempe*, *quippe*, *ille*, *inde*, *mitte*, etc.; see Introd. § 77, also App.

244. quom . . . imperitabam : an adversative clause, *though*, etc.; for the mood, see note on *quom feras* in 146. See App.

245. te erga : *erga* commonly precedes its case, but exceptions to this rule are found in Plautus and Terence.

246. perque : probably read metrically as monosyllabic *perq;* see App. **quód hŏstica** : cf. *quíd ĕxprobras* in *Trin.* 318. See App.

247. ne . . . secus honore honestes, etc.: i.e. that you continue to *feel* just as much respect for me as hitherto, though the part you play will compel you to *treat* me like a slave. **quom seruibas mihi** : the normal position of words is here inverted merely to give *seruibas* an emphatic position ; the fact that such an inversion in short sentences brings a word (here *mihi*) to the end of the sentence does not necessarily make it emphatic ; see Introd. § 99. Such forms as *seruibas* (for *seruiebas*) are common in early Latin ; e.g. *scibam* for *sciebam*, *audibam* for *audiebam*, etc. For the construction, see note on *quom* in 146.

248. qui fueris : for *quis fueris;* see note on *qui* in 206ᵇ. Notice that in indirect questions which cannot be separated from their context and treated as independent, the subjunctive is the rule in early Latin, as in classical times. **ut . . . ut memineris** : the repetition of the *ut* is for the purpose of getting a new start, as it were, after the intervening clause.

249. istuc : in an emphatic position.

250. inest : in an emphatic position, *there is̲ hope*, etc., the emphasis upon *inest* contrasting with previous doubts and uncertainties. **in hăc** : see Introd. § 84 ; also App.

ACT II. SCENE 2.

251. iam : *directly*, the idea of *already* applied to the future. **his** : i.e. Philocrates and Tyndarus.

252. ubi sunt : the captives had stepped to one side (cf. 218) and were not seen at once.

253. Philocrates now adopts the saucy, happy-go-lucky tone characteristic of slaves. **edepol tibi ne**, etc.: the position itself of *tibi* gives a tone of pertness: *you've taken mighty good care that we shouldn't turn up missing — I see that;* this emphasis upon " that " reproduces the emphasis brought out by the position of the clause *ne . . . essemus,* which would normally follow the word upon which it depends (cf. 255, *cauet ne,* etc.).   **in quaestione**: *in quaestione esse* is used in the sense of *to be missing;* literally, *to be (the one sought) in a search.* Similar expressions are common in Plautus; e.g. *Pers.* 52; *Pseud.* 663; *Mil.* 1279; *Trin.* 278ᵃ; *Cist.* 593; *Cas.* 530.

254. uinclis: such forms, *uinclum, saeclum, periclum,* etc., are the earliest forms and are more common in Plautus than *uinculum, saeculum, periculum.* The parasitic *u* between the *c* and *l* arose from an (unconscious) effort to facilitate the pronunciation.   **circummoeniti** : with *moenire* for the later *munire,* cf. *coerauit* for *curauit* (*C. I. L.* I. 600), *loedos* for *ludos* (*C. I. L.* I. 567), etc. Instead of *oe* in such words, *oi* is frequently found, and both *oi* and *oe* continued to be used in inscriptions even in classical times.

255. The humor from this point on throughout the scene cannot fail to be appreciated by any one who keeps in mind the general situation.

256. cautor captus est: *the catcher* (literally, *the wary one*) *finds himself caught.* One must not mistake *captus est* for a gnomic perfect (aorist), a use of the perfect tense that is first found in the poets of the classical period, who borrowed it from the Greeks. Here *est* alone is the verb, the *captus* being used in the predicate to express the state.

257. an: *an* commonly introduces the second part of a disjunctive question, but in early Latin and even in the poets of the classical period it is frequently used as a simple interrogative. The same use is occasionally found in Livy and later prose.   **ut** : *cur* would be more common after *causa.*

258. sim mercatus : the subjunctive may be due to any one of these causes (or to all combined), viz.: (1) to a desire to represent the *quos*-clause as the indirectly reported thought suggested (by the question) to the minds of the persons addressed ; (2) to a desire to emphasize the causal relation of the *quos*-clause to the clause upon which it depends (see App.); (3) to the fact that it depends upon another subjunctive.

259. tibi . . . uitio uortere: *to lay it up against you;* literally, *to turn it unto you for a fault.*   **quia** : *(the fact) that;* see note on 153.

260. sī ăbĕamus : for the hiatus, see Introd. § 85.   **fuat** : an old form of the present subjunctive used in the sense of *sit;* see Introd. § 88 (*a*).

261. apŭd uos : i.e. in your country.   See note on 193.   **meus** : *mĕus.*

262. ignaui : refers to their having allowed themselves to be taken alive.   **fūimus** : the original length of the *u* is here retained.

263. ex te solo : i.e. without being overheard.

264. quarum rerum : objective genitive, depending upon *falsi-loquom.*

265. quod sciam : see note on 173.   **nescibo** : an old form for *nesciam ;* cf. note on *seruibas* in 247, and the forms *ibo, quibo,* and *nequibo,* found even in classical times.   See App.   **siquid nescibo, id nescium tradam** : Philocrates is indulging in a sly trick of words.   Hegio will understand him to mean, *If there is anything I am ignorant about I'll frankly tell you so;* but there lies in the words also the meaning, *If there is anything I don't know, I'll tell you all about it just the same* (literally, *I'll give it to you, unknown though it be*).   Tyndarus enjoys this bit of fun, as the next words show.

266. est in tostrina : i.e. the fleecing has begun.   The form *tostrina* is for the later *tonstrina;* cf. *cesor* (for *censor*), *Pisaureses* (for *Pisaurenses*), etc., in early inscriptions.   **cultros adtinet** : *is putting the clippers on him;* the change of subject seems strange, but the subject of this verb is easily supplied.

267. inuolucrum inicere : *to put the napkin on him.*   He will handle him " without gloves " and regardless of consequences.

268. utrum strictimne . . . dicam . . . an per pectinem : Such uses of -*ne* after *utrum* form reminiscences of the original meaning of the interrogative particle *utrum*, viz.: *which of the two?* The questions introduced by -*ne* were in apposition with it : *which of the two (shall I do), say this or that?* *Vtrum,* however, came at an early period to be felt as merely an interrogative particle, whereupon the -*ne* was of course no longer regarded as necessary.   This use is distinct from that represented by *utrumne,* where the *ne* seems to be appended only because *utrum* has also an indefinite use (= *either one or the other of two*); the -*ne* makes it clear at once that the inter-rogative use is intended ; see App.   **strictimne . . . an per pectinem** : *give him a close shave, or merely trim him up a little.*

269. uerum : *but.*   It is possible that such a use of *uerum* origi-nated in some accusative construction with the meaning *as to the truth* (cf. "as a matter of fact"). Such an expression following a statement implies that what has been already alleged is not true, but that what follows is. This relation between what follows and what has preceded is thus one of opposition, and *uerum* at length came to be felt merely as an adverb equivalent to *but*.   **frugist** (i.e. *frugi est*): *is good for anything; frugi* was originally felt merely as a dative of service from *frux* (cf. *Pseud.* 468, *tamen ero frugi bonae*), *for use;* but as *for use* practically meant *useful*, this dative came to be regarded, and used, as an indeclinable adjective, meaning *proper, honest, discreet,* etc. Cic. *Verr.* II. 3. 27. 67, *homines frugi ac sobrii; Cluent.* 16. 47, *seruos frugi atque integer;* Ter. *Heaut.* 580, *hominis frugi et temperantis;* Hor. *Sat.* II. 5. 77, *(Penelope) tam frugi tamque pudica;* Plin. *Ep.* II. 17. 4, *atrium frugi nec tamen sordidum.* See note on 956.   **usque admutilabit probe**: *will get right down to the skin in fine style;* with this use of *probe*, cf. the English expression "a *good* thrashing."

270. quid tu: *quid* and *quid tu* are frequently used merely to secure the close attention of the person addressed to a question about to be asked, performing the same function as the English "how is it?" "say!" "by the way!" or the like.   With *tu*, probably no particular verb was felt to be omitted; it merely stands in a general way as the subject of action.   **mauelis**: represents exactly the same use of the subjunctive as in *uelim* (*I should like*).

271. quod sit: *which would be.* If the *quod*-clause were used in the sense of *which is*, the indicative would here be used, as it would then be either a determinative clause (*the particular one of these alternatives which*, etc.), or one equivalent to *si* with the indicative (*whatever is,* i.e. *if anything is*, etc., *that is what I want*). In the latter case the characterizing idea, no matter how prominent, would not give rise to the subjunctive. See *Appendix to Bennett's Latin Grammar,* § 402, with the references there given.   **longissume**: one would expect *longissumum;* the adverb gives the degree to which the idea of *sit a malo* is true, the adjective would ascribe to the antecedent of *quod* a characteristic (*a malo longissumum*).

273. erat: Philocrates used the perfect *fuit* in the preceding verse; the imperfect here shows that his mind is wandering back and dwelling, as it were, amid the former scenes.   **quam si essem**: one might expect *fuissem*, but *quam si* here follows the same construction as when it means *as if* (cf. note on *quasi* in 181), the imperfect here representing the present tense thrown back into the past. In early Latin, however, the present subjunctive is apparently frequently used in unreal present conditions and the imperfect in unreal

H

past conditions.   **familiaris** : *of the family*. As Philocrates actually
was a "son of the family" in Elis, the *nec secus erat*, etc., was
literally true and the condition *si essem . . . filius* was not contrary
to fact at all. The spectators of course are thoroughly enjoying this
hoodwinking of Hegio.

274. eugepae (εὖ γε, παῖ): *capital! Good, by Jingo!*   **Thalem
talento** : this pun is interesting as an item of proof that the Θ of Θαλῆς
was pronounced much like *t;* the only difference was that between
th in *rat-hole* and *t* in *top*. As the Latin originally had no aspirates
of its own, Θαλῆς was, if we may judge from similar words in inscriptions, transliterated *Tales*. See note on *colaphos* in 88. Thales was
the earliest of the Greek philosophers, and one of the seven wise men.
talento non emam : *I would not take* (literally, *buy*) *at a talent*, i.e.
if I could get him for a talent (I have a far better wise man in Philocrates).   Notice that the present subjunctive here, by implication, as
a result of an omitted protasis, seems to mean *I would buy* (involving
the will).   Strictly speaking, the idea is *I should buy* (merely a conclusion to an "ideal" "less vivid future" condition, i.e. *should do
so, if any one were to make me the offer*). The Attic silver talent was
worth about $1100. A small amount, instead of this large one, would
seem more natural in such a connection, but "big talk" was frequently indulged in by slaves, just as ragamuffins nowadays are
always ready, on the slightest provocation, to "bet a hundred dol-
lars." Furthermore, in using *talento*, Tyndarus is probably thinking
of the pun more than of anything else. But see App.

275. ad : *in comparison with*, a meaning developed from the use
of *ad* to denote *direction toward; ad sapientiam huius* would strictly
mean *directing our attention toward* (i.e. *if we speak with regard to*)
this man's wisdom.   **nimius nugator** : *egregious simpleton*. A
word has apparently dropped out of this line.

276. ut facete . . . contulit : not *how cleverly he has adapted*
(which would be *quam facete*), but *how he has cleverly adapted!*

277. The richer the captive and the higher his birth, the brighter
would be Hegio's prospects of exchanging him for his son. Philocrates, in the character of Tyndarus, is willing to give him every
encouragement, and proceeds to paint himself in very satisfactory
colors.   **genere** : *family*.   **Polyplusio** (πολύ, πλούσιος): *the
Money-bags family; Polyplusio* is an adjective, modifying *genere*
understood, the preceding *de* still governing the case. Plautus himself probably wrote *Poluplusio; y* does not seem to have been
introduced till the time of Cicero.

278. unum : i.e. the one above all others.

279. ipsus : common in early Latin for *ipse*.　　**hic :** like *tu* in 270, is felt as subject in the most general indefinite sense, no particular verb being present to the mind. An accusative is often used to denote the object of action in a similarly indefinite sense ; e.g. Ter. *Phorm.* 755, *Quid illam alteram ?*　　**ab summis uiris :** to be taken with the passive verb (*is held in honor*) suggested by *quo honore est.*

280. tum igitur : *in that case then.*　　**quom . . . gratiast :** for the mood, see note on 146. The metrical structure of this line is doubtful. It seems barely possible that we should read *Āleîs.* See App.

281. quid diuitiae : on the case of *diuitiae*, see note on *hic* in 279.　　**unde excoquat sebum senex :** this is a play upon *opimae*, which originally meant *fat.* The entire line might be rendered : *How about his purse ? Is it a fat one ? Fat enough to keep him in grease as long as he lives.*　　**senex :** in apposition with the subject, *till old age ;* literally, *as an old man.*

282. pater : for the construction, see note on *hic* in 279.

283. id Orcum : notice the force of the position of *id, that's a matter which*, etc.

284. philosophatur : I have followed the custom of editors in writing *ph* instead of *p*, though it is probable that *ph* was not used in the time of Plautus. See notes on 88 and 274.

285. quid . . . nomen : *what was his name ?* literally, *what was unto him as name.* "What name?" would commonly be *quod nomen ?*　　**Thensaurocrysonicocrysides :** a name manufactured from θησαυρός, *treasury ;* χρυσός, *gold ;* νίκη, *victory ;* χρυσός, *gold ;* and the patronymic termination *-ides : Goldy Goldman, Jr.*

286. uidelicet : *clearly enough*, from *uidere licet*, literally, *it is permitted to see* (cf. *scilicet* and *ilicet*, from *scire licet* and *ire licet*). **inditum id nomen quasist :** *that has been applied to him as his name, so to speak (as a sort of name)*? Hegio naturally enough infers that such a compound could not be his real name, but must have been used as a substitute for it, in allusion to the riches he had acquired. *Quasi* is often thus used to apologize for an expression that might seem out of place (*nomen* in this instance) ; cf. *philosophia artium omnium quasi parens* (Cic. *de orat.* I. 3. 9). See App.

287. immo edepol : see note on *immo* in 209.　　**ipsius :** *ipse* regularly implies contrast ; here the avarice that characterized the *father himself*, implying a desire not to make such a charge against the son.　　**audaciam :** *greed* (for money). The word is connected with *auidus*, *aueo*.   Cf. Festus, p. 20, *Audacia ab auide, id est cupide, agendo dicta est.*

288. germano : *real*.

289. quid tu ais : the pronouns *tu* and *ego* are commonly emphatic, and indicate contrast with some one else, but occasionally, like *tu* here, they seem to be used without special emphasis.   **eius** : *ẽius*.   **immo** : see note on 209.

290. ut . . . noscas : this clause depends upon some words to be supplied : "I will mention the following fact," or the like.   **genio suo** : the effect is heightened by the prominent position of these words.   By *genius* is meant a sort of guardian spirit that was supposed to be one's constant companion from the cradle to the grave, representing in fact one's very existence, and watching over one's welfare.   The allusion here is to some ceremony in honor of this spirit.   **quando** : this indefinite use of *quando* is extremely rare in Plautus.   It is not recognized at all by some scholars.   See App.   **sacruficat** : ante-classical for *sacrificat*.

291. quibus est opus Samiis uasis utitur : *the vessels he needs are Samian ware*, literally, *the vessels of which there is need he uses of Samian ware*.   **Samiis** : a cheap kind of earthenware came from Samos ; cf. *Bacch.* 202 ; *Men.* 178 ; Cic. *Mur.* 36.

292. ne : (*for fear*) *lest*.   **ut** : *how*.   **uide** : *judge, conclude*.

293. hac : sc. *uia* ; cf. 953.   **eadem** : ablative agreeing with *opera* understood, *at the same time* ; literally, *by the same effort*. *Opera* is expressed in *Bacch.* 60 ; *Capt.* 450 ; *Most.* 1039.   **ego** : see note on *tu* in 289.   **exquaesiuero** : *I'll get out of this man* (*in a twinkling*) ; the future perfect emphasizes the promptness with which the act will be accomplished.   It betrays the self-confidence of Hegio, who "means business" with these captives, and has no time to dilly-dally.   See the note on *iuero* in 194, App. on that passage, and Introd. § 95.   *Exquisiuero* would be the more regular form, but *-quaero* for *-quiro* is occasionally found in composition ; see B. App. § 87. 1.

294. frugi : modifying *hominem* ; see note on 269.

295. ego : another instance of an unemphatic *ego* ; see note on *tu* in 289.

296. tua ex re : *to your own advantage*.   **feceris** : a true future perfect (*will have acted*), not one used like *iuero* in 194 and *exquaesiuero* in 293, to indicate promptness of accomplishment.

297.   What Tyndarus has hitherto said in this scene has been "aside."   He now cleverly changes his tone and bearing to suit the rôle of master, that he here begins to play.   **tamen** : i.e. even if you are not willing to confess.   **scio** : if this is the correct reading, this must be pronounced *scĭo*. Perhaps Plautus wrote *aio*.

298. uolui : *did want;* see Introd. § 99.

299. meam: *mḗam*.

300. perdidi : differs from *amisi* in that it commonly implies culpability.

301. istunc me potius quam te metuere, etc.: the intentional ambiguity of these words would be thoroughly enjoyed by the audience. They may mean: (1) I see no reason now why I should fear him rather than you ; (2) I see no reason why *he* should fear *me* rather than you, i.e. that I would be untrue to him ; (3) I see no reason why I should fear him more than you should ; or (4) I see no reason why he should fear me more than you should.

302. cum istoc : strict logic would require *cum istius opibus*.

303. memini : see note on *memineris* in 240.   **audebat**: sc. *laedere* from the following *laedat*.   **laedat licet** : the two verbs in such cases were originally felt as syntactically independent, *laedat* being a subjunctive of permission : *he may offend. It is permitted.* In the course of time the verb in the subjunctive came to be felt as dependent upon the *licet*. Thereupon, to make this dependence clear, *ut* was occasionally used before the subjunctive.

304. uiden : i.e. *uidesne*. With the loss of final *e*, compare *quin?* for *qui nĕ ? (why not ? nĕ* being used in the sense of *non*); *sin* for *si nĕ ; duc* and *fac* for the earlier forms *duce* and *face ;* etc., etc. An intermediate step is seen in *nempe* and *quippe*, which were probably sometimes pronounced *nemp* and *quip* (see App.), though the *e* continued to be written.   **humana** : accusative plural.

305. fueram : i.e. had been prior to the time of my capture. See App. As Tyndarus is the son of Hegio, he is in reality telling the truth, though he thinks he is uttering falsehoods.

306. alterius : to be read *altríus ;* cf. note on 8.

307. proinde ut : where we should expect *talem qualis*, or the like ; *proinde ac* is unknown to Plautus.   **familiae** : with especial reference to the slaves of a household.

309. hoc . . . uolueram : *this* (i.e. what I am about to say) *is a matter about which I had* (i.e. before the present opportunity presented itself) *been wanting you informed* (and I will now proceed to improve the opportunity), *unless perchance you yourself wish me not to.* See App. on this passage and also on 305.   **hoc te monitum** : for *monere* with two accusatives, see B. 178. 1. *d* ; A. & G. 238. *b* ; G. 376. Rem. 1 ; H. 412. The accusative *hoc* is one retained from the active construction.

312. apŭd nos, apŭd te : see note on 193 and App. thereon.

313. est : the emphatic position of this word is due to the fact that the truth here asserted is sometimes disputed or doubted.   **-que et** (instead of the *et . . . et*, or the *cum . . . tum* of classical prose): a combination chiefly confined to poetry and Silver Latin prose.

314. habueris : *habeo, have, keep,* easily comes to be used, as here, in the sense of *treat*.

315. bene merenti bene profuerit : *the man who does his duty will find himself well rewarded;* literally, *to the well deserving it will have profited well.* The future perfect *profuerit* regards the result as one to be looked back upon from a future point of view ; the following *erit* regards a future result from the present point of view.   **par** : *a corresponding return.*

316. The effect is heightened by the fact that, although Tyndárus intends to deceive and believes his words to be false, the audience knows that he is unconsciously telling the truth.

317. faterin : i.e. *faterisne.*

320. ne . . . faxint : a more energetic and emotional form · of expression than *ne faciant.* See note on 172.   **tuom animum . . . diuitiae meae** : notice the chiasmus and the strongly contrasted positions of these phrases, *your* mind, *my* riches.   **auariorem** : with reference to the ransom that he expected Hegio would exact.

321. patrĭ : for the shortening, see Introd. § 84.   **magis** : with *decere.*

322. saturum : *well supplied.*

323. potius : repeating the idea of *magis* (321), but adding to it the further idea of personal preference.   **illi** : adverb = *illic.*   **mendicantem** : alluding to the results of paying an excessive ransom.

324. Notice the repetition of the emphatic *ego* in this and the following lines. It seems to indicate conscious superiority over the vulgar crowd with their false ideals.   **uirtute** : *kindness.* The term *uirtus* covers all the qualities of an ideally perfect *uir* (from which word it is derived), i.e. *manliness, virtue, strength, bravery, worth, goodness,* etc. It should be translated in each case according to the particular quality uppermost in the thoughts of the speaker.   **nostrum** : including other members of his family. One might, however, have expected **meorum**.

325. non ego : *I'm not the man to.*

326. scio ego, etc.: the tone conveyed by the position of words should not be lost : *full well do I know, many are the men whom, before now,* etc.

327. est: emphatic by position, *there <u>are</u> occasions when*, etc.
ubi . . . praestet: expressions of this type commonly have the
indicative in Plautus (cf. 263, *sunt quae uolo*), and this construction
is found also in later poets. The subjunctive of characteristic, however, is the regular usage of classical prose.

328. odi ego aurum: *as for gold, I despise it* (see Introd. § 99).

329. hoc: probably an adverb = *huc;* cf. *Pers.* 605, *iube hoc
accedat; Truc.* 531, *adduce hoc istas.*

330. Alide: see Introd. § 93 (*d*).

331. eum si reddis mihi: *if you restore him to me.* For this
loose use of the present tense (*reddis* where strict accuracy would
require *reddideris*), see Introd. § 95 (*a*. 1). *Eum* should be read *ẽum.*
mĭhĭ prāe|tĕrĕā | ūnum: for the hiatus in the diaeresis, see Introd.
§ 85 (*a*).   **ne duis**: *ne* with the present subjunctive in prohibition
is used only in prohibitions of a mild type (as compared with *ne* and
the perfect); see note on 186.   Here it is hardly stronger than *you need
not give.* For the form *duis*, see Introd. § 88 (*a*).

332. amittam : see note on 36.

333. oras: here, as often, with its original meaning, *say.* Similarly
orator originally meant *spokesman; ambassador, orator, pleader* represent specialized applications of the original meaning.

335. cluens: allusions to Roman customs and institutions are very
common in Plautus, though very rare in Terence.   In Greece the social
position of a physician would not have been likely to be such as is here
indicated.   Plautus has in mind the condition of things at Rome, where
in his time physicians were commonly freedmen or slaves.   Upon being
manumitted, a slave became the *cliens* of his former master.

336. hoc: i.e. the restoration of the lost son.   **in procliui**:
easy; literally, *on the incline;* cf. our expression, "uphill work."
One is reminded of the saying, "as easily as falling off a log."
Tyndarus apparently forgets, for the moment, to preserve the tone of
the aristocratic gentleman he is supposed to be, and falls into the free
and easy style of the slave that he really is.

337. fac: *see to it.*   **ōrō Hēgio**: this is not to be regarded as
an instance of hiatus; see Introd. § 74, and notes on 152, 169.

338. ab re: *against my interests;* cf. *Trin.* 238; *As.* 224.   The
contrary idea, "in one's interests," is sometimes expressed by *ex re,*
or *in rem;* cf. 296, 386, etc.

339. ego me: *as far as I'm concerned*, contrasted with the *hunc*
in the next line.   **donicum**: a common form of *donec* in early
Latin.   **ille**: with a gesture toward Philocrates.

340. **aestumatum**: *with a price set upon him;* literally, *appraised;* the amount thus fixed was to be forfeited to Hegio in case the supposed slave failed to return. See App.   **des**: the rule commonly given, that the present subjunctive in commands is used chiefly of an indefinite person, is not true for any period of Latin. In Plautus and Terence there are only twelve instances of this use addressed to an indefinite person, while there are 128 instances addressed to a definite person. In Cicero there are only four instances (not counting those used as protases, e.g. *roges, respondeam*) addressed to an indefinite person, while there are twenty-two (all in the *Epistulae*) addressed to a definite person. See App.

341. **illi**: adverb.   **immo**: see note on 209.   **misero**: on this rhetorical, energetic use of the future perfect at the end of a line, see note on *iuero* in 194, with the App. on that passage.

342. **tuom**: this word and *tua* in the next line are emphasized by their positions; cf. also the emphatic *tu* that follows. This emphasis is apparently explained by the fact that Hegio is contrasting his son, Philopolemus, and *his* (i.e. Philopolemus') father with Philocrates and *his* (Philocrates') father. By the proposed plan, communication would be established in both directions.

343. **uelis**: the subjunctive is due to its dependence upon another subjunctive.

344. **nil est**: *it's no use,* i.e. it is labor lost.   **luseris**: *will have frittered away,* a true future perfect, referring to what *will have resulted* when the *opera* is finished; it is thus a different use of the tense from that found in 194, 293, 341, etc.

345. **omne**: *the whole thing.* See App.   **transactum reddet**: differs from *transiget* in calling attention to the state resulting from the act; *transiget* would refer merely to the act itself. Cf. the English phrase, "get a thing finished," instead of "finish a thing."

346. **quoi plus credat**: *in whom he has more confidence,* a predicating characterizing clause of the developed type ("clause of characteristic"); see note on 12.   *Plus* is the accusative of "the inner object," or of "the result produced." A. & G. 238. *b;* B. 176; G.-L. 332, 333; H. 409.

347. **magis . . . ex sententia**: *more to his mind.*

348. **neque adeo**: *nor yet, and furthermore not. Adeo (ad + eo)* follows rather closely the meaning of its constituent parts: —

(1) *to that (such a) point (of space, time, or degree); to a high degree, very* (see note on *mirum adeo* in 824);

(2) *just, precisely*, a meaning developed from a restrictive application of the one just indicated (*to that point, and no further*, which would easily come to suggest the general idea of precision) ;

(3) *to that* (*end*), *with a view to that;*

(4) *in addition to that*, i.e. *furthermore, moreover, besides.* In this last sense, the thing added is sometimes (especially in the phrase *atque adeo*) opposed to the preceding context, when it may be translated *still*.

quoi concredat: a predicating characterizing clause of the original type ; see note on 12.   **hodie** : this particle seems to be often used in early Latin as a mere formality, without temporal force. Perhaps the nearest English parallel is the colloquial use of "now " in such expressions as "he did not say so at all, now," "you'll never get off like that, now." Sometimes this colorless *hodie* seems untranslatable ; in this passage it is commonly translated *ever*, though it probably has no temporal force.   **audacius** : *with greater confidence.*

349. **ne uereare** : see note on 331.   **periclo** : *risk.*

350. **ingenio** : *disposition.*   **eius** : $\widehat{eius}$.   **erga** : this postpositive use of *erga* is chiefly ante-classical, and is most common with *me, te, se.*

351. **fide** : *guarantee.*

352. **quam citissume potest, tam** : for the more common *quam potest tam* with a positive, or *quam citissume* alone.   **cedere ad factum** : *be carried out, put into execution;* literally, *come to a deed.* See App.

353. **causa quin . . . des** : *reason why you should not give.* *Quin* is composed of *qui, how?* or *why?* and the negative particle *nĕ* (which in early times was used in the sense of *non*) ; it here retains its original meaning.   **quin . . . des** : *why you should not give*, an indirect question of obligation, or propriety. See note on 208. **uiginti minas** : about $360. Such estimates, however, in terms of modern money are based merely on equivalence in weight of coin, without any reference to the relative purchasing power of the amount in question.

354. **optuma — immo** : *not at all — the best of reasons rather* (*why I should*), *optuma* agreeing with *causa* understood, with which *cur dem* is easily supplied. This position of *immo* is very unusual before Livy ; in answering a question it commonly stands first.

355. **atque** : *and in fact*, introducing a sort of afterthought. He has been so much pleased with his interview with the supposed Philo-

crates that he proposes to be indulgent and kind to him, quite unconscious of the fact that he is being sadly duped. The pathos about all
this cannot fail to be appreciated.

356. quom honestas : for the indicative in a causal *quom*-clause
in Plautus, see note on 146.

357. haud molestum : litotes.   **iam** : emphatic by position, *so
soon*. He pretends he had not expected such consideration until the
return of the supposed Tyndarus.   **quod** : *that*.   **collus** : ante-
classical for *collum*.   **caret** : *is rid of*.

358. The alliteration in this line is noteworthy.   **quod bonis
. . . bonis** : *every kind deed done a good man — a good man will
regard such a deed as its own abundant reward;* literally, *whatever
kindness is kindly done to the good, that reward* (= *reward for that*) *is
full for the good.* Notice the strongly contrasted positions of *bonis*.

359. dic(e) : for the classical *dic;* cf. *duce, face*, etc., for *duc, fac,*
etc. *Dice* should probably be read here with silent *e*, which afterward
came to be omitted also in writing. For other instances of silent *e* at
the end of a word, see Introd. § 77. See App.

360. ad patrem : with reference merely to the act of carrying to
the father, *as limit of motion; patri* would express interest on the
part of the father, including the *for*-idea as well as the *to*-idea.
uin : *uisne*.   **uocem** : such a subjunctive depending upon *uin* is
common in Plautus, but only in the first person. Such uses are
reminiscences of parataxis (*uisne? uocem? do you wish it? shall I
call him?*), but the subjunctive came at an early date to be felt as
dependent. See note on 121.

ACT II. SCENE 3.

The manuscripts indicate here the beginning of a new scene. There
is no change in the characters upon the stage, but Philocrates has,
during most of the preceding interview, been standing apart. Hegio
now crosses over to talk with him, and this makes the forming of a new
scene not unnatural.

361. quae res bene uortat : a regular formula for invoking a
blessing upon a proposed undertaking; the *quae res* refers to the plan
that was now to be put into execution; cf. *Pers.* 329; *Aul.* 218, 787;
Curc. 729; also Hor. *Ep.* I. 7. 94, *quod te obsecro et obtestor, uitae me
redde priori,* where *quod* refers to *uitae me redde priori.*

362. uolt : the emphatic position of this word seems to imply some
doubt on the part of Hegio.

362–363. erus has more particular reference to a man's relation toward his slaves; **dominus** to his relation toward the family as a whole, with all its belongings. Hegio seems to use them here, however, without any particular distinction in mind. **operam dare ... fideliter**: *to obey faithfully.*

363. quod: *in what; quod* strictly has its antecedent in the ellipsis of some such idea as *in that matter*, or *in those matters.* **uelit**: *uolt* in the preceding line has suggested an *indirect reporting* of the speaker's own ideas; hence the subjunctive.

364. aestumatum huíc: *h* here "makes position"; see note on 169.

365. uelle: i.e. *se uelle.* **ad patrem**: notice the double meaning: (1) your father, (2) his father; cf. 375, 379, etc.

366. meum: *my own;* note the position.

367. filiis: probably dative.

368. In what follows one should notice how cleverly, in word and thought, Philocrates acts the part of a slave. **utroque uorsum**: *in both directions*, an adverbial expression sometimes written *utroque-uorsum.* **rectum**: a participle, *directed.*

371. Hegio's change of tone should be noted, as he begins to address the supposed slave; the emphatic *tute tibi* and *tuopte,* for instance, are not deferential. **tute**: *you're the one that.* **tuopte**: this emphasizing *-pte* is appended in Plautus to *me, mea, meo, tuo, sua, suom, suo.*

372. Notice the hiatus. In early poetry, however, final *m* is frequently not elided; see Introd. § 85.

373. em tibi hominem: *here's your man!* literally, *behold the man for you.* **hominem**: accusative after the verbal idea implied in *em. Em (en)* must be distinguished from *hem;* the former means *lo! behold! look you!* the latter, *well, I declare! ahem!* or the like. See note on 183. **gratiām hăbeo**: here again the *h* makes the preceding syllable long; see notes on 169, 364. *Gratiam habere* means *to feel grateful;* literally, *to have gratitude (in one's heart); gratias agere, to express gratitude.*

374. quom: probably an instance of the explicative *quom, in that,* or *the fact that;* see note on 151. **facis**: *afford.*

376. qui me quid ... agitem ... perferat: *me* is grammatically construed as the object of *perferat*, with *quid agitem* as a sort of secondary object; literally, *who will report me what I am doing;* logically we should expect *quid ... agitem* alone. Such a use is common in Plautus and Terence; e.g. *Heaut.* 84, *fac me ut sciam,* for *fac ut ego sciam.*

377. omnem rem: *the whole story*, loosely added as an appositive to the *quid*-clauses.

379. patrem: the reference of this word in this and the following lines is intentionally left ambiguous.

380. rebitas: from *re* and *bĭtĕre* (*to go*) ; *adbitere, perbitere, interbitere*, and other compounds also occur in Plautus. See note on *arbiter* in 211. **si non rebitas**: the protasis of *dem*. Notice the loose use of the present tense. **ut . . . dem**: *with the understanding that*. Bennett calls such clauses "stipulative."

382. The hidden meaning should not be missed.

383. animum aduortas uolo: such uses originally consisted of two independent sentences, *animum aduortas! uolo, pay attention! I wish it*. See note on 360.

385. adhuc locorum: *hitherto ;* literally, *up to this point of time*, *locorum* being a partitive genitive, and here referring to time, rather than place; cf. *postea loci, afterward* (Sall. *Jug.* 102); *interea loci, meanwhile* (Ter. *Eun.* 126); *ad id locorum, hitherto* (Sall. *Jug.* 63. 6); *post id locorum, afterward* (Plaut. *Cas.* 120); *inde loci, since then* (Lucr. 5. 437).

386 f. ut . . . petam: explanatory of the *faciam ;* for *faciam ut petam* one might expect merely *petam*. **in rem tuam**: see note on 338.

387. This line is corrupt. Perhaps Plautus wrote *idque persequar* instead of *id persequarque*.

389. salutem dicito: *remember me to.*

392. me honore honestiorem . . . fecit: *has shown me unusual consideration ;* literally, *has made me more honored than honor*. Again the double meaning should be noted. Hegio would understand the words to mean *more honored than honor itself*, but Tyndarus chooses words that may also mean *more honored than my real station as a slave calls for.* See App.

393. ne praecipias: for this mild form of prohibition, see note on 331. **tamen**: i.e. even without instructions from you.

394. nam quidem: the only instance in Plautus of *nam quidem* instead of *nam equidem ;* see App. **nisi quod**: *aside from the fact that. Nisi* in such expressions was originally felt as introducing a conditional idea, and the explicative *quod*-clause was the subject of the verb to be supplied with *nisi*. The expression originally meant *if it were* (*was, is*) *not a fact that*, or something similar, but it drifted away from this original meaning.

395. quo pacto . . . conuenerit: *of the agreement that has been*

made ; literally, *in what way it has been agreed.*   **mĭhĭ cŭm hōc :**
see notes on 169, 364, 373.

396. mora : *waste of time.*

397. ut . . . redimat : *that he is to redeem.*   **nostrum . . . ambo-
rum uicem :** *in exchange for both of us, nostrum* being a partitive
genitive. Tyndarus is slyly pleading for himself, without arousing the
suspicion of Hegio. Compare such expressions as *meam uicem, in my
stead, on my account* (Plaut. *Most.* 355), *tuam uicem* (Cic. *Fam. XII.*
23. 3). Bennett (*Lat. Gram., Appendix,* 310. 3) thinks that *uicem*
was originally an accusative of apposition (= *as an exchange*), and
cites the present passage and *Most.* 355 as supporting this view.

398. The metrical structure of this line is uncertain.   **in rem :**
see note on 338.

400. suos quoique carus : *every man loves his own son ;* literally,
his own son is dear to each.   **numquid aliud uis,** etc. : a common
formula for closing an interview ; see note on 191.

401. me hic ualere : Tyndarus wants to put in an effective plea
for himself, but has some hesitation as to how he can proceed without
arousing the suspicion of Hegio. He is accordingly somewhat confused
at first by Philocrates' question, indicating, as it did, that the interview
was about to close. This confusion causes him to repeat aimlessly the
same words he has just used (391), *me hic ualere ;* but he suddenly
rises to the occasion, and launches boldly out into words that will sound
innocent enough to Hegio, but which are intended as a plea to Philocrates to remember the fidelity of his slave, thus left a prisoner. This
effort of Tyndarus is a masterpiece. It is fully matched, however, by
the reply of Philocrates.   **tute,** etc. : *tu* alone would commonly be
emphatic ; the enclitic *-te* makes it doubly so. The unusual emphasis
seems to imply that the information about to be given would commonly
be furnished by the master about his slave, rather than by the slave
about himself. In this case, however, *you (slave though you are) are
to put on a bold face and tell him yourself.*   **dicito :** see note on 11.
Here the act is not to take place till the supposed Tyndarus has reached
his destination.

402. fuisse : i.e. *nos fuisse.*

403. me aduorsatum tibi : see App.

404. gessisse morem : *have done the will (complied with the
wishes) of.*   **tamen :** i.e. in spite of the *aerumnae.* With this position of *tamen,* cf. 187, 393.

405. neque . . . umquam deseruisse : *have never been false to.*
med is the object, **te** the subject ; they are intended to be ambiguous.

Hallidie compares Shaksp. *Henry VI.* 1. 4, "the duke yet lives *that Henry shall depose*," and the oracle's reply to Pyrrhus : *aio te, Aeacida, Romanos uincere posse.* *Med* is an accusative formed after the analogy of the ablative, which originally ended in *d*.

407. ut fueris : in apposition to *haec*, which itself refers to what has preceded.

408. quin te gratus emittat manu : *that he will not (but that he will), in his gratitude, set you free.* For *quin*, instead of *ut non* or *qui non*, introducing a consecutive clause, when the principal verb is negatived, see A. & G. 319. *d* ; B. 284. 3 ; G.-L. 552. 3 ; H. 595. 5. **emittat manu :** for the classical *manumittat ;* literally, *release from the manus*, the *manus* representing the power of the master. This giving up of all claim to a slave was symbolized by a ceremony in which the master first took hold of the slave, as still his own, turned him about, and then released him from his grasp, a free man.

409. mea opera : *by my own efforts*, contrasting with *tua opera* in the next line.

410. uirtute : see note on 324.

411. liceat : *will be permitted.* He regards the success of the plan as assured.

412. genus : *family*, i.e. high birth.

414. ego : without any particular emphasis ; see note on 289.

415. nam : with reference to the *merito*.

417. quasi . . . esses : the tense of *esses* serves as a further blind upon Hegio. **meus esses :** probably to be read *meŭ' sses ;* see note on 94, and App. **nihilo setius :** (i.e. than as if you were a slave) loosely thrown in without influencing the construction of the rest of the sentence.

418. míhĭ ōbsequiosus : for the hiatus, see Introd. § 85 (*g*). See App. **di uostram fidem :** *for heaven's sake !* literally, *ye gods, your protection !* An accusative of exclamation, to be accounted for as the object toward which the speaker's emotion is directed.

419. liberale : *generous.* *Liberalis* is a term that covers all the qualities of an ideal *liber* (*freeman*), who is supposed to represent a higher type of man than a slave; it is accordingly to be translated by *gentlemanly*, *noble*, *kind*, *generous*, etc., according to the particular quality uppermost in the speaker's mind in each case.

420. uideas : probably used in the sense of *you (any one) would see (at a glance).* It is sometimes regarded as meaning *you can see*, but there is doubt whether the Latin subjunctive ever has such a force.

See App.   **corde**: literally, *from the heart*.   **amare**: sc. *hos.*
quantis laudauit: the text is corrupt.

421. conlaudauit: *has heaped praises upon;* the *con-* is intensive.
istic: for the classical *iste;* see Introd. § 87 (*c*).

421f. **haud centesumam partem**: *not a hundredth part* is apparently felt as meaning *a hundred times less*, and is therefore followed by *quam, than;* cf. the use of *quam* after *dimidium*, e.g. Liv.
45. 18, *dimidium tributi quam quod regibus ferre soliti erant*, etc.;
after *multiplex*, Liv. 7. 8, *multiplex, quam pro numero, damnum est*,
i.e. *many times greater than*, etc.   *Partem* is an adverbial accusative,
as in the phrases *meam partem* (*on my part*), *maximam partem* (*for
the most part*).

423. quom: see note on 146.   **occasio . . . cumulare**: for
occasio cumulandi.   An infinitive rarely depends upon a substantive
except when a verbal idea is prominently involved in the substantive.
The infinitive with *occasio*, however, occurs several times in early
Latin; e.g. *Poen.* 1212 ; *Pers.* 725–726 ; *Curc.* 59–60 ; Ter. *Phorm.* 885.

424. erga hunc: to be taken with *fideliter*.   **ut . . . rem
geras**: *by conducting things;* literally, *so as to conduct things.*

425. Philocrates means that his efforts for the success of the plan
will be as earnest as his wishes are sincere.   **opera**: *by my efforts.*
Possibly, however, *opera* here means *in reality*, *actually*.   **experiar
persequi**: *experior* with the infinitive, in the sense of *conor*, is a rare
construction.

426. id: i.e, the sincerity of the words just uttered.   **laudō|
Hēgĭo**: the *H* prevents elision ; see Introd. § 74.

427. me . . . Philocrati: a bit of humor which the audience
would be sure to appreciate.   **probus . . . homo**: *fine fellow.*

428. ei: *ei*.   **memet**: one might expect *ego* as subject of
faciam, understood ; in *memet* the *Iouem testem do* is allowed to
control the construction, with *facturum* (*esse*), understood.   For the
intensive -*met*, see grammars.

429. experiri: *prove*, *put to the test*.   **opera**, **factis**: the former refers to the effort put forth, the latter to the things actually
accomplished.

430–445. See App.

430. quo minus: one might expect a corresponding *eo magis* before *animum aduortas uolo;* the meaning is, *I want you now as much
more attentive as my previous words have fallen short of what I have
wanted to say;* literally, *by how much less I have said than I wanted
to,* (*by so much the more*) *do I want you now to listen.* See App.

de te : to be taken with *dixi*, though the position of the phrase is unusual.

431. horunc uerborum causa : *causā* very seldom means *on account of*, except where this phrase virtually means *for the sake of*. It is used in such sentences as "I left the city on account of important business," but not in such as "I left the city on account of disaster." The present passage presents one of the extremely rare exceptions to this rule.   **caueto** (?) : see App.   **fuas** : common in early Latin for *sis;* see Introd. § 88 (*a*).

432. cogitato : see note on 11.   **fide** : *guarantee.* See App.

433. pignori : *for security.*

434. ne = *lest.*   **meo é** : *meo͡ e.*

435. te hic : the *h* prevents elision ; see App., and Introd. § 74.

436. ducas, deseras : introduced, like *ignores*, by the *ne* (434).

437. neque des : *neque* instead of *neue*, because it is equivalent to *et non* instead of *et ne;* it negatives merely the word *des*, *ne . . . deseras neque des* meaning *lest you . . . forsake and fail to give.* **reducem facias** : *restore;* literally, *make returned.*

439. fac fidelis sis : originally in such cases the two words formed independent clauses, *fac! sis fidelis! be faithful! do so!* In the course of time the subjunctive came to be felt (as in passages like the present) to be dependent upon the *fac*. Later, a desire to make this dependence clearer led sometimes to the insertion of *ut*, e.g. Cic. *Att*. II. 4. 4. It is therefore incorrect to say that *ut* is "omitted" in expressions like *fac sis;* such expressions merely represent an earlier stage, nearer to parataxis. Cf. notes on 121, 360, 383.   **caue fidem fluxam geras** : i.e. *be sure to keep good faith with me.* See B. 305. 2.

440. omnia : the emphatic position of this word is intended as a sly hint to Philocrates that nothing less than manumission should be the reward for the self-sacrifice that Tyndarus is making.

441. hunc : i.e. Hegio's son, whom you are to bring back. The use of *hunc* in referring to the son is justified by the fact that the son is the main object of thought, at least from Hegio's point of view, and Tyndarus is choosing his words with especial reference to the presence of Hegio. *Hunc* is commonly taken as referring to Hegio himself, but this makes it impossible to interpret *inuentum inueni* satisfactorily.   **inuentum inueni** ; the son has already been "found" (*inuentum*) in the sense that they have learned of his whereabouts (see 335) ; he is now to be "found" (*inueni*) in the sense that a messenger is going to seek him out and bring him back. In the latter sense (though not in the former) he is still "lost" to Hegio.   See the preceding note.

442. haec . . . opsecro : *I make these entreaties.*

443. fuas : see 431 and Introd. § 88 (*a*).

444. tu (before *hoc*) another instance of an unemphatic *tu;* see note on 289.   The *h* prevents elision in *tu hoc;* see Introd. § 74, and notes on 55, 152, 169, 337.   **hoc age** : *mind you!* These words are not to be translated literally.   The phrase was originally used by the priest in charge of a sacrifice, as an order to the proper official to despatch the victim.   It was accordingly the signal for all to observe a sacred silence.   From this it came to be used merely to invoke attention.   **tu mihi** : strongly contrasted.   **patronus . . . pater** : because the speaker depended upon Philocrates to get him out of his trouble.   See App.

446. satin habes : *will you be satisfied ?* literally, *do you consider it sufficient ?*   **facta si refero** : *if I turn to accomplished facts;* literally, *if I bring back done.*   For this loose use of the present tense (*refero*) for the future perfect, see Introd. § 95 (*a*).

447. ornatus : *equipped, provided,* i.e. accompanied by Hegio's son.   **ex sententia** : *to your liking;* see note on 347.

448. numquid aliud (sc. *uis*) : *nothing more is there ?*   See note on 191.   **ut . . . redeas** : depending on the *uis* understood (and frequently expressed) with the preceding formula *numquid aliud ?* **possis** gets its modal coloring from the subjunctive clause in which it stands.   **res monet** : *the nature of the case warns* (*me to do that*).

449. a trapessita : we should say *at the banker's,* an idea which would be expressed in Latin by *apud trapezitam* (*argentarium*); but the Latin is fond of using phrases with reference to the point of view from which an act emanates, or a state is presented ; e.g. *a Romanis, on the side of the Romans; a tergo, in the rear; ab animo, in his mind* (cf. Ter. *Phorm.* 340).   For the spelling of *trapessita,* see note on 193.

450. eadem opera : *at the same time;* literally, *by the same exertion;* cf. the proverb "kill two birds *with one stone.*"   **a praetore** : *from the commanding general; praetor* is here used, apparently, in its original sense (*prae + itor = the one who goes before*).   **syngraphum** : *passport.* Aetolia and Elis were at war.   Plautus probably wrote *sungrapum;* the character *y* was first introduced in the time of Cicero ; see note on 88.

451. legionem : *army.* This word comes from *lego,* and originally meant *a gathering;* then, in a military sense, *a levy, an army;* its common meaning, *legion,* represents a still further specialization.

I

452. bene ambulato: *fare you well; fare* in "farewell" originally meant *go, travel*.

454. expediui: receives the emphasis.

456. sultis: i.e. *si uoltis* (later *uultis*) ; cf. *sis* for *si uis*, and note on 110.

457. ecferat: with *ec*, instead of *ex* (= *ec-s*), cf. the Greek ἐκ. **apparebo**: i.e. am to be found.

458. ad fratrem: *inuisere* means *to go to see; ad fratrem* is to be taken with the idea of *going* involved in the verb, while the idea of *seeing* governs the accusative *captiuos*.   **modō**: *only*, making an unimportant qualification of the statement just made. He says that he is *only going to call at his brother's;* with the exception of the time necessary for this, he *will be found at home* (*apparebo domi*). He means, of course, after the matter in hand is finished, and he therefore disregards the moment or two (cf. 505–506) spent at the praetor's. This adverb has both vowels short almost invariably in classical times, but occasionally, as here, in early Latin the final ō retains its original quantity.   **inuiso**: for the loose use of the present for the future, see Introd. § 95 (*a*), and cf. the similar English use, "I *am going* to-morrow." See App.

459. eadem: sc. *opera;* see note on 450.   **adulescentem**: Tyndarus.

460. tu: i.e. Philocrates.   **amittam**: *despatch*.   **ei rei primum praeuorti uolo**: *that's the thing I want to attend to* (literally, *turn to*) *first in preference* (*prae*) (*to all else*). The reference is to the procuring of the necessary passport (see 450 f. and 505 f.).

ACT III.   SCENE 1.

461. edit: subjunctive for the classical *edat;* see Introd. § 88 (*a*).

463. esse: infinitive of *edo*.   **quod edit**: *to eat*. The idea *which he can eat* would be expressed by *quod esse possit*. Something has apparently dropped out of this line, as it cannot be read metrically.

464. hercle: *gad!*   **lubens**: notice the emphatic position, *and gladly, too*.

465. malignitate: *stinginess; malignus* is sometimes used as the opposite of *largus*, e.g. *Bacch.* 401.   **mihi**: *as far as I'm concerned*.

466. ieiuniosiorem: a word coined for the occasion ; it agrees with *hominem*, which (with *quam me*) is easily understood.   **mag(is) ecfertum**: probably *s* is here elided before the following *e*, just as *m* would commonly be. This is apparently a common phenomenon in Plautus (see App.). Possibly, however, *neque* should be pronounced with silent final *e*. See note on 359 and Introd. § 77.   **ecfertum fame**: literally, *stuffed full of hunger.* The word *ecfertum* is of course chosen with reference to the usual propensity of a parasite. For *ec-*, see note on 457.

467. minus procedat: *meets with less success.*   **occeperit** (for *inceperit* or *coeperit*): attracted to the subjunctive.

468. resident: *resideo* originally meant *to sit back* (*and do nothing*), *to take a rest;* then, as this was a way of celebrating a holiday, it came to mean *to keep* or *celebrate*, but this transitive use of *resideo* is extremely rare.   **esurialis ferias**: *hunger-holidays; esurialis* is one of the many words coined by Plautus for humorous effects.

469. ilicet . . . crucem: *the parasite business may go and be hanged!*   **ilicet**: see note on 286.   **arti**: dependent upon the *licet* in *ilicet*.   **malam crucem**: limit of motion after the idea of *ire* in *ilicet*. Probably at one time the accusative was freely used without a preposition to express limit of motion, but in historical times only comparatively few reminiscences of this use are preserved, e.g. *domum, rus*, names of towns and small islands, and such expressions as *exsequias ire, infitias ire, malam crucem ire*, and a few others; see Bennett, *Lat. Gram.* App. 311. 3. The *crux* was originally a pole upon which offenders were impaled; later, a cross to which they were bound or nailed. Often *mala crux* is used as a stereotyped expression, felt as a single word, which in turn could be modified by *maxima, magna*, etc.

470. ridiculos inopesque: (*us*) *poor fools* (*merrymakers*). It was the business of a parasite to entertain the company in return for his dinner.

471. nil morantur: *care naught for;* literally, *make no delay* (*over*); *nil* is the accusative of the "inner object," or of the "result produced." A. & G. 238. *b;* B. 176. 2; G.-L. 332, 333; H. 409.   **iam**: *any more.*   **Lacones**: parasites are thus called, apparently because they need all the fortitude and endurance of the Spartans to withstand the ill-treatment they get.   **unisubselli**: a word humorously coined by Plautus. The *triclinium* was the couch extending around *three* sides of the table for the guests to *recline* on; the parasites frequently had to *sit* on a bench (*subsellium*) that stood by itself, which Plautus calls the *uni-subsellium* in playful allusion to the make-up of the term *tri-clinium* (cf. his similar coinage of *ueriuerbio* in 568); cf. *Stich.* 488. See App.   **uiros**: *heroes;*

notice the choice of *uiros* instead of *homines*, and also its emphatic position.

472. Plagipatidas : *us Whipping-posts* (as if referring to members of a prominent family); literally, *the Buffet-bearer sons.* **quibus sunt uerba** : *who furnish amusement;* see note on 651.

473. ederint : probably future perfect indicative. **qui . . . reddant** : *people who will return the compliment.* One should be on his guard against translating such clauses as this by *who can return*, an idea which probably lies outside of the sphere of the Latin subjunctive. See note on 346.

475. ipsi : i.e. instead of sending a parasite to do their disreputable errands. **aperto capite** : *boldly, unblushingly;* literally, *with uncovered head;* cf. the expression "bare-faced."

476. in tribu : referring to the *comitia tributa*. The purely Roman allusion is to be noted ; also the hiatus.

477. terrunci faciunt : *count worth a cent;* literally, *make of (the value of) a quarter of an as.* *Terruncius* is sometimes spelled with a single *r*.

478. dudūm hīnc : the *h* prevents elision, and makes the preceding syllable long.

479. quo imus : for the indicative in questions of deliberation, see note on 208. Probably the *s* is here elided before the following *una*. See note on *mag(is) ecfertum* in 466, and App. **prandium** : the first substantial meal of the day, taken between the *ientaculum* (a slight repast soon after rising) and the *cena*, the dinner proper, which commonly came at about three o'clock. Perhaps *luncheon* makes the best translation for *prandium*.

480. hoc : the adverb, = *huc*. Both *hoc* and *huc* were probably different forms of the accusative singular neuter of the pronoun *hic*, just as *istoc* and *istuc* were both used as the neuter singular of the pronoun *istic* (= *iste*). This accusative was originally felt as expressing limit of motion, but after a time the two forms came to be regarded sometimes as adverbs ; still later they were differentiated, *hoc* being retained as the pronoun and *huc* as the adverb. **profitetur** : *volunteers.* **silent** : when used strictly *silere* means *to make no noise;* *tacere, to say nothing.* *Silere* therefore includes the idea of *tacere.*

481. neque me rident : the parasite expected them to laugh at the good-natured impudence of his question. **ubi cenamus** : see notes on *quo imus?* and *prandium* in 479. **abnuont** : *shake their heads;* for the *-ont*, see Introd. § 86 (*a*), and notes on 8 and 81.

482. unum: hardly stronger here than an indefinite article; English *an*, German *ein*, French *un*, etc., are kindred with the Latin *unus*. **dictis melioribus**: *choice jokes.*

483. menstrualis: *for a month.*

484. compecto: from *compeciscor* (*compaciscor*).

486. saltem: to be taken with *dentes restringerent*.   **si . . . arriderent**: subjunctive apparently because the speaker is indirectly reporting the thoughts he himself had at the time of the experience referred to.   **dentes ut restringerent**: *by showing their teeth;* literally, *so as to bind tight the teeth* (i.e by stretching the lips over them in a forced laugh).   For the *ut*-clause, see note on 424.

487. me . . . ludificarier: *that they are making fun of me;* literally, *that I am being made fun of.*

488. una res: *always the same story.*

489. in Velabro olearii: another distinctly Roman allusion. The *Velabrum* was a quarter of the city famed particularly for its provision markets.   Oil formed one of the most important staples, and merchants frequently conspired together to keep up the prices to the detriment of the people.   Ergasilus thinks that there is now a conspiracy against parasites.

491. obambulabant: *were hanging around.*

492. barbarica lege: *barbarica* means *foreign*.   Here, in the mouth of a Greek character, it virtually means *Roman*, just as in the mouth of a Roman it might mean Greek.   The particular law to which reference is here made is the one in the Twelve Tables, which prohibited combinations against public interests.   **certumst**: *I'm determined; certum est* (in which expression *certum* is the participle of *cernere*) strictly means *it has been decided* (*by me*).   The regular participle of *cernere*, however, is *cretus* (found chiefly in compounds); the other form, *certus*, except in the expression under discussion, came to be used merely as an adjective.   See note on 215*a*.

493. concilium iniere: i.e. have joined the conspiracy.   The second foot of this line is a proceleusmatic, but the line may be corrupt. **uictu et uita**: *from getting a living*.   *Victus* refers to the sustenance which makes life (*uita*) possible.

494. is: for *iis* (*eis*); cf. *gratis* for *gratiis*.   **diem dicam**: i.e. set a day for their trial.   **ut . . . dent**: in apposition with *multam*.

495. meo arbitratu: *at my pleasure*.   **quom . . . sit**: the subjunctive is due to indirect discourse.   **sic egero**: *that's the way I'll fix 'em, have it out with them*.   The tense of *egero* is not a true future perfect, but is used for rhetorical effect to indicate energetic action and unceremoniousness ; see notes on 194, 293, 341.

496. est illic : the emphatic position of *est* calls into prominence the idea that elsewhere there is *not*. Ergasilus proposes now to try his fortunes among the new arrivals at the harbor.

497. decolabit : *shall fizzle out.*

ACT III. SCENE 2.

499. bono publico : ablative of attendant circumstance. Hegio thinks his act will not merely give him back his son, but will redound to the public good by rescuing a citizen from slavery.

501. uident : the subject is indefinite, "they," "people," "my friends," or the like, and *quisque* is in partitive apposition to this subject ; cf. "*they each* took one."

502. ita : anticipating the result expressed in 504 ; see note on that line.

504. uix . . . iam eminebam : *I scarcely kept my head above board any longer, wretch that I was, in consequence of (the flood of) congratulations.* The result of *ita . . . reddiderunt* is here expressed paratactically, where we might have had *ut uix . . . iam eminerem ;* cf. "I was so tired I could hardly hold up my head," for "so tired *that* I could," etc.

505. abii : *got away.* **ad praetorem** : see note on 450.

506. ilico : *on the spot ; ilico* is probably from *in* and *sloco,* the old form of *loco.*

510. protinus : *forthwith.* **inde** : i.e. from his brother's.

511. Philocratem : the object of *nouerit.* Its emphatic position serves to concentrate the attention at once upon the individual himself ; the particular question asked about him follows as a matter of minor importance. **ecquis** : *whether any one.*

512. hic : with a gesture toward Aristophontes, another captive from Elis, who is accompanying him.

514. hunc : i.e. Aristophontes.

515. ut conuenias : in apposition with the antecedent of *quod.*

ACT III. SCENE 3.

516. nunc illud est, quom : *illud* refers to *tempus,* understood as the antecedent of *quom,* which was in its origin a case form of the relative pronoun. The more remote demonstrative *illud* seems to

indicate a time previously anticipated and pondered over.   **fuisse** :
i.e. *to be no more, to be dead;* literally, *to have been.* See note on
243.   **nimio** : *very much;* in its origin, *nimio* is ablative of degree
of difference, but it came to be felt as an adverb.   **mauelim** : the
fuller form of *malim;* the subjunctive would be used here even in an
independent clause ; incidentally it may serve here to characterize
the antecedent of *quom* (forming a predicating characterizing clause
of the original type ; see note on 12), as in Enn. *Ann.* 383 (Vahlen),
nunc est ille dies quom gloria maxima sese Nobis ostendat, si uiui-
mus siue morimur, though this latter is a clause of the developed
type.   Cf., however, 518, where the indicative is used in a similar
clause.

517. spernunt : here in its original sense of *separate,* a rare use.
518. hic illest dies, quom : see note on 516. See App.
meae : *mēae.*   **sperabilist** : i.e. *sperabilis est;* for the disappearance of the final *s* and the initial *e,* see note on *captust* in Argumentum, 1.

519. neque exitium exitio : the accusative *exitium* is governed
by the idea of *exire* (construed with the accusative in the sense of *evade,*
avoid), that is present in the verbal substantive *exitio* (nominative
case), *an evading.*   A similar phenomenon is occasionally met with
in English, in expressions like " there's no evading death," where the
use of "no" shows that "evading" is felt as a substantive, while
the use of " death," instead of " of death," shows that " evading" is
felt as partaking also of a verbal nature ; see Introd. § 92 (*a*).   The
pun in *exitium exitio* is inimitable.   **neque adeo** : *nor yet ;* see note
on 348.   **quae . . . aspellat** : *to drive away,* or perhaps *which shall*
drive away.   Such clauses are commonly explained as akin to purpose
clauses ; but perhaps they are developed from an anticipatory use of
the subjunctive, — a use common in Homeric Greek, but not preserved
in Latin except in certain subordinate clauses (e.g. in subjunctive
clauses introduced by *antequam, priusquam, donec,* etc.).   See App.

521. See App.
521 ff. **sycophantiis, perfidiis** : *acts of cunning, acts of treachery.*
Plautus is fond of plurals of abstract nouns ; cf. *Trin.* 490, *opulentiae ;*
Most. 348, *industriis.*   Plautus probably wrote *sucopantiis ;* see notes
on 88 and 450.   **obuiam** : *at hand.*

522. neque deprecatio perfidiis, etc.: i.e. the consequences
(to me) of my treachery cannot be averted by prayer and there is no
escape from the consequences of my misdeeds ; literally, *neither is*
there unto my acts of treachery (any) averting by prayer, nor is there

unto my misdeeds (any) escape. Malefactis and *perfidiis* (both in the dative case) are, in a sense, personified; cf. 523, *confidentiae hospitium, deuorticulum dolis.*

523. nec confidentiae . . . hospitiumst : i.e. there is no longer anything for me to depend upon ; literally, *nor is there any hospitality (refuge) unto (for) my confidence;* cf. *Most.* 350, *nusquam stabulumst confidentiae.* **deuorticulum** : *place of refuge;* literally, *a turning-aside place, an inn.*

524. See App.

525. palam est : *is out.* **neque de hac re negotiumst** : *nor is there anything to do about this matter.*

526. quin male occidam : *to save me from a miserable fate;* literally, *but that I should basely perish; quin* follows the idea of prevention implied by *neque . . . negotiumst.* **oppetamque pestem eri uicem meamque** : *from meeting with disaster on account of my master and on my own (account).* In saying *meamque (uicem),* Tyndarus apparently refers to his expectation that what he was doing for his master would result also in his own manumission (cf. 406 ff.). Perhaps our poet intended *meamque* to be uttered under the breath, as a sort of afterthought. *Vicem* with the genitive and *uicem* with the possessive pronouns (*meam, tuam, nostram,* etc.) are both common constructions, occurring sometimes together, e.g. here and *Truc.* 158, *et nostram et illorum uicem.* **meamque** : *mĕamque.*

527. The only way to read this line metrically as it stands is to admit an anapaest and hiatus in the seventh foot ; see App.

528. Philocrati : probably dative ; but it may be a genitive, as Plautus forms the genitive of such nouns in *-i* as well as in *-is ;* e.g. 975; *Philocrati ; Rud.* 86, *Euripidi ; Rud.* 822, *Herculi ; Bacch.* 938, *Achilli,* etc.

529. Salus : *Salvation (herself).* This divinity had a temple on the Quirinal, and the summit on which it stood was called *Collis Salutaris.* **si uolt** : i.e. *etsi uolt.* **nec copiast** : *and there is no chance (for me).*

530. nisi si : is common where *nisi* alone would have sufficed. **corde** : we should say, *in my mind.* **machinŏr** : the final syllable here retains its original long quantity ; see Introd. § 82 (*f*). **astutiam** : (*some) clever scheme.*

531. quam : i.e. *quam astutiam.* **malum** : *confound it! malum* is an accusative of exclamation ; cf. "the mischief!" **quid machiner** : *what shall I devise?* a question of deliberation, anticipating, in reply, some expression of the will either from the speaker

(cf. *incipisse* in the next line) or from some one else. One should
be careful not to use " can " in translating such questions.

531-532. maxumas . . . haereo: *set on foot (some) huge piece*
of nonsense, (some) tomfoolery.   **nugas inepti(as)**: if the text is
correct, the *s* must be elided, or else we must read *ineptĭas*. See App.
incipisse: the speaker thus addresses himself in answer to the
questions he has just put to himself. No promising plan of action,
however, suggests itself at the moment, and in his despair he ejacu-
lates *haereo, I'm stuck!* But at the critical moment, as will be seen
below, a happy inspiration comes to him, and he rises to the occasion
(547 ff.). The initial *h* of *haereo* prevents elision.

ACT III.   SCENE 4.

533. quo . . . dicam: i.e. I wonder in what direction that fellow
has hustled himself out of the house now ! literally, *in what direction*
shall I say that that fellow has, etc.; but the use of a word of saying
under such circumstances is foreign to the English idiom. Cf. 268,
541, etc.   **nunc**: the position of this word makes it probable that
it is to be taken with *proripuisse;* the use of *nunc* seems to indicate
that Hegio has had previous experiences with runaways and was sus-
picious (cf. 456 f.).

534. enim uero (also written *enimuero*): *in very truth.*   *Enim*
alone commonly means *indeed*, in Plautus and Terence, and occasionally even in Cicero and Caesar.   **eunt ad te** : *are after you.*

535. quid loquar: *what am I going to say?*   The following
fabulabor and *negabo* make it probable that *loquar* also is here a
future indicative, but the present subjunctive is much more common ;
cf. 531, *quid machiner?* In early Latin the indicative (but commonly
the *present* indicative) is very common in deliberative questions ; see
note on 208.

536. omnis ín incerto : *omnis* sometimes seems to have the value
of only two *morae* and to have been pronounced *ŏ-mnis*.   **quid . . .**
confidam? *what confidence shall I put?*   See App.

537. utinam . . . perderent : one might expect *perdidissent* of
an unfulfilled wish referring to the past.   **prius . . . quam**
periisti : as *perire* frequently serves as the passive of *perdere*, there
seems to be here a play upon words : *O that the gods had taken you*
away before you were " taken away " from your fatherland.

538. qui . . . facis : the indicative is about as frequent as the
subjunctive in causal *qui*-clauses ; the indicative calls attention merely

to the fact, without emphasizing its causal relation to the main clause ; the subjunctive serves to emphasize this relation and force it upon the attention.   **parata** : *well arranged;* **imparatam** : *disarranged.*

539. atrocem : *outrageous.*

540. hominem : for the construction, see note on 373.

541. quid . . . quod . . . te dicam fugitare : *how* (literally, *what*) *is this, that I should say*, etc.; an awkward circumlocution for *quid* (*cur*) *fugitas?* Cf. a similar use of *dicam* in 533. *Dicam* is probably a subjunctive of obligation or propriety ; see App.

542. quasi . . . noueris : for the construction, see note on 181 ; *noueris* is of course equivalent to a present subjunctive (see note on 240).

546. qui . . . appelles : see note on 538 *qui . . . facis.*

547. hīc homo : the *h* of *homo* seems here to make the preceding syllable long ; the vowel of *hic* (the pronoun) is regularly short in Plautus.   **in Alide** : the emphatic position of this phrase is intended to convey the impression, " his true character is not known *here.*" See App.

548. auris immittas tuas : *give ear to ;* literally, *send* (*let*) *into your ears,* the *auris* being felt as the object of *in* in *in-mittas,* while *-mittas* takes as its object the antecedent of *quod.*

550. illic : i.e. *ille.*   **isti** : dative.   **qui sputatur** : *which keeps spitting,* i.e. the foaming-at-the-mouth disease (epilepsy). *Sputatur* is probably from a deponent *sputor* not recognized in dictionaries (see App.).

551. ultro : *further away,* a meaning of the word preserved only in Plautus. *Ultro* originally meant *beyond, to the further side* (cf. *citro, intro = to this side, to the inside*); then *besides; beyond what is necessary,* i.e. *of one's own accord ; beyond what one would expect,* i.e. *actually.*   **istum** : the accusative is governed by the general idea of *taking away* that is suggested by *ultro.* No particular verb is to be supplied.   **ain** : i.e. *aisne,* but it is merely a common formula expressive of indignation, wonder, or the like, and not a question to which any answer is expected : *what do you mean ! what's that !* or the like.   **uerbero** : *you whipping-post* (*uerberare = to flog*).

553. eum morbum mi esse, ut qui, etc.: *that I have such a disease* (literally, *that disease*) *that it is necessary to spit on me;* literally, *that there is need me to be spit upon.* Epilepsy was apparently supposed to be cured by spitting upon the person who had it. With this superstition compare the practice, still in vogue among boys, of spitting upon their fish-hooks " for luck," while angling.

People of some localities similarly believe that spitting on coins will
bring good fortune.   Interesting in this connection are certain passages
in the New Testament, e.g. St. Mark 8. 23, " And he took the blind
man by the hand . . . ; and when he had spat on his eyes, . . . he
asked him if he saw aught "; see also St. John 9. 6.   The *qui* here is
not the relative, but merely an intensifying particle, as in *atqui*
(at qui); see notes on 28 and 243.   **me**: possibly Plautus wrote *med*,
in which case the *d* would be due to false analogy with the ablative ;
see notes on 240, 405.   **insputarier**: *to be spit upon.*

554. multos : *many are the men whom,* etc.

555. quibus : dependent not upon *insputari*, but upon *fuit.*
fūit : the original length of the *ū* is here retained ; cf. *fúimus* in
262 ; *As.* 782 ; *Mil.* 754 ; 1364 ; etc.   **is** : dative ; see note on 494.
Notice the change, very common in Latin, from the relative to the
demonstrative construction.

556. quid tu : *how* (literally, *what*) *about you?*   With *tu* probably no particular verb was felt to be omitted.   **autem** : starting
with the meaning *on the other hand, but, autem* came to be frequently
used (as here) by the comic poets, in questions prompted by a feeling
of opposition, or reproach.   It may be better translated by giving the
question a proper tone than by the use of any particular word.
etiam credis : *can it be that you believe?* literally, *you even believe?*
Etiam is often thus used in impatient questions, implying incredibility.
Possibly, however, *etiam* is here a temporal particle, equivalent to
adhuc, still.

557. uiden : i.e. *uidesne.*   For the force of *-ne*, see note on 121.
tu hunc : the *h* prevents elision.   **intuitur** : from the archaic *in-
tuor* (= *intueor*) ; cf. *Most.* 836, 837 (*optuĕre*), 838 (*contui*) ; for the
mood, see note on 206ᵇ.   **concedi**: *for us to withdraw ;* literally, *it
to be withdrawn (by us).*

558. Hegio : probably to be read with synizesis, *Hḗgiŏ*, though
synizesis of *io* in nouns is rare.   **fit**: *is coming on.*   See App.

559. credidi, extemplo : both emphatic by position, *I thought
he was crazy right away.*

560. quin . . . ignorat : *why, he doesn't know.*   *Quin* (*qui* + *nĕ*
= *why not?*) and English *why?* came to be used merely to attract
attention to surprising, or incredible, or particularly emphatic statements that are about to be made.   It will be noticed that *why*, when
thus used, is commonly pronounced *w'y.*   **qui siet** : the later distinction between *quis* and *qui* does not seem to have been observed in
early Latin.   Even in classical times it is sometimes disregarded.   The

indicative in indirect questions (see note on 206 *b*) is most common
in questions with an imperative, or with some form of the verb that
makes it possible to treat the question as independent, e.g. *dic quis
est.* This seems to indicate that such questions were not felt distinctly as indirect questions, but as not yet far removed from parataxis (*dic ! quis est ?*). Three stages of development may be assumed :
(1) *dic ! quis est ?* (2) *dic quis est;* (3) *dic quis sit.*   **siet** : for the
form, see Introd. § 88 (*a*).

561. aibat: we use the imperfect in the same way, e.g. "some
one *was telling* me the other day that you had been robbed. Is it
so ?" The view that *aibat* sometimes has the force of a perfect is
quite unjustified. For *aibat* instead of *aiebat*, see note on *seruibas* in
247.   **haud uidi magis**: a phrase used much like our ironical "I
dare say !" literally, *I have not seen* (*any one*) *more* (*so than he is*).

562. Alcumeus, Orestes, Lycurgus : famous madmen of antiquity.   **Alcumeus** : the Greek form is Ἀλκμέων (Ἀλκμαίων). In
Latinizing Greek forms, the Romans frequently introduced vowels
lacking in the Greek word ; with the first *u* in *Alcumeus*, cf. *Aesculapius* (Ἀσκληπιός), *techinae* (τέχναι), *mina* (μνᾶ), *drachuma* (δραχμή).
Alcumeus killed his mother.   **Orestes** : he murdered his mother,
Clytemnestra, and was driven mad by the Furies.   **Lycurgus** : the
Thracian king who was driven mad by Dionysus.   **postea**, *then;*
literally, *afterward*, i.e. after admitting that he is a comrade of mine,
we must admit that all madmen are.

563. una opera . . . qua : *just as much as ;* literally, *by one* (*and
the same*) *agency . . . by which ;* see note on 293.   **at** : *at* sometimes
introduces an expression of surprise, indignation, or the like ; such
feelings involve an adversative relation — opposition to what was
expected.   **furcifer** : *gallows'-bird;* literally, *yoke-bearer*. The
furca was a fork-shaped frame which, for purposes of punishment,
was put on the neck, and to the two arms of which the culprit's arms
were bound.

564. non ego te noui ? *I do not know you* (*you say*)*?* *Non* in
questions frequently differs from *nonne* in implying surprise at the
thought that a thing is *not* so, while *nonne* implies confidence that the
thing *is* so ; cf. "you do not think so ?" with "do you not think so ?"
Nonne, however, is rare in early Latin.   **pol** : *gad !*

566. The chiasmus in this line is noteworthy.   **eum ignoras** :
eum ignoras.

567. immo : see note on 209.   **ait** : *ăit.*   **qui non est** : in
early Latin a relative clause in indirect discourse, unless it depends

directly upon another subjunctive, commonly takes the same mood as in direct discourse, e.g. 720 ; Ter. *Phorm.* 4, 9, 21, 251, 424, 481 ; *Adelph.* 14, 67 (*bis*), etc.

568. **tu**, etc. : emphatic, *in you, no doubt, is found a man, who,* etc.   **enim** : see note on 534.   **qui superes** : *who surpasses,* a predicating characterizing clause of the developed type (clause of characteristic) ; see note on 12.   **ueriuerbio** : a word coined apparently by Plautus.

569. **uera . . . conuincas** : *pervert* (literally, *overcome*) *the truth.* **uanitudine** : *empty lies.*

570. **agedum** : *come now.* This enclitic -*dum* is akin to the *dum* which means *while*, etc., and was probably, in its origin, an accusative expressing duration of time, *a moment.* With imperatives it came to be used merely to emphasize the command. Cf. the German *mal, einmal* with imperatives ; e.g. *warte mal, just wait, wait once.* **em** : *well! here you are!* calling attention to the fact that he has complied with the request just addressed to him.

571. Cannot be read metrically as it stands.

573. **Alidem** : for *in Alidem;* see Introd. § 92 (*d*).

574. **quem patrem, qui** : loosely constructed, as frequently in colloquial speech ; the real meaning is "*father*" (*say you*) *of one who is a slave ?* and the *qui* has for its antecedent the genitive that is suggested in the *quem*.   The father of a slave was not legally recognized as such ; a slave was designated not as the *filius* of anybody, but as the *seruos* of his master.   **et tu quidem** : *you, too, for that matter.* Notice the clever manner in which Tyndarus turns the taunt of Aristophontes.

575. **fuisti** : *are no longer;* literally, *were,* see notes on 243, 516. **fore** : sc. *liberum;* while the preceding *liber fuisti* seems best translated by *are no longer free,* it strictly means, of course, *you were free* (the virtual meaning represented by the translation being due merely to the contrast with present time suggested by the tense); the construction *fore* (*liberum*) is therefore a natural one.

576. **reconciliasso** : equivalent to *reconciliauero, shall have brought back;* for the meaning of this word, see note on 33; for the form, that on 124 (*faxis*).

577. **gnatum** : sc. *esse,* which has possibly dropped out after *gnatum,* as the line is not complete as it stands.

578. Tyndarus purposely misconstrues what Aristophontes meant by *liberum*.   **Liberum** : this suggested identification of Tyndarus with Bacchus is a touch that the audience would be sure to appreciate.

579. **ut** : *how.*   **te ludos facit** : *is making game of you;* literally, *is making you* (i.e. *causing you to be*) *games.*

581. **qui uiuas** : (*anything*) *to live on;* literally, *whereon you may live,* a volitive characterizing clause ; see note on 12. For the ablative (or instr.) *qui,* see note on 28.

582. **omnis similis** : accusative plural.   **inueniri** : i.e. *to be made out to be.*   **tui** : for the *similis* constructions, see note on 116.

583. **miserorum** : A. & G. 214. *d;* B. 198. 3 ; G.-L. 366. Rem. 1 ; H. 447.   **bonis** : opposed to *miserorum.*

584. **sis** : i.e. *si uis.*   **insistas credere** : *persist in believing.*

585. **aliquid pugnae edidit** : a slang expression, *has been putting up some game* (*on you*) ; literally, *has put forth something of a fight.*

586. **filium tuom quod**, etc. : *this son of yours — his talk about ransoming him by no means pleases me;* literally, *as to the fact that he says he is going to ransom your son, it,* etc. ; for the loose use of the present (*redimere*) referring to the future, see note on 194.   **se ait** : *s(e)ait.*   **ne utiquam** : a reminiscence of the time when *ne* was used in the sense of *not;* these two words are sometimes written *neutiquam,* but as the *e* of *ne* is regularly elided in Plautus, *n(e)ut-* being always short, it seems better to write *ne utiquam.*

587. **scio** : notice the exasperating emphasis. Aristophontes, in saying *id ne utiquam mihi placet,* intended the *id* to refer to the *quod-*clause (*the fact that he says,* etc.) But Tyndarus at once takes the *id* as referring to the return of Hegio's son : "of course you don't want his son returned ; I am well *aware* of *that* without your telling me."   **si di adiuuant** : a loose use of the present tense for the future. It would be possible, however, to conceive of this as referring to present aid.

588. Tyndarus is trying to give Aristophontes a hint of what is really on foot.

589. **propterea** : *that is the reason why.*   **quin** : *w'y;* cf. note on 560.

591. **esse** : depending upon the idea of saying in *exprobrare.*

592. **enim** : see note on 534.   **iam nequeo contineri** : *can no longer contain myself* (literally, *be held together*).   **heus** : *look out there;* Tyndarus construes Aristophontes' words as meaning that he could *no longer restrain himself* (*contineri*).   **audin quid ait** : see note on 560.   **quin fugis?** *why don't you run?* This line is unmetrical as it stands.

593. iam: *in a minute.*   **insectabit**: *will be chasing;* cf. 552, where the verb is deponent.   **illunc**: see Introd. § 87 (*b*).   **iubes**: another loose use of the present for the future perfect.

594. conprehendi: *arrested.*   **fit opus**: *the fit is on, es geht schon los;* literally, *the work is being done.*

595. uiden: for the non-committal force of *-ne,* see note on 121. **maculari**: *is getting speckled.*

596. atra bilis: such a condition of the bile was supposed to indicate madness; cf. μελαγχολία, *melancholy,* which etymologically means *black bile.*   **at**: see note on 563.

597. pix atra: the inverted order of words, as compared with *atra bilis,* serves to heighten the contrast. The allusion is to a mode of punishment by which a slave was covered with pitch and then set on fire; cf. Juv. 1. 155; Lucr. iii. 1017. See App.

598. laruae: *evil spirits;* the word is always trisyllabic in Plautus, though dissyllabic in classical times.

600. habere: logically this has a causal relation to *crucior;* the infinitive depends upon the idea of thinking that is involved: *I'm going distracted that I have not* (i.e. *at the thought of not having*).

602. quaeritare: sc. *eum;* the subject of an infinitive is frequently omitted in colloquial Latin, even when it is not the same as the subject of the principal verb.   **solus . . . uolo**: i.e. I want a private interview with you.

603. istinc: *from where you are.*   **tamen**: with reference to the *procul* (*though at a distance, still*).

604. denasabit: a word invented by Plautus, and not found elsewhere: *will de-nose.* We should expect the present subjunctive in the apodosis; the future indicative is used to emphasize the certainty of occurrence.

605. insanum Hegio: initial *H* here prevents elision of the preceding syllable.   **creduis**: archaic for *credas;* see Introd. § 88 (*a*).

607. uerum: see note on 269.   **uolo**: *I am willing,* as often.

608. dum: *provided that.*

609. qui uolt: *since he wants to.* Tyndarus mischievously pretends to understand the *uolo* of Aristophontes (see 607) as meaning *I want* (*to be bound*). For the indicative in causal *qui*-clauses, see note on 538.

611. quid mi abnutas? *why do you keep shaking your head at me* (*abnuto,* frequentative)? Tyndarus is making desperate attempts to give Aristophontes a hint.   **quid agat, si**: i.e. his behavior even

now is betraying his guilt.   Nothing but your presence prevents him
from confessing the truth.

612. quid si adeam : Hegio's confidence in the supposed Philocrates begins to weaken.   **nugas** : accusative of exclamation.   **lu-
dificabitur** : *will make game* (*of you*).

613. garriet, etc. : *will rattle off what you will never make head
or tail out of;* literally, (*that*) *to which neither foot nor head will ever
be visible.*

614. quoi . . . compareat : a clause of characteristic (predicating characterizing clause ; see note on 12), referring to the future.

615. ornamenta absunt : **Aiacem**, etc.: *the characteristic dress
*(*of an Ajax*) *is lacking* — (*otherwise*) *when you behold the fellow,
you behold a very Ajax himself,* i.e. he is as much of a madman as
Ajax ever was.   **Aiacem . . . ipsum** : alluding to the madness of
Ajax, caused by this hero's defeat in the contest for the arms of
Achilles.

616. nihili facio : *I don't care a fig;* literally, *I make* (*it*) *of nothing* (i.e. *of no account*).   **tamen** : i.e. in spite of all the risk which,
you say, is involved.

617. inter sacrum saxumque : *between the altar and the stone,*
a proverb that originated at a very early period, when the victim for
sacrifice was despatched by means of a flint-stone (Liv. 1. 24) instead
of a knife.   For another instance of *sacrum* in the sense of *altar*, see
Curc. 471.   **quid faciam** : an indirect deliberative question.

618. quod me uelis : *uolo* here, as often, takes two accusatives.

619. audibis : archaic for *audies;* see note on *nescibo* in 265, and
cf. note on 247.

620. hoc : ablative.   **me** : object of *expurigare*.   **expurigare** :
for the classical *expurgare;* cf. *Mil.* 497, *Am.* 909, *Cas.* 944; *obiuri-
gare, Trin.* 70.   **tibi** : *in your eyes.*   **insaniam** : subject of *tenere.*

621. neque . . . neque : The infinitives are not in apposition
with *hoc*, but depend upon the ideas of saying and proving involved
in *me expurigare uolo;* hence *neque . . . neque*, instead of *aut . . .
aut.*   **nisi quod** : *except that;* for the original force of this phrase,
see note on 394.

622. at : see note on 563.   **ita . . . ut** : *as certainly as.*
deorum : *deōrum.*   **faxit** : for the meaning of the perfect (aorist)
tense in prayers, see note on 172.

625. quin : see note on 353.

626. deliquio : a nominative, occurring only here.

627. tu : emphatic.

628. fuistin : *fŭistin.*

629. Tyndarus is now on the defensive.   **qui tu scis?** *how do you know?*

630. qui : *how.*   **puerum . . . puer** : *I knew you when we were boys together;* literally, *I (when) a boy saw you (when) a boy.*

631. ego . . . maior maiorem : *I know you when we are men together (maior,* literally *older).*   **em rursum tibi** : *there you have it, right back at you!* an expression which is intended by Tyndarus to sound defiant, but which really betrays the desperation to which he is driven.

633. fuitne, etc.: *was the father,* etc.   For the long *ū* in *fuit,* see note on 262.

635. Philocrati : the position of this word again forces upon the attention the fact that the man they have been talking with is *not* Philocrates.

636. quin quiescis : *be still!* literally, *why aren't you still?* See note on 592.   **i dierectum . . . ac suspende te** : *go straight and hang yourself; i dierectum* seems to mean, literally, *go stretched!* (cf. *abi dierectus, Poen.* 160), and is itself sometimes equivalent to *go and be hanged!* In the present passage, the words seem to indicate despair rather than anger.   *Dierectum* is probably to be pronounced *dĭerectum.*

637. tu sussultas (*subsultas*), **ego . . . uix asto** : addressing his heart in a melancholy attempt at a joke, *here you are dancing a jig, while I am so badly frightened I can hardly stand up (asto,* literally, *stand by).*   Notice the strongly contrasted pronouns.   **sussultas** : frequentative ; literally, *you keep up a jumping (throbbing).*

638. satin . . . exquisitumst : *may I depend upon what you say?* literally, *has that been sufficiently ascertained by me?*

640. ubi ego minume (sc. *eum esse uolo*), etc.: i.e. here with me instead of on the way to Elis, as I supposed Tyndarus was, and as I wished him to be.   Aristophontes' question was apparently caused by the fact that Tyndarus had for the moment dodged out of sight, but Hegio, by his answer, gives the question a different turn.

641. tum igitur : *in that case then.*   **deruncinatus, deartuatus** : *buncoed and bamboozled;* literally, *planed down, dismembered.*

642. huius : *hŭius.*   **techinis** : this was probably spelled *tecinis* in the time of Plautus ; see note on 88.

643. uide sis : i.e. be sure not to mislead me ; these words are here somewhat threatening in tone, like our " you'd better look out." **quin** : see note on 560.

K

644. quin: as in 643.   **magis hoc certo certius:** *more surely*
"for sure" than this, the *certo* being merely a repetition of the preceding adverb.   Such a double comparative as *magis certius* is
not uncommon in colloquial language; cf. *Stich.* 704, *magis dulcius;*
Men. 978; *Bacch.* 500; and Shakspere's "the more better assurance,"
(*Midsummer Night's Dream*, III. 1. 21), and "the most unkindest
cut of all" (*Julius Caesar*, III. 2. 187).

645. inde . . . **a puero puer:** *from the time when we were boys*
together; literally, *thence from a boy, a boy (himself).* The phrase
a puero is merely a closer definition of *inde.*   **puer:** in apposition
with Philocrates.   This construction would commonly indicate that
Philocrates is still a boy at the time the sentence is uttered, but the
appositional construction is sometimes loosely used; cf. Cic. *de senect.*
9. 30, *Metellum memini puer ita bonis esse uiribus,* where *puer* does
not indicate that the speaker is a boy, but that he remembers that,
when he was a boy, Metellus had, etc.

647. corpore: *complexion.*

648. crispus, cincinnatus: *with hair curly and well crimped.*
Crispus refers to hair naturally curly; *cincinnatus* to flowing locks
artificially curled.   **conuenit:** *it tallies,* i.e. your words correctly
describe the appearance of the supposed Tyndarus, who has been sent
to Elis.

649. ut quidem hercle, etc.: *that I, confound it all, came out*
to-day under auspices most unfortunate! Such a clause is exclamatory in feeling, but is conceived of as also expressing the result (hence
ut) of circumstances; cf. Ter. *Phorm.* 772, *ut stultissime quidem* . . .
rem gesserimus! that we have managed things like consummate fools!
The *ut*-clause in our passage is sometimes explained as depending
upon *conuenit,* which Tyndarus is then supposed to use for his own
purpose with the sense of *it is agreed,* but after *conuenit* in this sense
we should have had *me* . . . *processisse* instead of *ut* . . . *processerim.*
Conuenit ut with the subjunctive might express agreement as to
purposes that shall be attained, or determination that shall be carried
out, but not agreement as to facts or events that are past.   **in**
medium . . . **pessume processerim:** the phrase *in medium pro-*
cedere is used of a man going out from the privacy of his home in the
morning to begin his day's work.   There was a common superstition
that a man began each day either under good or under bad auspices,
the influence of which lasted throughout the day; cf. "getting out of
the wrong side of the bed."   *Pessume* here has reference to these auspices; cf. *Stich.* 459, *auspicio hercle hodie optumo exiui foras; Epid.*

183, *liquido exeo auspicio foras, aui sinistra;* Ter. *Adelph.* 979, *processisti hodie pulcre.*

650. morientur : i.e. will be broken.

651. uerba mihi data esse : *I have been imposed upon; uerba dare* means *to give words (and nothing but words — words without any basis of fact),* i.e. *to practise deceit.*

652. ut uos custodiam : Tyndarus is not so badly frightened that he cannot indulge in a bit of humor.

653. satin : i.e. *satisne.* This and similar passages are commonly interpreted as questions, but such an interpretation makes the use of *satis* seem very unnatural. The enclitic *-ne* has two distinct uses in early Latin : —

(1) as an interrogative particle ;
(2) as an emphasizing particle with the sense of *uero, indeed.* Cf. e.g. *Trin.* 634, Lɣ. *Egone?* Lᴇ. *Tune*; Ter. *Phorm.* 153, *adeon rem redisse, to think that things have come to such a pass!* and many similar passages.

Satin is probably an instance of the latter use.   **illi hodie** : the *h* prevents elision here, as often ; see Introd. § 74, and App.

655. nuculeum = *nucleum;* cf. *periculum* with *periclum, Aesculapius* with Ἀσκληπιός, etc.; see note on *Alcumeus* in 562.

656. stolido : an adjective agreeing with *mi, fool that I was.* **sursum uorsum** : *upturned.* Probably *uorsum* is here a participle modifying *os,* though the two words *sursum uorsum* are frequently used together as an adverbial expression meaning *upwards.*   **os subleuere offuciis** : an expression said to have originated in the practical joke of painting the face of a sleeping person. It thus came to be used in the sense of *make a fool of, hoodwink.*

657. quidem : spends its force on *hic* and adds a contemptuous force.   **Colaphe, Cordalio, Corax** : *Cuff, Club, Knocker* (modelled after κόλαφος, κορδύλη, and κόραξ). Plautus probably wrote *Colape.*

658. lora : the thongs with which Tyndarus was to be flogged. **lignatum** : supine. *Lora* were also used for binding together sticks of wood into a bundle suitable for carrying. The slaves, as a bit of pleasantry, asked whether, by ordering out the straps, Hegio intends to have them fetch wood.

ACT III. SCENE 5.

660. quid . . . negoti : *what kind of business, what piece of nonsense?* literally, *what of business?*

661. sartor : *cultivator ;* literally, *hoer.*   **et messor maxume** : *and particularly (as you will soon learn to your sorrow) the reaper.*

662. audebas : here used apparently in its original sense, *to wish, to choose ;* see note on 238.

664. at : see note on 563.   **ut confidenter**, etc.: not *how boldly he has*, etc. (which would be *quam confidenter*), but *how he has boldly*, etc.   **astitit** : not from *asto*.

666. confidentem : *trustful.* Tyndarus plays upon the meaning of *confidenter*, which Hegio has just used in the sense of *boldly, impudently.*

667. sultis : see notes on 110 and 456.

668. has quidem : the use of the contrasting *quidem* implies that the speaker considers the hands of no account.   **uel** : *if you want to ; uel* was originally an imperative of *uolo*, and it commonly carries with it some suggestion of its origin, i.e. it indicates *choice* between things.

670. quod . . . fuit : *so far as lay in your power alone.*

672. deartuauisti : *deártuauisti ;* see note on 641.

678. fallaciis : emphasized by its position, *that it was all through trickery that.*

679. opera atque astutia : hendiadys.

680. id . . . suscenses mihi : *are you angry with me over that?* The *id* is difficult to explain. Possibly it is a loose use of the " inner object," *is that your anger ?* though *id* strictly indicates the cause rather than the substance of the anger.

681. cum cruciatu : referring to the consequences to Tyndarus of his deed, not to anything attending the performance of it.   **tuo** : in translating, one should bring out the emphasis attained by the position of this word.

682. parui : A. & G. 252. *a* ; B. 203. 3 ; G.-L. 380. 1 ; H. 448.

683. ast : seems to have meant, originally, *furthermore ;* in early Latin it is chiefly associated with *si* clauses and used, as here, to add a second condition ; cf. *Trin.* 74, *si demutant mores ingenium tuom neque eos antiquos seruas, ast captas nouos*, etc. ; *Lex Serv. Tull.* (Festus, p. 230), *si parentem puer uerberet, ast olle plorassit ; XII Tables*, V. 7 (Schoell), *si furiosus escit, ast ei custos nec escit.* In the Augustan poets and later prose, the word is used as a synonym of *at ;* cf. also *Merc.* 246, *Atque oppido hercle bene uelle illud uisus sum, Ast*

non habere quoi commendarem capram.   The condition here introduced by *ast* would logically precede the condition *si . . . peribo.*
redit : for this loose use of the present tense, see note on 446.

684. at : *still.*

688. ponere : *expose.*

689. Acherunti : locative.

690. The verb of the *qui-*clause is easily understood from the following *periit;* cf. Cic. *Verr.* IV. 53, *cum aliquid a priuato nonnumquam, occulte auferebant.*   **per uirtutem** : i.e. in a noble cause ; literally, *by reason of his nobility.*   **periit, interit** : there is commonly no essential difference of meaning between these words, but *interit* is here used in a pregnant sense, implying that he still lives in the memory of his survivors.

691. exemplis = *modis,* as in *Epid.* 671, and often elsewhere ; *exemplum* originally meant a *model* ; literally, *something taken out (eximo).*   Such a phrase as *istoc exemplo (As.* 389), *after that model,* easily came to mean *in that manner ;* thus *exemplum* took on the meaning of *modus.*   The word is frequently used of punishments that make "examples" of the victims.

693. uel . . . uel : i.e. I care not for the particular word you use. *Vel* was originally an imperative from *uolo,* and indicates freedom of choice.   **praedicent** : from *praedicare ;* the quantity of the penult (see Introd. § 39), as well as the sense, shows that it is not from *praedicere.*

694. The metrical structure of this verse is uncertain.   The line is apparently corrupt.   **dicant** : already felt as dependent upon *interdico,* but having its origin in an independent expression of permission, *they may say (let them say, if they choose).*   **uiuere** : i.e. *te uiuere.*   The subject of the infinitive is much more freely omitted in colloquial Latin than in more careful styles.

695. faxis : see note on 124.

696. affore : i.e. *eum affore ;* see note on *uiuere* in 694.

697. pro : the interjection.

699. ad patrem : for *apud patrem ;* see note on 49.   See App.

700. aeque melius quoi uelim : *for whom I have better wishes,* literally, *for whom I wish equally better.*   There is apparently a fusing together here of two expressions, viz. *melius* alone and *aeque bene ;* cf. 828, *adaeque fortunatior ; Merc.* 335, *miserior nullust aeque ; Mil.* 551 ; *Cas.* 860.

701. mihi aegrest : cf. "makes me sick," in the sense of "disgusts me" ; adverbs are frequently thus used with *est ;* e.g. *bene est,*

frustra est, palam est, etc. **dedisse operam malam** : *have done a
bad turn.*

703. uotuin: archaic for *uetui* (cf. *uorto, uoster,* etc., for *uerto,
uester,* etc.). The answer "yes" is of course expected, but *-ne* itself
contains no suggestion of this answer ; the effect is much the same as
in *did I, or didn't I, forbid you ?* cf. 713, *emitteresne necne ?* and see
note on 121. It was Philocrates, rather than Tyndarus, whom Hegio
had warned (264) that he must tell the truth.

705. uera obessent : the pluperfect tense might have been expected, but the evil that would have resulted from telling the truth
would have continued into the present.

708. custodem : i.e. *paedagogum,* whose duty it was to look
after the children of the family. **erus maior** : i.e. the father of
Philocrates.

710. sorsum : i.e. *seorsum.*

711. siquis . . . faxit : the speaker starts out as though he were
about to make his whole thought refer to future time, i.e. as if he were
about to say, *think, in case any one should do this for your son, how
thankful you would feel;* the future imperative *cogitato* makes this
the natural course of thought, hence *si faxit (fecerit)* instead of *si
fecisset.* With *haberes,* however, the character of the thought is
changed, and *haberes* is used as though *si fecisset* had preceded. Such
mixed conditions are common in colloquial language. This *si faxit
(fecerit)* is commonly explained as an instance of the perfect subjunctive in an unreal past condition, corresponding to the early use of the
present subjunctive in unreal conditions, but no parallel instances of
such a use of the perfect *in protases* seem to be found.

713. emitteresne necne : this is interesting as showing the really
non-committal force of *-ne* in certain passages in early Latin where it
is said to be equivalent to *nonne;* see notes on 121 and 703. For the
meaning of *emittere manu,* see note on 408.

717. quid tu : see note on 270.

718. recens : an adverb. **nuperum** : no sure instance of this
adjective occurs elsewhere.

719. te perdocere : for *postulare* with the infinitive and a subject accusative referring to the same person as the subject of the
principal verb, cf. *Trin.* 237 ; *Cas.* 141 ; etc.

720. quicum . . . exegeram : relative clauses in indirect discourse, unless they depend directly upon another subjunctive, commonly take, in early Latin, the same mood as in direct discourse ; see
note on *qui est* in 567. **una** : an adverb.

721. ab eo : note the emphasis on this phrase, — *'tis from him, then, that you should seek, etc.*   **petito** : see note on 11 ; the interval to elapse before the carrying out of the command is that between the time of speaking and the next meeting of Tyndarus and Philocrates. **gratiam istam** : *thanks for that* (literally, *those thanks*), i.e. for your fidelity to him.

723. latomias lapidarias : *lapidarias* seems superfluous, but is perhaps added to make it clear that *latomias* here refers to a stone-quarry and not, as it sometimes does, to a prison. Hard work in the stone-quarries was regarded among the severest punishments to which slaves were subjected ; cf. 730, 1000, etc.

724. octonos : i.e. eight each day.

726. Sescentoplago . . . tibi : *your name will be The Thousand-Striped-Man. Sescenti, six hundred*, is frequently used in Latin to indicate an indefinitely large number, where we say "a thousand," "ten thousand," or the like. For the construction of *Sescentoplago*, see A. & G. 231. *b* ; B. 190. 1 ; G.-L. 349. 5 ; H. 430. 1.

727. Aristophontes, who now understands the situation, no longer feels as he did toward Tyndarus.

728. perduis : for *perdas* : see Introd. § 88 (*a*).   **curabitur** : *will be looked after.* Hegio pretends to understand *perduis* as meaning *lose*, instead of *destroy*, as Aristophontes intended.

729. custodibitur : for *custodietur;* see notes on 265 and 619.

730. interdius : ante-classical for *interdiu.*

732. moriri : for the classical *mori;* this verb is often treated in early Latin as belonging to the fourth conjugation.

733. fabrum : *blacksmith.*

734. huic : *istum* has just been used referring to the same person. For similar changes of pronoun, see 2, 112, 547, 1014 ; *Mil.* 22 ; *Rud.* 810 ; etc.

736. facite deductus siet : originally each of the verbs in such cases was independent, *do (as I tell you) ! let him be led away !* In the course of time the subjunctive came to be felt as dependent, as in the present passage, whereupon *ut* came to be sometimes used ; see notes on 121, 360. The perfect *deductus siet*, instead of the present *deducatur*, is characteristic of energetic utterance ; cf. notes on 172 and 622.

737-738. ita curarier, nequi : *to be so taken care of that he shall not fare worse in any way.* It must not be supposed that *ne* in such clauses is equivalent to *ut non. Vt non* in the present passage would mean, *that he will not ; ne* must be translated *that he shall not* (an expression involving the will).   Bennett regards *ita* (737) as meaning *with this plan in view* (viz. *that*, etc.).   For the *qui* in *nequi*, see note on 28.   **quoi pessumest** : *who fares worst.*

740. tuo stat periculo : *stands at your own risk*, i.e. if you do any injury to me, you will suffer for it when my master gets back ; *periculo* is an ablative of price.   For *stare* in this sense, cf. the English expression "stand one in " for any amount, and Verg. *Aen.* 10. 494 ; Hor. *Sat.* 1. 2. 122, *magno stet pretio ;* Liv. II. 36.

741. quod metuam : *that I should fear*, a characterizing clause of obligation or propriety ; see note on 12.

742. summam aetatem : *extreme old age ;* literally, *extreme of life.*   Life is at best so short that it matters little what I suffer here during my remaining years, as compared with the time after death when there is nothing to fear (cf. 741).

743. perferundi : for the more common *perferendi.*

744. salue : *God bless you !*   **ut dicam** : object of *meres.*

745. ut meruisti, ita uale : *may you fare as you have deserved.*

749. peristis : *you are dead men.*   **nisi hunc** : the *h* prevents elision.   See Introd. § 74 and App.

750. uis : *an outrage ;* cf. Suet. *Iulius*, 82, *ista uis est.*

751. illic : this is to be scanned, probably, as a monosyllable *īllc* (see Introd. § 83) ; perhaps, however, *īllĭc.*   **recta** : (sc. *uia*) *straight.*   **phylacam** : φυλακή was probably transliterated *pulaca ;* see note on 88.   **ut dignus est** : i.e. as he deserves.

754. quod absque hoc esset : *and if it were not for this man here* (viz. *Aristophontes*); literally *suppose that it were without this man ;* cf. Cic. *Off.* 3. 19. 75, *dares hanc uim M. Crasso . . . , in foro . . . saltaret.*   *Absque* is thus used in Plautus and Terence only before a personal or a demonstrative pronoun, with the imperfect subjunctive, to form the protasis of a conditional sentence.   After Terence, there is no certain instance of this use of *absque* before Quintilian (7. 2. 44), and then not again till Gellius.   The *quod* is the same *quod* that appears in *quod si*, etc., for which see A. & G. 156. *b*, 240. *b* ; B. 185. 2 ; G.-L. 610. Rem. 2 ; H. 510. 9.   **mihi hoc** : the *h* prevents elision ; see Introd. § 74.

755. usque : *right along.*   **offrenatum** : *with a bit in my mouth ;* cf. our expression "lead by the nose."

756. quicquam credere : *to put any trust.*

760. surpuit : i.e. *surripuit ;* see note on 8.

762. maior : sc. *natu.*   **potitus hostiumst** : see note on 92. **scelus** : *calamity* (originally *crime ;* then, as here, the result of crime).

763. quasi . . . produxerim : see note on 181.   **in orbitatem** : *only to be childless still ;* literally, *unto childlessness.*

764. hac : an adverb.   **neminis** : in classical times the genitive *neminis* and the ablative *nemine* were no longer used; their places were taken by *nullius* and *nullo.*

765. mei : *meî.*

766. exauspicaui : *I set out with good omens.* His release from his chains seemed to be an omen that this temporary freedom might become permanent. For the superstitious belief in auspicious beginnings, see note on 649.

767. redauspicandum esse . . . denuo : *I must omen myself back again* (Morris). *Redauspicandum* is a new coinage of Plautus, made for the sake of playing upon *exauspicaui*, which itself is not elsewhere found.

ACT IV.   SCENE 1.

769. opimitates : the plural of abstract nouns is not uncommon in Plautus (see 522 ; *Stich.* 300 ; *Trin.* 490 ; *Most.* 340, etc.) ; here it seems to refer to the various kinds of property enumerated in the next two verses.

770. laudem : Ergasilus was to be the first to announce the good tidings.   **ludum** : *sport.*

771. pompam : referring apparently to a procession of slaves loaded with provisions for a feast. See App.

772. nec : *and not,* but the " *not* " is to be taken with *supplicare* rather than with *certumst : and it is settled that I shall not,* etc.

773. Ergasilus could now procure for his friends opportunities to feast. By withholding such privileges he could (from a parasite's point of view) ruin his foes.

774. The effect of the chiasmus and the alliteration should not be lost. Ergasilus now thinks better of the day than he did when (in 464–467) he felt like digging its eyes out.

775. sine sacris hereditatem : the reference in *sacris* is to private religious rites observed by individual families. The performance of these rites was a sacred duty which heirs were wont to inherit. As this duty naturally entailed trouble and expense, an *hereditas sine sacris*, an inheritance which did not carry with it any such duties, is an expression that came to be used of any unalloyed blessing, cf. *Trin.* 484.   **aptus** : from *apiscor* (= *adipiscor*).

778. certa res est : *the matter is settled.*   **eodem pacto ut** : *in the same way as ; quo* would be more regular than *ut.*   **comici** : *in* *comedy;* cf. Cic. *De Amicit.* 99, *comicos stultos senes, foolish old men in the play.*

779. coniciam ... pallium: one who was in haste would gather up his cloak and throw it over his shoulders, in order to allow freer movement to his legs. A slave on the run, with his cloak thus gathered up, is a common figure in comedy. Free men were expected to be more dignified than to run; see *Poen.* 522, *liberos homines per urbem modico magis par est gradu ire.* **me hanc:** the *h* here prevents elision. Possibly, however, Plautus wrote *med.*

780. aeternum ... cibum: *permanent board.* There is hiatus in this verse after the fourth foot, and the final syllable of the foot in such cases has the privilege of *syllaba anceps;* see Introd. § 85 (*a*).

ACT IV. SCENE 2.

782. auctior: for the length of the *ō,* see Introd. § 82 (*f*).

784. id perspicere: *see through it.*

785. scibitur: for *scietur;* see notes on 247, 265.

786. extemplo: seems logically to go with *loquentur.*

787. doctus: *wise* (ironical, of course). **verba data sunt:** see note on 651.

788. The position of *Ergasilus* indicates surprise. Upon suddenly catching sight of him, the name comes first to his lips, and then the question: *but Ergasilus — is this he, or isn't it?* etc.

789. conlecto quidemst pallio: *and in such a hurry, too;* literally, *he is of a gathered cloak indeed* (*he has his cloak gathered indeed*); see note on 779. *Conlecto pallio* is an ablative of quality; the *quidem,* as usual, spends its force upon the word immediately preceding.

790. aps: *abs* (*aps*) is a form confined (except in compounds) almost exclusively to its combination with *te.* Even in this combination, it was almost entirely supplanted, in the last years of the Ciceronian period, by *a.* Later, when used at all, it was in affectation of archaic style.

791. nequis mihi obstiterit obuiam: *that no one shall for an instant put himself in my way; obstiterit* is from *obsisto,* not from *obsto.* Such uses of the perfect (aorist) subjunctive, referring to the future, are more common in dependent clauses than is generally supposed, e.g. *Curc.* 559, 764; *Bacch.* 598; *Cas.* 628; *Mil.* 333; Ter. *Phorm.* 554; Cic. *ad Att.* 2. 21. 1; Ovid. *ex Pont.* II. 3. 52. Though the perfect in such cases is commonly translated in the same way as the present tense would be, the Romans felt a very distinct and important difference between the two tenses ; the perfect is energetic, emotional (see App.).

792. nisi qui . . . homo: *unless any fellow.*

793. ore sistet: *will be put on his face* (punning on *obstiterit*), *will get laid out.* This is commonly translated, *will stand* (*get stood*) *on his head*, but the reference is clearly to a knock-down ; cf. *pugilatum incipit* and 796. *Sisto* is here intransitive, as in *Curc.* 287 ; *Mil.* 850, etc.

794. proinde: *therefore.*   **ut . . . sua**: *let all travel ways of their own;* the emphatic position of *sua* seems to mean *this way belongs to me.* For the use of *ut* with the jussive subjunctive, see note on 115.

795. sui: the emphatic position of *sui* suggests, by way of contrast, *this street is reserved for me;* see note on *sua* in 794.

796. meus . . . pugnus: *my fist;* the emphatic position of *meus* is in keeping with the swaggering tone and manner of the parasite. The terms *ballista* and *catapulta* commonly designate the machines used for hurling missiles, but sometimes, as here, the missiles themselves ; cf. *Trin.* 668 ; *Pers.* 28.   The fist is here likened to the stone hurled by the *ballista;* the forearm, to the arrow shot from the *catapulta.*

797. genu . . . iecero: *against whomsoever I shall have set* (*cast*) *my knee.*   For *ad* in the sense of *against*, see Ter. *Heaut.* 545 ; Prop. 3. 19. 9 ; Caes. *B. G.* 2. 5, 7. 70 ; an early poet in Cic. *Nat. Deor.* 3. 29. 73, etc.   **quemque**: for *quemcumque*, just as *quandoque* is found for *quandocumque;* cf. 798 ; *Mil.* 156, *ni hercle diffregeritis talos posthac, quemque in tegulis uideritis alienum, ego uostra faciam latera lorea; Mil.* 160 ; *As.* 404 ; *Merc.* 20.

798. dentilegos . . . faciam: i.e. I'll knock out their teeth for them ; literally, *will make them all tooth-collectors.*   **quemque**: see note on 797.   **offendero**: *fall in with, come across* (literally *strike against*), a very common use in Plautus.

799. quae . . . nam? *nam* is used to emphasize a question, and denotes emotion of some sort in the questioner ; *quaenam ?* differs from *quae?* much as "what in the world?" differs from "what?" The position of *nam* in the present passage is unusual, but cf. *Bacch.* 1114, *quid tibi ex filio nam, obsecro, aegrest ?*   Truc. 938, *quae tria nam ?*

800–802. See App.

800. huius: *huĩus.*   **meī**: genitive of *ego*, not of *meus.*

801. qui, etc.: i.e. the man who gets in my way will suddenly find that he has got in the way of his own life.   **opstiterit**: (a future perfect indicative) this is primarily the verb of the principal clause, though it is felt as doing duty also for the *qui*-clause; cf. the position of *periit* in 690, with note.   **faxo**: (i.e. *fecero*) *I'll settle that in a hurry;* for the form, see note on 124; for the energetic force of this use of the future perfect (not a true future perfect), see note on 194. *Faxo* is here parenthetical, without influence upon the construction of the rest of the sentence, as in 1010 *faxo uenies; Men.* 950, *potabis faxo; Mil.* 463, *iam faxo hic erit; Am.* 355, *accipiere faxo;* and often elsewhere; cf. *Aul.* 578, *faxo perdiderit; Trin.* 64, *faxo dederis; Men.* 521, *faxo comedereis.*

803. Ergasilus adopts the airs and the language of a magistrate issuing an edict.

805. mira . . . sunt ni, etc.: *well I declare, this fellow must have swallowed bumptiousness;* literally, *strange things exist, by Pollux, if this fellow has not,* etc. *Mirum est, it's a wonder if not (I shouldn't wonder if),* is more common than *mira sunt;* but cf. *Pseud.* 1216; *Trin.* 861; *Poen.* 839; *Am.* 431.   **ni hic**: the *h* prevents elision here, as often.   **in uentrem**: *confidentia* would properly be taken *in animum* instead of *in uentrem*, but as the parasite is more likely to put things into his stomach than into his head, *in uentrem* is humorously used with reference to this characteristic.

806. uae misero illi: i.e. I am sorry for the unfortunate man who has had to give this fellow enough to eat and drink to put him into his present condition — he can't have much left.   **quoius**: *quoius*.   **imperiosior**: i.e. so ridiculously imperious; literally, *more imperious (than there's any sense in, than is often seen,* or the like), *too imperious.*

807. tum: *in the next place*, with reference to *prius* in 803.   **pistores scrofipasci**: *pig-breeding millers;* the case is attracted to that of *qui;* the genitive might have been expected, with *eorum* in agreement.

810. ex ipsis . . . exculcabo furfures: *I'll knock the stuffing out of the owners themselves* (instead of out of their pigs); literally, *I'll stamp, or tread, out with my fists;* the use of *exculcabo* in connection with *pugnis* adds a humorous touch. *Furfur, bran,* was frequently fed to pigs.

811. edictiones: for the usual *edicta.*

812. satur homost: exactly like our *the fellow's full*, except that *satur* has reference to the effect of food, rather than to that of

drink.   **profecto** : contrasted with *mira edepol sunt ni* in 805.
confidentiam : see note on 805.

813. **piscatores** : for the construction, see note on *pistores* in 807.

814. **aduehuntur** : *ride up.*

815. **odos** : early form for *odor;* cf. *arbos, labos,* for *arbor, labor.*
An original *s* between two vowels regularly became *r* ; hence the original *odosis, odosi,* etc., became *odoris, odori,* etc., and after the analogy
of such forms in the other cases the nominative *odos* became *odor.*
Monosyllables like *flos, mos,* etc., resisted this change in the nominative.

subbasilicanos : *the arcade-loungers, sub-* calling attention to the roof
above them.   A *basilica* was a large open building, the floor space of
which was divided into aisles by rows of colonnades, and which was
used as a hall of justice and as a public meeting place, serving, in some
respects, the purposes of a modern "town hall."   The first basilica
mentioned as existing in Rome was the Basilica Porcia, built by Cato
the Censor in 184 B.C., the year in which Plautus died.   Plautus must
here have in mind an earlier basilica, of which no account has been
preserved.   For Roman allusions in Plautus, see note on 34.

817. **alieno naso** : *to other people's noses.*

818-822. See App.

818. **concinnant** : not uncommon in Plautus in the sense of *red-
dere, make, render.*   **liberis** : *little ones;* literally, *children;* used
here of the young of sheep to give a touch of pathos.   Ergasilus is
trying to heighten the enormity of the offences of which the *lanii* are
guilty and thus enhancing his own merits in proposing to trounce
them.

819. **qui locant caedundos agnos** : i.e. who contract to furnish
the public with lambs that are to be fat and tender ; literally, *who
contract for lambs as fit to be slaughtered.*   The emphatic position
of *locant* is due to a design to contrast strongly the idea of *locant* with
that of *danunt* — what they agree to do, with what they actually do.
For another instance of *caedundus* in this sense, see *Aul.* 567, where
Megadorus, upon being accused of having bought a lean and unsuitable
lamb for a feast, replies *caedundum conduxi ego illum, I bought (contracted for) that lamb as one fit for killing* (i.e. for eating).   See App.

duplam agninam danunt : *give the public twice as much lamb (as they
agreed to),* i.e. lamb twice as old — old sheep instead of genuine lamb.
Another interpretation is commonly given, but see App.   **danunt** :
archaic for *dant; nequinont* occurs for *nequeunt,* and *obinunt* (for
obeunt) is mentioned by Festus ; cf. also the *n* in *cer-n-o, li-n-o, si-n-o,*
etc., as compared with their perfects *creui, liui, siui,* etc.

820. **petroni** : Ergasilus probably has in mind the connection of this word with *petra* (πέτρα), *a rock*, implying that the flesh is tough.

822. **mortales** : *beings, creatures ;* as the word, however, is commonly used only of human beings, *mortales* may be intended as a touch of humor.

823. **eugepae** : | **edictiones** : for the hiatus, see Introd. § 85. **aedilicias** : the duties of the aediles included the regulating of the traffic in the markets (the testing of the weights, measures, the quality of goods, etc.) and the care of the streets. Ergasilus has been talking as though these things were in his charge. **hicquidem** : always *hĭcquidem* in Plautus. **habet** : *is issuing ;* cf. *orationem habere, to deliver an oration.*

824. Plautus seems to forget for the moment that his Hegio is himself supposed to be an Aetolian. **mirum adeost** : *it is strange enough ;* literally, *it is strange to that degree ;* cf. the similar English use of "so" in the sense of "very," e.g. "it is *so* strange !" For the different senses of *adeo*, see note on 348.

825. **regalior** : *right royal.*

826. **tantus . . . commeatus . . . cibus** : *such abundant supplies in the line of eatables ;* literally, *so great supplies, food (I mean) ; cibus* is in apposition with *commeatus.* **in portu** : cf. such English expressions as "my ship has come in," in the sense of "I have received a supply of money" ; but the expression may be chosen here because it is by bringing to Hegio the news of Philopolemus' arrival in port that Ergasilus expects to fare so handsomely.

828. **qui** : ablative ; see note on 28. **adaeque . . . fortunatior** : see note on 700. This line is probably corrupt. As it stands, it can be read metrically only by supposing it possible to scan *quī hŏmĭ|nē ă|daeque,* or *quī hŏ|mĭnĕ ăd|aeque.* With *hominē* may be compared *milĭtē* (?) in *Pseud.* 616; *carnē* in *Capt.* 914; *pumicē* in *Pers.* 41; *parietē* in *Cas.* 140.

829. **illaec** : for *illa ;* see Introd. § 87 (*b*). **illic** : for *ille ;* see Introd. § 87 (*b*). **mihi** : the emphatic position betrays Hegio's surprise at hearing his own name connected with the parasite's strange behavior.

830. **aperit** : for the present tense, instead of the future, see 446 and 683. This line is apparently incomplete. Probably something has dropped out.

831. **hic** : this pronoun is regularly short in Plautus. Here the syllable is made long by the following *h.* For the hiatus see note on 331 and Introd. § 85. **ambas foris** : referring, of course, to the two leaves of the door. Ergasilus needed plenty of room in his present inflated condition.

833. perlubet : *I should like very much.* **hominem colloqui :** the construction of *colloquor* with the accusative is rare except in Plautus. Other writers would say *cum homine colloqui.* **Ergasilum :** the position of this word gives much the same emphasis as in " Ergasilus ! — who calls Ergasilus ? " **qui :** the later distinction between *quis* and *qui* does not seem to have been observed in early Latin. Even in classical times it was sometimes disregarded.

834. nec facit nec faciet : plays upon the two meanings of *respicere;* (1) *look back at*, in which sense Hegio has just used it; and (2) *have regard for, be propitious to.*

835. mihi : *I assure you.*

836. quantumst . . . optume : (where one might expect *omnium hominum qui sunt optumorum optume*) *thou best of all the best men who exist;* literally, *as much as exists of men, thou best of the best (of them)* ; cf. *Rud.* 706 ; *Ps.* 351 ; Ter. *Phorm.* 853. Similar expressions of quantity, where one might expect an expression of number, are common in Catullus and elsewhere. **in tempore :** *in the nick of time.* See App.

837. nescioquem : *nescio quis* came to be felt merely as forming an indefinite pronoun. In this use all consciousness of *nescio* as a verb seems to have been lost ; even in Ciceronian Latin the expression is followed by the indicative, rather than by the subjunctive of indirect question. In this use the *o* of *nescio* is short ; as an independent word, *nescio* forms a cretic (*nēscĭŏ*), though exceptions to this rule may be found. **ubi cenes :** *(some one or other) to dine with;* literally, *with whom you may dine,* a volitive characterizing clause ; see note on 12. *Ubi* is frequently used in the sense of *apud quem,* just as *unde* is used for *a quo.* **eo fastidis :** *that is why you are putting on airs.*

838. cedo : an imperative form, *give here, here with, out with,* or the like ; plural *cette* (for *cedite* ?).

839. quid . . . gaudeam ? a question of obligation or propriety ; see note on 353. **gaude modo :** *modo* is frequently thus added to an imperative for emphasis, where we use " just."

840. This line is apparently incomplete. See App.

841. iam : see note on 251. **omnis maculas :** corresponding to the English " every speck."

842. quod gaudeam : *on account of which I should rejoice,* a characterizing clause of obligation or propriety ; see note on 12. As the ablative case originally ended in *d, quod,* in cases like this, may be a reminiscence of this early ablative form, though it is sometimes explained as an accusative; see App. The antecedent of *quod* is certainly felt as the cause of the rejoicing; cf. Ter. *Phorm.* 263, *nihil fecit quod suscenseas, he has done nothing on account of which you should be angry;* Cic. *de Senect.* 5. 13, *nihil habeo quod accusem senectutem.* If *quod* is an ablative, cases like *istuc* in *Am.* 1100, *istuc gaudes,* and *id* in Ter. *Phorm.* 259, *an id suscenses illi?* are you angry at him for that? will have to be explained as due to analogy with *quod* which was wrongly understood as an accusative.

843. bene facis: this phrase is commonly used in the sense of *thank you,* but it seems here to retain something of its literal meaning. **quid iubeam?** *order what?* **ignem ingentem**: Ergasilus is thinking of the dinner he is going to have. **fieri**: for the length of the *i,* see Introd. § 82 (*i*).

844. magnus ut sit: *that it is to be (shall be),* depending upon *dico,* which is here a verb of ordering; we use "tell" in the same sense.

846. iuben: i.e. *iubesne.* **astitui**: *to be put in position.* **aulas**: old form for *olla.*

847. laridum atque epulas: this use of *atque* to add a general to a special term is not uncommon; see App. **foculis**: from *fōculum* (*fouiculum,* from *fouere*) *a warming pan,* not from *fŏculus* (diminutive of *fŏcus*), *a little fireplace.* This form with long *ō* is not properly recognized in dictionaries.

850. scis bene esse: *you know how to have a good time;* with *bene esse* compare *Men.* 485, *minore nusquam bene fui dispendio; Truc.* 741; *Merc.* 582. **unde**: *the wherewithal;* literally, *whence, (that) from which;* the subject of *sit* is the antecedent of the relative pronoun involved in *unde.* **pernam**: here probably the name of a fish; see *Plin.* 32. 11. 54. Observe the hiatus after *pernam.* **ophthalmiam**: probably Plautus himself wrote *optalmiam;* see notes on 88 and 274.

852. nominandi istorum . . . copia: *a chance to name those dishes;* literally, *a chance of the naming of those.* The gerund partakes of the characteristics of both a verb and a noun; in *nominandi* (with an objective genitive) the noun-characteristic appears more prominently, the gerund approaching the meaning of *nominationis;* cf. Ter. *Heaut.* 29, *nouarum spectandi copiam; Lucr.* 5. 1225; Cic. *Inv.* 2. 1; *Fin.* 5. 7. The English present participle shows a tendency toward a similar development; cf. "he believes in *doing good,*" and "he believes in *the doing of good*"; in some localities are heard expressions like this last, without the definite article, e.g. "in doing of it."

853. mea : emphatic, *that it is on my own*, etc.; i.e. it is the good news I am bringing to *you* that makes me so elated.

854. ne frustra sis : *don't fool yourself*. Perhaps, however, this *ne*-clause is subordinate.

855. tui cottidiani uicti uentrem : *an appetite for everyday fare;* literally, *the stomach of your daily living.* **uicti** : substantives of the fourth declension commonly in early Latin have their genitive in -*i* (rarely -*uis*), e.g. *senati, quaesti*, etc.

856. quin : for this use, see note on 560. **ita faciam ut . . . cupias** : *I will make you desire;* literally, *I will bring it about so that you would desire; cupias* serves as the apodosis of *etsi uetem*, as well as to express the result of *ita faciam*. If the text is correct, *faciam ut* is to be read without elision. See App.

857. tu ne : *yes, you; ne* seems to be the asseverative particle *nē*, instead of the enclitic -*ne;* cf. *Most.* 955; *Stich.* 635. The particle, however, commonly precedes the pronoun. **tum . . . igitur** : *in that case, then.* **tu mi . . . erus es** : i.e. *I am yours to command.* **immo beneuolens** : *nay, your well-wisher (rather)* ; on the meaning of *immo*, see note on 209.

859. cedo : see note on 838. **em manum** : for the construction of *manum*, see note on 373. **nil sentio** : literally, *I have no perception of the fact (nil* being accusative of the "inner object," or the "result produced ")* ; for the sake of preserving the pun, one might translate this, *I do not think it*, and the next line, *to be sure you are not in a thick-et, that's why you do not think it.*

860. For the pun, see note on *nil sentio* (859). Probably *esse in senticeto* was proverbial, meaning *to be in trouble; non es in senticeto* would then have much the same force as "you are out of the woods," i.e. your troubles are over — Philopolemus has returned. It can hardly be supposed that such an expression is dragged in merely for the sake of the pun.

861. ad rem diuinam : i.e. for the performance of sacred rites in honor of the son's return.

862. proprium : *special.*

863. deorum : *deōrum.* **summus** : *most high.*

864. idem ego sum : *I am also;* literally, *I the same am.* **Laetitia** : *gladness*, that shows itself in the face, manner, etc. **Gaudium** : *joy*, that may be too deep-seated to be seen by the observer. Both are here personified as deities.

865. deum : the *h* prevents elision. Probably *deum* is here monosyllabic by synizesis. See App.

L

866. uidere : i.e. *uideris*.   **miquidem esurio** : *it's for myself (in my own interest) that I'm hungry*.   Ergasilus, in jest, pretends to misunderstand Hegio's *mihi* as modifying *esurire* (instead of *uidere*, as Hegio intended).   Notice that *mi* in *mĭquidem* is short; cf. *sĭquidem* (920).

867. tuo arbitratu : *as you please, at your pleasure*, expressing a willingness to acknowledge the truth of the last words of Ergasilus.
facile patior : meant by Hegio in the sense of *I readily grant it*, i.e. I know you well enough to grant that, when it comes to eating, you are "in it" for yourself only.   **consuetu's puer** : Ergasilus pretends to understand Hegio's words (*facile patior*) in an obscene sense, *I readily submit*, and replies *I suppose so ; you had the habit when a boy*.

868. Iuppiter . . . perdant : the use of *perdant* (*perdat, perduint*, etc.) in curses, though extremely common, is confined almost exclusively to make-believe curses, that are not really meant by the speaker; hence the present tense is regularly used instead of the perfect; see note and App. on 172.   **te hercle** : Ergasilus begins as though about to utter a curse against Hegio, in reply to the latter's curse against him.   All of this is of course good-natured raillery, and Ergasilus, after an insinuating pause, substitutes for the expected *perdant* an utterance of a very different character; *te* becomes the subject of *agere*, instead of the object of *perdant*.   **aequomst** : an English-speaking person would be likely to say, *it would be proper*, but it must not be supposed that *est* in such an expression was felt as we feel "would be."   The Latin *est* means merely *is ;* in the present passage, for instance, the conception is *the proper thing to do is to thank me* (*thanks are due me instead of curses*).   See note on 61.

870. nunc tu . . . places : i.e. I am now ready to accept your invitation.   Heretofore Ergasilus has had his doubts about the character of the dinner he was likely to get at Hegio's (cf. 179 ff. and 497) and has been waiting and hoping for a more promising invitation.   Now, however, he feels sure that the good news he is about to announce to Hegio will incline the latter to give him of his best.   **post tempus** : *behind time ;* Hegio means that his misfortunes have left him in no mood for a feast.

871. igitur : connected with the demonstrative pronoun *is*, and originally meaning, *in that case, at that time ;* the *si*-clause seems here to be in apposition with the demonstrative idea in *igitur : in the following case*, viz. *if I had come some time ago, then*, etc., cf. *Mil.* 772, *quando habebo, igitur dabo*.   *Igitur* is sometimes used in connection with *deinde* and *demum ;* e.g. *Rud.* 930, *ubi liber ero, igitur* *demum instruam agrum.*   **olim**: *formerly, sooner,* i.e. before I had heard good news for you.   **istuc**: referring especially to *abi.*

873. saluom et sospitem: *safe and sound;* *et* must be regarded as connecting merely the two terms of this couplet, the couplet itself being added as a unit to *uiuom;* *et* is seldom used to add the last term of a series, when the other terms are without connectives.

874. publica celoce: *packet boat.*   **illum adulescentulum**: i.e. Philocrates.

875. una: *with him.*

877. in malam rem: *to the deuce.*   **ita . . . amabit, . . . ut**: this is a common formula for solemnly certifying to the truth of an assertion, though the subjunctive *ita . . . amet, ut* is more common. In the present passage the future indicative and the subjunctive are found side by side; cf. *condecoret* in the next line.   In the case of this future indicative, the conception seems to be, *is going to bless (love) me according as I have actually seen (and, therefore, speak the truth),* implying that if I am saying that I have seen, when in reality I have not, then I have no hope of being blest; hence, you may be sure my words are true.   **sancta Saturitas**: *St. Cramfull;* humorously personified as the goddess whom the parasite serves.

878. itaque . . . cognomine: i.e. may I always be called Cram-full with as much truth to the reality; Plautus probably has in mind here such names as Saturio (a parasite in the *Persa* has this name).   *Cognomine* seems here used as a general term, without reference to its distinction, when strictly used, from *praenomen* and *nomen.*

879. genium: *good angel;* see note on 290.   In calling Philopolemus his *genius,* Ergasilus is thinking of the sumptuous dinner he is expecting to get in consequence of the former's return.

880. Alidensem: *Elean;* from *Alis* for *Elis,* corresponding to the Doric ᾿Αλις for ῾Ηλις.   μὰ τὸν ᾿Απόλλω: μά in Attic Greek is used chiefly in negative oaths, *no, by —,* but occasionally, as here, it is used affirmatively, *yes, by —.*

881. gnatum: see note on 19.   ναὶ τὰν Κόραν: *(yes) by Cora.* Cora is another name for Proserpina, the queen of the lower regions; but it was also the name of a town in Latium, a coincidence which suggests to Ergasilus the idea of swearing by several other towns in Latium (Praeneste, Signia, Frusino, and Alatrium), as though they, too, were goddesses.   Ergasilus' indifference to the real gender of these town names and the consequential airs he gives himself by swearing in Greek, instead of Latin, add touches of humor to the scene.

882. iam diu : *now long since*, to be taken with the preceding *surripuit*. The idea is so improbable that Hegio thinks there must be some mistake about it. *Diu* commonly means *for a long time*, but frequently in early Latin, and occasionally later, it is used as in the present passage, in the sense of *long ago*. See App.

883. uide sis : *careful now;* literally, *see to it, please* (*that you do not deceive me*).

884. tu : emphatic.   **barbaricas** : i.e. Italian ; see note on 492. **enim** : see note on 534.   **asperae** : *rude,* "*tough,*" a joke at the expense of the towns mentioned, which were at the time very unpopular at Rome. *Asperae* may refer to the rude character of the people or their language, or possibly to the rugged character of the sites of the towns.

885. autumabas : viz. in 188 ; cf. 497.   **uae aetati tuae** : *woe be unto you!* literally, *woe to your life. Vae* here forms an exception to the rule that monosyllabic interjections are not elided.

886. quippe quando : (*you may well say* "*woe be unto you*") *since, indeed,* etc. *Quippe* is frequently thus used with causal particles and causal relative clauses, for greater emphasis.   **mihi nil credis, quod,** etc.: *you grant me no confidence in what I say in all earnestness; nil* is the accusative of the " inner object " (" result produced "); that with reference to which no confidence is felt is the antecedent to be supplied for *quod.* Such an antecedent might be in the genitive case, as seen from passages like the following : *Asin.* 459, *quoi omnium rerum ipsus semper credit ; Truc.* 307, *numquam mihi quisquam posthac duarum rerum creduit.*

887. Stalagmus : the person is thrust upon the attention first, the question about him follows, just as in English we might say, " this Stalagmus — of what nationality was he ? "   **quoius** : q͡uoius. **abit** : in early Latin the historical present is often found after *quom*, as well as after *postquam ;* see 282 ; *Am.* 668 ; *Stich.* 511 ; *Epid.* 217 ; *Most.* 25 ; *Men.* 1054, etc.

888. boiam terit : *he's a captive;* literally, *he wears a boia,* i.e. a wooden or iron collar put about the neck of prisoners ; but *Boia* means also a Boian woman (the Boii were a people just south of the Po), and *Boiam terit,* therefore, means also *he has a Boian wife,* or *a Boian woman has taken him captive ;* it is with reference to this double meaning of the phrase that Ergasilus playfully says, *Boius est, he's a Boian now.*

889. liberorum quaerundorum : alluding to his propensity for acquiring children, shown in his having stolen Hegio's little boy.

891. gnatus: (sc. *esse*) here a participle ; see note on 19.

892. ain tu : (i.e. *aisne tu !*) merely a formula expressive of indignation, wonder, or the like, *what do you mean, sir ?* It is here prompted by Hegio's *si uera autumas.*   **etiam, sancte quom . . . iurem** : *when I would take even a solemn oath* (*if asked to do so*) ; *etiam sancte* is given an emphatic position for the purpose of contrasting his present mood with his previous inclination to jest in taking oaths (881 ff.). For other interpretations, see App. The mood of *iurem* is due to the fact that it is felt, virtually, as the conclusion of a "contingent" ("less-vivid-future," "ideal") condition ; it is uninfluenced by *quom*, which in Plautus takes the indicative (see notes on 146 and 244).

896. nam : (*a very proper thing to do*) *for.*   **nisi mantiscinatus probe ero** : *if I shall not* (*prove to*) *have given an honest report ;* the meaning, however, of *mantiscinatus* (a word occurring only here) is doubtful.

898. unde id : *at whose expense is that to be done ?* literally, *whence is that ?* The *id* refers to the whole idea of *dapinabo uictum*, rather than to *uictum* alone (hence *id* instead of *is*), but the question seems rather pointless after the assurance just given by Hegio. Ergasilus is, however, using the formalities of a legal bargain (*stipulatio*) and he wants to make sure that there will be no misunderstanding.

899. ego tuom tibi : notice the emphasis obtained by the juxtaposition of these pronouns.   **respondeo** : *I promise* (*assure you*) *in return ;* the word here has its etymological meaning, with a play, of course, upon its usual sense.

900. cura : used absolutely, *manage.*   **quam optume potes** : *as best you can ; potes* is frequently omitted in such cases.   **bene ambula** : see note on 452.

ACT IV. SCENE 3.

901. illic : probably to be pronounced *illc ;* see note on 751. See App.

902. iam : see note on 251.   **ut** : *how.*   **collos** : *collus* is an anteclassical form for *collum.*   **tegoribus** = *tergoribus* (from *tergus*).

903. The alliteration is noteworthy in this and the following verses.

905. laniis lassitudo : because the *lanii* will be kept so busy.

906. nam : (*enough of this*) *for.* This is the usual interpretation, but it is possible that *nam* in such cases is, like *enim*, used in the sense of *indeed*.   **morast**: see note on 61 ; cf. *Poen.* 921 ; *Men.* 760.

907. pro: *in virtue of*.   **ius dicam larido** : *pass sentence upon the bacon*.

908. indemnatae : *unsentenced*.   **auxilium ut feram** : i.e. release them from their present predicament ; they were hanging up, like so many culprits.

ACT IV.   SCENE 4.

909. Diespiter: an old name for Jupiter.   B. App. 180. 4.

911. -que: joining *clades* and *calamitas* into a unit, to which *intemperies* is added without connective.

912. Something has apparently fallen out of this line.

913. nimis . . . male formidaui : *was very badly frightened at*.

914. adueniens : *upon his arrival*, i.e. after his arrival ; see note on 9.   If strictly used, the participle should here mean *while in the act of arriving*.   The English present participle is frequently used of action prior to that of the principal verb ; the Latin only rarely. **carnē** : the quantity of the *ē* should be noticed ; see Introd. § 82 (*c*), and note on 828.

916. nisi quae : *except those which* (literally, *unless any*) ; cf. note on 394.

917. percontabatur : *kept asking*, implying impatience.   **possentne seriae feruescere** : as shown by the position of the words, the emphasis lies on *possent*, and betrays some such tone as in "*can we by any possibility* set the pickle jars to boiling just as they are ? " *Seriae* were apparently large jars used for storing meats, as well as wine and oil ; Ergasilus wanted to cook their contents whole.

918. rēclusit : a mute with a following liquid does not make quantity in Plautus ; the length of the *rē* here is probably due to the fact that the fuller form was *redclusit ; rēduco, rēlatum* also occur.

919. adseruate: *watch*.

920. sĭquidem : for a similar shortening of a long accented syllable before *quidem*, see *mĭquidem* in 866.   **sese uti** : *uti* alone would be more common with *uolet ; sese* is apparently used to heighten the emphasis and contrast already produced by *sibi*.

921. nam hic : the *h* prevents elision ; *hic* is an adverb.

ACT V. SCENE 1.

922. deis: *deîs.*

923. quom : *that;* this explicative *quom* must not be confused with the causal *quom*, from which it is distinct in origin and development; the latter, in classical times, regularly took the subjunctive, while the former was at all periods of the language construed only with the indicative. See note on 151.   **reducem** : *redux* is probably not from *re(d)ducere*, but from *redeo;* cf. *trux* from *terreo.* See App.

926. hunc : Stalagmus.

927. haec . . . fides : i.e. the *fides* of Philocrates. Cf. *eam potestatem* (934) for *eius rei potestatem.* See App.

928. ex animo et cura : *from deep-seated anxiety* ; literally, *from the heart and from anxiety*, apparently a case of hendiadys. With *ex animo* cf. the English expression, "from the bottom of my heart." **lacrumis** : earlier form of *lacrimis.*

930. hoc : *the business in hand; hoc agamus* is apparently used here in its literal sense, but see note on 444.

933. immo : see note on 209.

933 ff. The meaning of *immo potes*, etc. (933 ff.) is as follows: *nay, not so, father; you are able to and always will be able, and so shall I, and the gods will always give us the power of suitably rewarding our benefactor, just as you, father mine, are able to do most suitably to this fellow here.*

934. dī ĕăm pŏtĕstātem : for *dī*, see Introd. § 85 (*h*), and for *pŏtĕstātem*, see Introd. § 84.

935. ut . . . muneres : in apposition with *eam potestatem.* **bene merenti nostro** : *our benefactor.* The phrase *bene merenti* is apparently felt as a substantive modified by *nostro.*

936. tu : the emphasis implies that the speaker himself would feel quite unable to invent a suitable punishment for Stalagmus ; but he is sure he can trust his *father* to rise to the occasion.   **huic** : i.e. Stalagmus ; cf. *hunc* in 926.   **pater mi** : *father mine;* this use of *mi* is chiefly confined to tender and affectionate expressions.

937. qua negem : a predicating characterizing clause of the original type (see note on 12): *with which I should refuse* (whatever you should ask, i.e. if you should ask anything whatever). The *negem*, besides being the verb of the characterizing clause, serves also as the apodosis of the protasis implied in *quicquid roges.*

938. postulo : Hegio's word had been *roges;* Philocrates substitutes a less deferential word, and he gives it the emphatic position, all of which seems to indicate that Philocrates now realizes that he is

master of the situation. In 942 Hegio uses *orabis*. **reliqueram**:
i.e. had done so prior to the time when he was hunting up Philopolemus in Elis. The perfect tense would seem more natural to us, but
see note on 305 and App. thereto.

941. quod . . . fecisti, referetur gratia: the *quod* is probably
relative, its antecedent being somewhat vaguely understood with
gratia, thanks will be rendered for your kindness; literally, (*for that*)
which you have done well.

942. id et: taking up again the *id* before *quod;* such repetition
is common in colloquial language.

943. quod ego . . . ei feci male: contrasted with *quod bene
fecisti* in 941.

945. data esse uerba: see note on 651.

946. euenisse: exclamatory infinitive, *to think that,* etc.

947. ne duis: a milder form of prohibition than *ne* with the
perfect subjunctive, and here meaning merely *you need not give;* for
the form *duis* see Introd. § 88 (*a*).

951. statua: i.e. Stalagmus.

952. quid sit factum filio: *what has become of,* etc. ; literally,
what has been done with, etc. ; *filio* is an instrumental ablative.

953. lauate: this reflexive use of *lauare* is not common. **hac**:
adverbial.

ACT V. SCENE 2.

955. talis uir: *a man of your station* (as compared with me, a
slave).

956. Stalagmus disregards the irony of Hegio's words. **fui**:
emphatic. **bellus**: *fine,* from * *benelus,* diminutive of *bonus;* cf.
bene. **frugi bonae**: *serving any good purpose;* literally, *for good
use.* See note on 269; in *frugi bonae,* the use of *bonae* shows that
frugi was nevertheless sometimes felt as a dative.

957. ne spem ponas . . . fore: *do not set any hopes on my ever
being,* etc. **bonae frugi**: instead of *frugi bonae,* as in the preceding line, to put greater emphasis on *bonae.*

958. propemodum ubi loci: *about where; loci* is a partitive
genitive depending upon *ubi.*

959. tua ex re: a significant look or gesture would easily suggest
the verb to be supplied ; for this use of *ex,* see note on 338. **facies
. . . meliusculam**: (sc. *rem*) *you'll be making a bad matter a little
better;* literally, *you'll be making (the matter), from a bad one, a
little better.*

960. If the text is correct, this line must be read with hiatus, *rectē | adhuc.*

961. **quod ego fatear . . . autumes** : *what I myself would (readily) confess, would that shame me (think you ?) when you affirm it ? credin* is parenthetical ; *autumes* subjunctive probably because dependent upon another subjunctive, though it might be conceived of as a subjunctive of the indefinite second person (*when any one says,* as you have just done).

962. **in ruborem te totum dabo** : *I'll set you to blushing all over ;* literally, *I'll put you into a blush whole,* i.e. I'll whip you till you are red all over.   *Dabo* is from the *dare* that is connected with τίθημι, *to put ;* see note on 124.

963. **credo ego** : notice the irony involved in the position of *credo* and *ego,* respectively.   **imperito** : *as though I weren't used to them ;* literally, *as one inexperienced.*

964. The metrical structure of this line is uncertain.   See App. **ista** : i.e. those airs you are putting on.   **quid fers**, etc. : i.e. what you want of me and what you propose to do with me, that you may get from me satisfaction for the evil I have done.   For the mood of *fers* see note on 560.

965. **iam fieri . . . compendi** : *to be cut short at once ;* literally, *to be made (a matter) of saving (abridgment) at once.*   For *iam* in this sense, see on 251, 841.

966. **bene morigerus** : *very compliant ;* an indelicate allusion is intended.

968. **ex tuis rebus**, etc. : *you will have bettered your prospects somewhat ;* literally, *from your (present) prospects you will have made somewhat better (prospects).*

969. **quid dignus** : *quid* is felt as the object of some verb of suffering vaguely suggested by *dignus ;* the full expression would be *dignus ut patiar,* or something similar (cf. *Mil.* 1140).

970. **ea . . . pauca** : *a few of those (punishments)* ; literally, *those (punishments) in small numbers.*   **potis es** : equivalent to *potes.*

971. **pauca** : notice that *pauci* may mean either *a few* (contrasted with none at all), or *few* (contrasted with many).   Hegio used *pauca* in the former sense, Stalagmus repeats it emphatically, but gives it the latter sense (*yes, few indeed will be the punishments that I shall escape*).   **et merito meo** : *and it will serve me right, too ;* literally, *and in accordance with my desert.*

975. **Philocrati** : for this form of the genitive, see note on 528. **quin** : see notes on 560, 589.

ACT V. SCENE 3.

978. quid me: *uolo* frequently takes two accusatives.   **gnatum meum**: the position of these words would regularly be occupied by the subject of the infinitive instead of the object; in the speaker's enthusiasm and excitement, *gnatum* forces its way to the front.

980. diu: for *diu* in the sense of "long ago," see note on 882. **incipit uicensumus**: literally, *begins as the twentieth, incipere* being here a neuter verb.

983. memoradum: in classical Latin this use of the enclitic *-dum* with an imperative is preserved only in *agedum*.

984. Paegnium: παίγνιον = *plaything, pet.*   **Tyndaro**: i.e. *ei nomen Tyndaro;* for the attraction of *Tyndaro* to the dative, see A. & G. 231. *b. c*; B. 190. 1; G.-L. 349. R. 5; H. 430. 1.

986. nili sit faciunda: *is to be regarded as of no account.* The subjunctive is apparently due to the influence of the infinitive; were it not for this, the *quoius*-clause, having the force of an indicative *si*-clause, would take the indicative; see Bennett, Appendix to Latin Grammar, § 401. 2.

987. istic: for the classical *iste* (see Introd. § 87 (*c*)). It is the antecedent of *quem*.

988. huius filius: Philocrates has just asked whether the boy sold by Stalagmus to Theodoromedes and the one given to himself when a boy were one and the same. Stalagmus answers this question with a nod, adding the further assurance *huius filius*.

989. is homo: the fact that Hegio here uses these words, instead of *filius (gnatus) meus*, seems to indicate that he still doubts whether the person in question was really his son ; however, he uses the same words in 337, in referring to his son.   **nil curaui**: differs from *non curaui*, as "I cared naught for," "I cared nothing for," differ from "I did not care for."   **ceterum**: substantive.

990. quin.: see note on 560.

991. ut . . . argumenta loquitur: i.e. judging by the proofs he offers.

993. sum | et: it seems simpler to admit hiatus here than to emend the text arbitrarily. See App.

994. male . . . feci: *I have misused.*

995. eheu, quom: *alas that, quom* giving the reason for saying *eheu!*   **plus minusue**: i.e. more in the way of ill treatment, less in the way of kindness.   **me**: subject of *facere*, understood. Possibly, however, it is ablative with *aequom* (after the analogy of the ablative with *dignus*); see *Bacch.* 488, *me atque illo aequom foret;* and cf. *Mil.* 619; *Rud.* 47.

996. **quod male feci**: *the wrong I have done; quod* is the relative. **modo si**: introducing a wish, exactly as "if only" may do in English; the usage must have originated in some such conditional sentence as "if it were only so, all would be well," from which the apodosis was suppressed, leaving merely "if it were only so!"   **possiet**: the present tense (instead of the imperfect) is not uncommon in early Latin in unreal present conditions; see Introd. § 95 (*a*), 2.

997. **eccum**: see note on 169.   **ornatus**: alluding to his chains and *upupa*.   **ex**: *in accordance with.*

ACT V.   SCENE 4.

998. **quae . . . fierent**: *which were taking place*, i.e. which were represented as taking place; the mood is due to the idea of indirect discourse suggested in *picta*, *represented*.   **Acherunti**: locative; cf. *ruri*, *Carthagini*, *Lacedaemoni*, etc.

999. **enim uero**: see note on 534.   **Acheruns**: commonly masculine, here feminine; cf. *altae Acheruntis*, quoted from an old poet, in Cic. *Tusc.* 1. 16. 37.

1000. **atque**: *as*, to be taken with *adaeque*.   **illic**: for the classical *ille*. With *illic ibi*, cf. the vulgar English, *that there (that 'ere)*.

1002. **monerulae**: the common form is *monedulae;* cf. *arbiter*, *arfuerunt*, for *adbiter*, *adfuerunt*.

1003. **anites**: for the usual *anates* (from *anas*).   **qui**: see note on 28.

1004. **haec**: Tyndarus had the *upupa* in his hand.   **upupa**: the name of a bird and also the name of a kind of hoe, or mattock; this twofold meaning offers to Tyndarus an opportunity to indulge in a grim jest, which may be reproduced by translating *upupa* by *crow* (*crow-bar*).   **qui**: ablative (feminine) of means; see note on 28.

1005. **eccum**: cf. 997.

1006. **quid 'gnate mi'**: *why (do you say) "my son"? Gnatus* is a less commonplace word than *filius*. For some reason, the vocative *fili* is never used in the dramatic poets; *gnate* is very common; see App.

1008. **lucis . . . tuendi**: *of beholding the light of day;* literally, *of the beholding of the light* (see note on 852); some editors, however, regard *lucis* as masculine and *tuendi* in agreement with it (cf. *claro* *luci* in Ter. *Ad.* 841). Tyndarus is contrasting daylight with the darkness of the stone quarries, from which (thanks to Hegio) he is now allowed to emerge (cf. 730).

1009. et tu : sc. *salue.*   **exigo** : here apparently in the sense of *endure.*

1010. faxo : parenthetical and without influence upon the construction of the rest of the sentence. For the force of the future perfect (instead of the future), see notes on 194, 293, 341, 495.

1011. surpuit : for the form, see note on 760.

1014. illic : probably to be pronounced *illc ;* see note on 751. The more remote demonstrative is here used to indicate a return to Stalagmus as subject (the *is* just used, had referred to the father of Philocrates) ; after the attention has thus been recalled to him, he is then referred to as *hunc.* But see App.   **reducimus** : one might expect the perfect tense.

1015. quid huius filium : *what of this man's son ?* At first thought, it may seem strange that Tyndarus receives the announcement that Hegio is his father with a question about Philopolemus, but it must be remembered that Tyndarus has been looking forward to and longing for the return of Philopolemus as the one thing that could rescue him from his suffering and restore him to freedom. Upon seeing Philocrates again before him, it is natural that his first thought should be whether Philopolemus had been brought back with him. As his attention is absorbed by this (to him) all-important question, the improbable announcement just made by Philocrates, that Hegio, the man who is responsible for his suffering, is his father, makes but little impression upon him. Even when Philocrates repeats his assertion, Tyndarus is still very indifferent about the matter ; indeed, at first he ignores the allusion to Hegio, and merely says (1019) that he will make trouble for the slave who stole him.   **quid huius** : the *h* makes the preceding syllable long. Possibly, however, we should read *hŭius ;* see G.-L. 104. 2.   **eccum** : see note on 169.

1016. aïs : treated in early Latin as *āis*, *aïs*, or *a͡is.*

1017. quin : see notes on 560, 589, 643, 856.

1018. tuos : used objectively.

1019. grandis : contrasted with *paruom* (1018).   **ad carnuficem** : differs from *carnufici*, in calling attention merely to the idea of motion, while the dative with *dabo* would connote the " for- " idea as well as the " to- " idea.

1020. Imperfect in metrical structure.   **meritam mercedem** : *a desert* (literally, *reward*) *deserved.*

1021. ēs (ess): for *ĕs*, as regularly in Plautus and Terence. **gnate mi**: see note on *pater mi* in 936.   See App.

1022-1023: such repetitions, on the part of one who is trying to recall something almost forgotten, are common phenomena.   See App.

1024. per nebulam: would be more appropriate with *in memoriam regredior*, but it is apparently felt as going with *audisse;* cf. *Pseud.* 463, *quae quasi per nebulam scimus atque audiuimus.* The *H* of *Hegio* makes the preceding syllable long.   **uocarier**: when used of personal experience, *memini* (to which *in memoriam regredior* is here equivalent) commonly takes the present infinitive instead of the perfect.   G.-L. 281. 2 ; H. 618. 2.

1025. sit leuior: *be relieved;* literally, *be lighter.*

1026. principio : strengthening the idea of *prae* in *praeuortier.*

1027. faber: *blacksmith.*

1028. quoi . . . feceris : as much as to say, you may well speak of "giving" to one who is penniless ; another attempt at a grim joke, in allusion to Hegio's proposal to "give" ("*dem*") him something. *Feceris* is future perfect indicative.

After the close of the play proper, it was customary for one member of the company to come forward, and, in the name of the company, ask the audience for plaudits of approval.   In Terence, the speaker does this very briefly, with the words, *ualete et plaudite*, or simply *plaudite;* but in Plautus, his address is commonly, as in the present play, somewhat elaborate.   It is possible that lines 1029–1036 were pronounced by the entire company in concert, instead of by a single actor.

1029. ad : *with due regard to.*

1031. pueri suppositio : as in the *Truculentus*, in which play Phronesium palms off upon Stratophanes a child, under the pretext that it is hers and that he is the father of it ; cf. also a similar case in the Andria of Terence.

1032. neque ubi: *nor (cases) where.*   **clam**: often a preposition in early Latin, but in Terence only with *me* and *te*.   In classical times it was used only as an adverb.

1033. reperiunt : i.e. in the Greek plays which serve them as their models.

1034. ubi, etc.: *whereby* (i.e. *through the influence of which*), a colloquial use.

1035. neque odio fuimus : *and have not bored you;* literally, *and have not been for annoyance (to you).*

APPENDIX.

THIS Appendix is devoted chiefly to references, comments, or explanations that seem called for by statements made in my notes, or by readings adopted in my text. It has been taken for granted that users of this book who are especially interested in the constitution of the text will have access to all the standard editions, with their manuscript readings, critical notes, and appendixes.

ARGUMENTUM. **4.** The various emendations of this line seem to me so uncertain that I have adopted none of them in the text. Possibly Plautus wrote *captum* after *natum* (Brugmann).

5. Editors commonly avoid the hiatus by writing *in ibus* for *inibi*.

LINE **2.** The most plausible emendation suggested for *illi qui astant* seems to me to be that of Speijer (*Mnemosyne*, XVI. p. 138), viz. *non uili quia stant*, but the reading is so uncertain that the best course seems to be to follow the Mss. See my note.

hi: editors commonly read *i*, but the manuscripts uniformly read *hi*, which (with Bach and Leo) I have retained. For parallel instances of *ille* and *hic*, both referring to the same person, see *Capt.* 1014, illic *indicium fecit; nam* hunc *ex Alide huc reducimus; Mil.* 22, *periuriorem* hoc *hominem siquis uiderit, aut gloriarum pleniorem quam* illic *est;* cf. *Capt.* 110–112, istos *captiuos duos, heri quos emi de praeda de quaestoribus,* his *indito catenas,* etc. (according to the manuscripts); *ib.* 733–734, *abducite* istum . . . *iubete* huic *crassas compedes inpingier.*

10. *patri huiusce:* this line has hitherto been considered corrupt and has been variously emended, but see my note, with references there given.

optumumst: Lindsay (*The Journal of Philology*, 52, p. 287) thinks that "absolute certainty is attached" to Leo's emendation, *optume est.* The latter certainly represents the regular usage in this sense, but under conditions similar to those in the text, we might in English say either "very well" or "very good," and it seems at least possible that *optumum est* was occasionally used in the sense of *optume est.*

159

11. See note.

39. For *illc* as a pronunciation of *illic*, see Skutsch, *Studien zur Plautin. Prosodie*, p. 113 ff.

53. On the force of the perfect subjunctive in expressions of contingent futurity, see *Cornell Studies in Classical Philology*, VI. There I have shown that the *uoluerim* in this line cannot be classed with such expressions. The perfect tense in such future uses of the subjunctive denotes *energetic action promptly performed and promptly completed.* Accordingly, no verb whose meaning is opposed to this idea is found with the perfect tense in this use. With *uos quod monitos uoluerim* in the sense of *which I have wanted you advised of,* cf. 309, *hoc te monitum uolueram ; Cist.* 299, *te uolo monitum.* With this use of a past tense of *uolo* where *uelim* would make equally good (though entirely different) sense, cf. also 430, *quo minus dixi quam* uolui *de te animum aduortas uolo.*

72-73. The repetition of *scortum* in 73 has caused most editors to suspect a corruption in the text. The repetition is sufficiently accounted for by Ergasilus' evident desire to lay all possible emphasis upon the point that he is making. He is contending that, in spite of what the *derisores* say, it is perfectly appropriate that he should be called *" Scortum" ; for,* he says, *it is his scortum that the lover invokes, when he throws the dice — it is his scortum, I repeat ; isn't a scortum then "inuocatum" ? Why then object to my being called Scortum ?*

74. *Scortum* is inserted by Bentley after *inuocatum.* I have not incorporated it into the text, but I believe it to be correct, for the following reasons : (1) it is certain that a word has dropped out ; (2) *scortum* has to be mentally supplied, in any case, to make sense, even if omitted from the text ; (3) the preceding lines show that the speaker is making the most of this word by constant repetition and by centering the thought upon it ; (4) the word would easily be omitted by a scribe, who, glancing up from his copy for a moment, after reading *inuocatum* would, upon turning again to his copy, mistake the *-tum* of *scortum* for the last syllable copied, and would begin writing again with *an non,* etc. The loss of ⟨*est ? est*⟩, supplied by Camerarius, could not be so easily accounted for.

77-83. Karsten (*Mnemosyne,* XXI. p. 296 f.) regards 77-79 and *rebus . . . miseri,* in 82 and 83, as interpolations.

77. This line is commonly regarded as spurious (see, for instance, Spengel, *Philologus* 37, 421 ; Brix, *ad loc. ;* Langen, *Plautin. Studien,* p. 271), but, it seems to me, without sufficient reason. Niemeyer defends it (*Zeitschrift f. Gymnasialwesen* for 1885, p. 361).

85–87. Rozwadowski (*Wiener Studien*, 13, p. 324), following Guyet, rejects these lines, but without sufficient reason. One is tempted to follow Speijer (*Mnemosyne*, XVI. p. 139) in retaining the *canes*, which the Mss. have at the end of 85, by letting it begin 86, *canés sumŭ(s) quándo*, etc., and changing *redierunt* to *rediere*. But it seems equally plausible to suppose that *canes* crept into the Mss. from the margin, where some scribe had written it to make unmistakable the meaning of *uenatici*.

89. *potest*: see Leo, *Plautin. Forsch.* p. 72.

90. Editors commonly omit *ire* and read *ilicet*, needlessly altering the Mss. Instead of reading *uĕl īre éxtra*, Speijer (*Mnemosyne*, XVI. p. 139) suggests *u'l īre éxtra*. See Skutsch, *Iambenkürzung und Synizese*, pp. 12–17.

94. This line is commonly considered corrupt, but see my note, with references. Karsten (*Mnemosyne*, XXI. pp. 296 f.) regards both 93 and 94 as interpolated. On the elision, before a following initial vowel, of a final syllable ending in *s*, see Leo, *Plautin. Forsch.* pp. 224 ff.

102–107. Langen regards these verses as spurious (*Beiträge*, p. 206 ; *Plautin. Studien*, p. 271).

102. A word must have fallen out from this verse, but it seems impossible to restore it with any degree of certainty.

104. *nullast*: Brix reads *necullast;* Leo, *nam nulla est;* but neither of these readings would have been likely to be corrupted into the reading of the Mss. (*nulla est*). Müller reads *in iuuentute;* Ussing, *iam iuuentutis;* others change the order of words. Possibly *ipsi* has fallen out after *sese*, the scribe having looked away from his copy after reading *sese*, and, upon returning, mistaken the *-si* of *ipsi* for the last syllable copied. The difference between *i* and *e* in capital Mss. is often almost indistinguishable. If *ipsi* originally stood in the text, *iuuentutis* must have been read *iŭuĕntutis* as in *Most.* 30, *Ps.* 202*ᵇ*, etc.

110. The colon is commonly placed after *tu*. As the caesura comes after *sis*, it seems more probable that *tu* is to be taken with what follows. Brix-Niemeyer suggests the possibility of this, but in the text retains the usual punctuation.

111. *de:* commonly changed to *a* by editors ; cf. *de quaestoribus* in 34.

112. *his:* most editors change this to *is* (*eis*), but the reading of the Mss. seems correct ; cf. 547–548, *hic . . . istic;* 733–734, *istum . . . huic;* 1014, *illic . . . hunc* (see note on *hi* in Prol. 2).

113. For the punctuation after *istas*, instead of after *singularias*, see Bach, *Studemund's Studien*, II. (1896) p. 322.

120–121. Karsten (*Mnemosyne*, XXI. p. 289) argues that a line must have dropped out between these lines.

121. Schrader conjectures *men* for *mene* and *ipsus* for *ipse;* see *Dissertationes Argentoratenses*, VII. p. 263. On the supposed use of *-ne* in the sense of *nonne*, see Morris in *Am. Jour. of Phil.*, XI. pp. 19 ff.

136–137. Regarded as interpolations by Karsten (*Mnemosyne*, XXI. p. 298 ff.).

139. For the justification of the statement made in my notes, to the effect that there is no such thing in Latin as a negative question of deliberation, see *The Latin Prohibitive* (*Am. Jour. of Phil.*, XV. pp. 313 ff.); also *Cornell Studies in Classical Philology*, VI. pp. 213 ff.

151. For *quom* (*cum*) in the sense of *the fact that*, see, e.g., Hale, *The Cum-Constructions*, pp. 79 and 242.

152. For the use of the subjunctive in expressions of obligation or propriety, see *The Latin Prohibitive* (*Am. Jour. of Phil.*, XV. p. 313), and *Cornell Studies in Classical Philology*, VI. p. 213. For a different view, see Bennett, *Cornell Studies in Classical Philology*, IX. pp. 1–30.

152–167. *Er. Eheu . . . bonum animum.* These verses are regarded by Karsten as interpolations. For *éheū huīc*, see note on 148, with references there given.

157. *quod optigerat:* the editors who retain this line at all, follow Camerarius in changing *quod* to *quoi;* but see my note. The reading of the Mss. seems as likely to be right as any one of the numerous conjectures.

169. *Intus* is commonly added before *Aleum*, on metrical grounds, but unnecessarily. See my note and Birt (*Rhein. Mus.* for 1899, p. 61).

172. For the force of the perfect tense in prayers, etc., see my *Studies in Latin Moods and Tenses* (*Cornell Studies in Classical Philology*, VI.). For an opposing view, see Bennett, *Cornell Studies in Classical Philology*, IX., and for an answer to this *critique*, see *American Journal of Philology*, XXI. (1900).

175. I follow Leo in retaining the reading of the Mss. *te uocari*. The usual emendation (*a te uocari*) misses the wit of Ergasilus' words, referred to in the next line, and is less in harmony with *num uocatus es ?* in 173. See note.

179–181. See Karsten (*Mnemosyne*, XXI. p. 303).

193. *apud:* Leo (*Plautin. Forsch.* pp. 226 ff.) argues that the *d* in *apud* was silent in cases like this.

trapessitam: this is probably the correct form for Plautus; see my note. Harrington (*Proceedings of the American Philological Association* for 1898, p. xxxiv.) argues that there was no letter *z*, even in the earliest Latin alphabet. See Hempl's article on *The Origin of the Latin Letters G and Z* in *Transactions of the Am. Phil. Ass.*, XXX. p. 24.

194. *iuero:* Meifart (*de fut. exacti usu Plaut.*) shows that this use of the future perfect, where one might expect the future, is found chiefly at the end of a line or in diaeresis, and that the choice of this tense is frequently determined by metrical convenience. It must not, however, be supposed that no difference was felt between the future perfect and the future. Very often the energetic and the calm forms of expression (e.g. "I'll *be off*" and "I'll *go*") are equally appropriate in the context. In such cases, metrical convenience may determine the choice, but the difference between the tenses nevertheless remains clear and distinct. See note.

199. Niemeyer (*Plautin. Studien*, pp. 6 ff.) favors the reading *et erili imperio eamque ingeniis*, etc. See Nettleship, *Lectures and Essays*, p. 343; Karsten in *Mnemosyne*, XXI. p. 304. The reading of the Mss., however, may be correct after all (see my note).

201. Speijer (*Mnemosyne*, XVI. p. 144) suggests *Éiulátióne múlta óculis múlta méra ciétur*. I have not been able to see what Schebor says of this passage in the *Journal des kais. russ. Ministeriums der Volksaufklärung*, Sept. 1891, pp. 57–84; Oct. pp. 1–7.

211. For another view regarding the etymology of *arbiter*, see Fay in Vinson's *Revue de linguistique*, 1898, pp. 373 ff.

217. The insertion of *atque* before *ea* seems the best of the various emendations of this line.

243. *esse nunc:* *nunc* is commonly dropped by editors; but see my note.

244. *quom:* perhaps Plautus wrote *quoi*. See Speijer in *Mnemosyne*, XVI. p. 144.

246. *perque:* for the pronunciation *perq* see Skutsch, *Studien*, p. 152. Lindsay apparently rejects the possibility of the scansion *quód hŏstica* (*Journal of Philology*, 22. p. 4).

250. It is quite possible that we should, with Speijer (*Mnemosyne*, XVI. p. 140), read *'n hăc*, instead of *ĭn hăc*.

258. The impression, sometimes given by grammars, that causal *qui*-clauses require the subjunctive, is a mistaken one. Such a clause may take either the subjunctive or the indicative. The difference between the moods seems to be that the subjunctive lays particular stress upon the causal relation, while the indicative merely states the fact, and leaves the logical bearing of the clause to take care of itself. See Hale, *Cornell Studies in Classical Philology*, I. pp. 97, 104, 118, 138.

265. *nescibo:* there is some doubt about the reading. Delaruelle (*Revue de Philologie*, 18. p. 265) argues for *quod nesciumst.*

268. On the appending of *ne* to interrogative words, see *Proceedings of the American Philological Association* for 1892, p. xviii.

274. Nettleship (*Lectures and Essays*, p. 343) suggests *Euge! prae tali Thaletem non emam Milesium.*

280. This line is considered corrupt. It is barely possible that the usual *Ālḗīs* may here be *Ălḗīs* (cf. *Āpŭlo* and *Ăpūliae* in Hor. *Od.* 3. 4 ; *Ītalus* and *Ĭtalus*), or that we should read *Ālеîs.*

286. *quasi:* it has been supposed that *quasi* must be taken with *propter diuitias*, but I can not see that it yields satisfactory sense when so understood. Furthermore, the position of *quasi* is a serious objection to such an interpretation. The explanation given in my note seems to me satisfactory, and the only one not open to objections.

290. Considered corrupt by some scholars, on account of the indefinite use of *quando.* See Scherer, Studemund's *Studien*, II. pp. 107 f. and 129.

304. On the probable pronunciation of *nempe* and *quippe* mentioned in my note, see Skutsch, *Forschungen zur lat. Grammatik und Metrik*, pp. 30, 93.

305. *fueram:* it is customary to say that the pluperfect in such cases is equivalent to the perfect or imperfect. Delbrück very properly dissents from such views, *Vergleichende Syntax der Indog. Sprachen, Zweiter Theil*, pp. 318 ff.) ; cf. Blase, *Geschichte des Plusquamperfectum*, pp. 9 ff., and my note on *dixeras* in Ter. *Phorm.* 613.

306. *alterius:* this is commonly changed to *altrius*, but see my note.

309. *uolueram:* Brix conjectured *uoluerim* for the *uolueram* of the Mss., but this conjecture is based upon a wrong conception of the force of the perfect subjunctive. This use of the perfect subjunctive of a verb belonging to the same class as *uolo* is impossible for either early or classical Latin. See note on *quod . . . uoluerim* in 53, and *Cornell Studies in Classical Philology*, VI. p. 173.

345. Skutsch (*Hermes*, 32, p. 92) suggests *ŏptime* for *omne.*

346. The expression "predicating characterizing," found in my notes, is adopted from Hale.

352. Mähly (*Zeitschft f. d. Oesterreichischen Gymnasien*, 38. p. 588) suggests *hic celere eat* for *hoc cedere ad*.

359. This line has heretofore been supposed to be corrupt. The supposed metrical difficulty is commonly obviated by writing *monstra* for *demonstra;* Lindsay retains *demonstra*, but writes *doce* for *dice*. The line is probably correct as it stands ; see my note and cf. Skutsch's "Ausblick," on pp. 147 ff. of his *Forschungen*.

387. See note.

392. Langen (*Plautin. Studien*, p. 274) would reject this line on the ground that *semper fecit* is absurd, coming from a prisoner captured only the day before (cf. 110 ff.), and that such expressions as are here found would not be used by a slave.

394. *nam quidem :* is commonly changed to *nam equidem*, on the ground that in the eight other passages where the phrase occurs it takes the latter form. In *Ps.* 260, however, C. has *quidem*, and all the Mss. have *quidem* in the present passage. There seems no sufficient ground for changing this reading.

395. Müller (*Rhein. Mus.* LIV. p. 385) suggests *mihi cum hoc* ⟨*nunc*⟩.

401. *me hic ualere :* see Langen, *Plautin. Studien*, p. 274 ; Speijer, *Mnemosyne*, XVI. p. 145. Nencini (*Studi Italiani di Filologia Classica*, 3. p. 84) suggests *ut alibi et tu te* for *valere et tute*.

403. *me aduorsatum tibi :* I see no sufficient reason for changing this reading of the Mss. It is in perfect harmony with (*nos*) *inter nos fuisse ingenio haud discordabili* in 402. Tyndarus is dwelling upon the *mutual* relations of good-will existing between them, and *neque me aduorsatum tibi* is needed to carry out this idea after the preceding *neque te commeruisse culpam*.

417. *meus esses :* commonly considered corrupt, but see my note.

418. The reading of the Mss. is commonly altered, but see my note.

420. *uideas :* for arguments in favor of the view that the subjunctive never has the power of expressing ability, and that this must not, therefore, be translated by *can see*, see *Cornell Studies in Classical Philology*, VI. p. 198. For a counter argument, see Bennett, *ib.* IX. p. 41.

430. *quo minus :* one is strongly tempted to write *quom minus*.

430–445. Karsten (*Mnemosyne*, XXI. p. 306) regards these lines as an interpolation.

431. *caueto :* editors are wont to follow Bentley in changing to *caue tu.* Nettleship (*Lectures and Essays*, p. 343) suggests *cauĭto* (see Serv. on *Aen.* IV. 409). It is barely possible, however, that the second syllable of a word of three or more syllables may be shortened, even when it is long by nature (see Introd. § 84, 4). At any rate, such phenomena are so frequently presented by Mss. that one cannot lightly dismiss them as not worth considering. See the readings of the Mss. in *Aul.* 482, *minŏre ;* 599, *herĭle ; Epid.* 338, *quiĕto ; Merc.* 841, *est cúpĭta ; Pseud.* 498, *ămŏris ; Stich.* 700, *ămĭca,* etc. Esch (*De Plauti correptione secundae syllabae vocabulorum polysyllaborum, quae mensura iambica incipiunt*) gives twenty-three such instances of shortening in Plautus, in trisyllabic words alone (though a few of these instances do not properly belong in his list), and many similar instances in longer words. When the second syllable is long by position, a similar shortening is very common. Esch gives seventy-seven such instances in trisyllabic words in Plautus, and many others in longer words. Under these circumstances, I have allowed the reading of the Mss. to stand, though not without misgivings. See Skutsch, *Iambenkürzung und Synizese*, p. 12 ; *Studien zur Plaut. Prosodie*, p. 108 ; Leo, *Plautin. Forsch.* p. 292.

432. *tĕ meã fĭdĕ mĭtti :* the *te* is commonly discarded but, in my judgment, without sufficient reason.

435. *te hic :* commonly written *ted hic* to avoid the supposed hiatus, but the reading of the Mss. may be correct. See my note.

444. This verse has been variously emended, but is probably correct as it stands. See note.

458. *modo captiuos :* Müller (*Rhein. Mus.* LIV. p. 385) regards Fleckeisen's *modo ⟨ad⟩ captiuos* as "absolut sicher" ; cf. 126.

466. On the elision of *s* before a following initial vowel in Plautus, see Leo, *Plautin. Forsch.* pp. 224 ff. For another possible explanation, see Spengel in *Philologus*, XXXVII. p. 436. Editors have commonly altered the reading of the Mss. here to *nec magis*, to make it conform to supposed metrical requirements. Similar changes have been made in numerous other cases of similar character. Leo now shows that the Mss. are probably right after all.

471. *unisubselli :* frequently changed to *imi subselli*, but even if this made the interpretation easier, the evidence in favor of the reading of the Mss., supported, as it is, by the Mss. in *Stich.* 488, is so strong that such an arbitrary alteration seems unjustified.

479. Editors commonly abandon the Mss. on account of the supposed violation of metrical requirements ; but see note on *mag(is) ecfertum* in 466, and Leo's *Plautin. Forsch.* p. 251.

518. Regarded by Karsten as an interpolation.

519. On the anticipatory subjunctive, see Hale's *The Anticipatory Subjunctive in Greek and Latin* (*Univ. of Chicago Studies in Classical Philology*, I.).

521. Regarded by Karsten as an interpolation.

524. *operta . . . aperta sunt:* Karsten regards these words as an interpolation.

527. *uenit modo | intro :* with our imperfect knowledge of the restrictions of hiatus, it is as well to allow it at this unusual place in the verse as to alter the reading of the Mss. Additional doubt, however, is caused by the anapaest in the seventh foot.

532. *ineptias incipisse :* Leo (*Plautin. Forsch.* pp. 224 ff.) shows that final *s* is much more frequently disregarded in Plautine verse than has been supposed. After a short vowel, it may not only be disregarded before an initial consonant of a following word, but it is often elided also before an initial vowel (see App. 466), as *m* continued to be in classical times. In lines like the present one (Leo cites numerous others, p. 297 f.), it may be that *s* was similarly elided, though preceded by a long vowel (just as *m* was elided, without regard to the length of the preceding vowel). Leo, however, excludes such an hypothesis as inadmissible. Possibly we should read *inép|tĩas ín|cipisse.*

536. I have followed Leo in letting *mihi* begin this verse. In the Mss. it ends the preceding line, where it cannot possibly stand.

541. See App. 152. There can be no doubt that the subjunctive is frequently used in Latin to express the idea of obligation or propriety, where the only correct translation is made by the use of *should*, *ought to*, or some equivalent expression ; see *Cornell Studies in Classical Philology*, VI. Part III.

547. It is not necessary to make any emendation here. See note. To change *hic* to *istic* destroys the alliteration, which seems intentional.

550. *sputatur :* it seems to me that editors have changed this to *insputarier* without sufficient reason. We know next to nothing about the usage of either of these words, and in the face of such ignorance it is wiser to let the reading of the Mss. stand. The fact that *sputo* occurs once in Plautus and once in Ovid in an active form is hardly sufficient evidence for rejecting *sputatur* here as a collateral deponent form. Verbs which are found in both active and deponent forms, even in the same author, are common ; see, for instance, dictionaries under *proficiscor*, *proficisco ; amplexor*, *amplexo ; sortior*, *sortio ; comitor*, *comito ;* and many others (see Introd. § 89). The interpretation in my notes was suggested by Fay (*Classical Review* for 1894, p. 391), who, however, accepts *insputatur* as a probable correction. He extends his interpretation to *insputarier* and *insputari* in 553 and 555. In this he may be correct, but his objection to the transitive use of *insputo*, though serious, is not insurmountable. Other similar compounds are found with the accusative, e.g. *inclamo*, *inuoco* (literally, *to call upon* or *at*).

558. Commonly considered corrupt, but see my note. Leo retains *ego*, but indicates an impossible scansion.

597. The Mss. read *atra pix*. Havet (*Revue de Philologie*, 18. p. 242) argues for *atra agitet pix.*

653. This line is commonly considered corrupt, but see my note. On the use of *-ne* in the sense of *uero*, *indeed*, see Warren, *Am. Jour. of Phil.* II. pp. 50 ff.

694. Apparently corrupt. The line can be read metrically as it stands only by scanning *ĭntĕrdīco*, which seems impossible.

699. This line may have originally ended in *redux*, the *bene est* then belonging to the beginning of the next line; see Speijer in *Mnemosyne* (1888), p. 152, and cf. 686, 923, and Prol. 43.

749. The reading of the Mss. is retained. See my note.

771. For other instances of *pompa*, see Knapp, *Classical Review*, X. p. 427.

791. For the proof that the Romans felt a distinct and important difference between the perfect and present tenses in expressions referring to the future, see *Cornell Studies in Classical Philology*, VI.

800–802. See Karsten (*l.c.*).

818–822. Regarded by Karsten as an interpolation.

819. Editors commonly read *dupla* instead of *duplam*, and interpret the line as meaning *who have lambs killed and then offer lamb for sale at double the price* (i.e. at double the price it is really worth).

This interpretation is open to the following objections: —

(1) *Lanii* means *butchers*, i.e. those who with their own hands slaughter animals; but the interpretation in question makes it necessary to suppose that the butchers employed some one else to do their butchering.

(2) The positions of *locant* and *danunt* clearly show that these two words are strongly contrasted. The interpretation in question disregards this contrast altogether.

(3) There is no authority of any kind for the reading *dupla*. The manuscript authority is unanimously in favor of *duplam*, and such

authority ought always to be respected until it has been clearly proved to be impossible. Furthermore, the presence of *duplam* in the Mss. would be difficult to account for, if we suppose that *dupla* was originally written, as *duplam* is the *difficilior lectio;* it would never have occurred to a scribe to write *duplam agninam, double lamb,* if he had found *dupla* in his Ms., since *dupla* and *duplum* were used of price commonly enough to have occasioned no difficulty.

(4) Finally, the parasite is complaining about the quality of things, not about the price ; note, for instance, *foetidos* (813), *petroni* (820). The price of food never worries a parasite.

The interpretation offered in my notes avoids all of these difficulties. *Agnos* is the object of *locant,* just as *statuam* is, in *locant statuam faciendam ;* the only difference is that the lambs are contracted for as *fit to be slaughtered;* the statue as one *to be made.* In neither case does *locant* imply that anything already in one's possession is to be *handed over* to some one else ; it implies, in either case, merely a contract for something not yet in one's possession. The *locator,* as Hallidie says, may be either the party who *pays,* or the party who *is paid,* according to the nature of the contract. In the present passage the *lanii* are the parties *to be paid* (by the public, with the understanding that the lamb is to be young and tender). For another instance of *caedundus* in the sense of *fit to be killed, fat,* see *Aul.* 567.

828. Kellerhoff, *de collocatione verborum Plautina* (*Studemund's Studien,* II. p. 80), conjectures *alter* before *fortunatior ;* see my note.

830. Bothe's conjecture of *hic est ? ecquis* after *ecquis* is commonly adopted, but it seems to me too uncertain to justify incorporating it into the text.

836. Abraham (*Studia Plautina, Jahrbuecher für Class. Phil.* for 1885, p. 202) holds that *in tempore* is not Plautine Latin.

840. The Mss. end this line with *noli irascier,* which both destroys the metre and is inappropriate. Probably these words have crept in from 845, displacing what originally stood here.

842. For comments upon the use of *quod* in passages similar to this, see Fay, *Am. Jour. Phil.* XVIII. p. 179.

847. *laridum atque epulas :* on this use of *atque,* see my dissertation on *The Copulative Conjunctions Que, Et, Atque, in the Inscriptions of the Republic, in Terence, and in Cato,* p. 31.

856. *faciam ut te :* editors commonly adopt Bentley's conjecture, *tute* for *te.* Probably, however, the reading of the Mss. is correct. See Appendix to my edition of Ter. *Phorm.* p. 156.

865. *deum :* I retain the reading of the Mss. See my note.

882. *iam diu :* Gray (*Proceedings of the Cambridge Phil. Soc.* for 1888, p. 6) revives Wagner's emendation, *tam modo.*

892. Brix-Niemeyer takes *etiam* with *quom* in the sense of *even when.* Kirk (*Am. Jour. of Phil.* XVIII. p. 26) takes it in the sense of *still.* But its position favors my interpretation. If Plautus did not intend *etiam* to be taken with *sancte,* he would be guilty of unnecessary ambiguity in assigning it to this position in the sentence.

901. I have followed the Mss. in making a new scene here, though editors commonly follow Spengel (*Scenentitel,* pp. 278 ff.) in recognizing no division.

923. *reducem :* on the derivation and form of this word, see Fleckeisen, *Neue Jahrbücher* for 1893, p. 196 f. and for 1895, p. 277 f. In the present passage it is customary to write *redducem,* but this is against all manuscript authority, and against the uniform usage of all poets from Naevius on, including Plautus himself (cf., in the present play, 437, 686, 931; also Prol. 43). In *Rud.* 909 there is similarly no authority for *redducem,* though editors adopt this reading. The simplest way to remedy the metre is to assume, with Fleckeisen, that *te* belongs after *tuo.*

927. *haec . . . repertast :* probably *rē* has fallen out before the *rĕ* of *repertast.*

964. Perhaps Plautus wrote *istaec* (Schmidt) instead of *ista ;* or *ac dic* (Camerarius) instead of *dic.*

993. *Vos* is commonly inserted, quite arbitrarily, after *si.*

1006. On the use of *gnatus* and *filius,* see Köhm, *quaestiones Plautinae Terentianaeque,* pp. 6 ff.

1014. For *illic,* Bach conjectures *ipse* (*Studemund's Studien,* II. pp. 343 ff.), but see my note.

1021. Havet inserts *tu* after *sed.* Perhaps *vero* was originally written after *oro.* See Speijer, *Mnemosyne,* XVI. p. 155.

1022-1023. One of these lines is commonly rejected, but, it seems to me, without adequate reason. See my note.

INDEX TO NOTES.

171

ALLYN AND BACON'S

COLLEGE LATIN SERIES

UNDER THE GENERAL EDITORSHIP OF PROFESSORS

CHARLES E. BENNETT, AND **JOHN C. ROLFE,**
of Cornell University, *of the University of Pennsylvania.*

CATULLUS. By Professor CHARLES L. DURHAM, of Cornell University.

CICERO. Selections from the Letters. By Professor SAMUEL BALL PLATNER, of Adelbert College.

HORACE. Odes and Epodes. By Professor CHARLES E. BENNETT, of Cornell University. (*Ready.*)

—— **Satires and Epistles.** By Professor JOHN C. ROLFE, of the University of Pennsylvania. (*Ready.*)

—— **Complete Edition.** The two volumes in one. By Professors BENNETT and ROLFE. (*Ready.*)

JUVENAL. By SIDNEY GEORGE OWEN, Fellow of Christ Church College, Oxford.

LIVY. Books I., XXI., XXII. By Professor JOHN H. WESTCOTT, of Princeton University. (*Ready.*)

OVID. The Fasti. By Professor JESSE BENEDICT CARTER, of Princeton University.

PLAUTUS. Captivi. By Professor HERBERT C. ELMER, of Cornell University. (*Ready.*)

—— **Mostellaria.** By Professor EDWIN W. FAY, of the University of Texas. (*Ready.*)

PLINY. Selections from the Letters. By Professor JOHN HOWELL WESTCOTT, of Princeton University. (*Ready.*)

QUINTILIAN. Selections. By Professor W. H. JOHNSON, of Denison University.

SUETONIUS. The Lives of Tiberius, Caligula, Claudius, and Nero. By Professor JOSEPH B. PIKE, of the University of Minnesota.

SUETONIUS. The Lives of Julius and Augustus. By Professor JOHN HOWELL WESTCOTT and CHARLES A. ROBINSON, of Princeton University.

TACITUS. Agricola and Germania. (*In one volume.*) By Professor ALFRED GUDEMAN. (*Ready.*)

—— **Agricola.** By Professor ALFRED GUDEMAN. (*Ready.*)

—— **Dialogus de Oratoribus.** By Professor ALFRED GUDEMAN. (*Ready.*)

—— **Selections from the Annals and Histories.** By Professor ALFRED GUDEMAN.

TERENCE. Andria. By Professor H. R. FAIRCLOUGH, of Leland Stanford Junior University. (*Ready.*)

—— **Adelphoe.** By Professor FRANK M. JOHNSON, of the University of Nebraska.

VIRGIL. Eclogues and Georgics. By Professor ARTHUR T. WALKER, of the University of Kansas.

Handbook of Latin Etymology. By P. GILES, Fellow of Emmanuel College, Cambridge.

Handbook of Latin Inscriptions, illustrative of the Latin Language. By WALLACE M. LINDSAY, Fellow of Jesus College, Oxford, Professor in St. Andrews University. (*Ready.*)

Handbook of Latin Style. By Dr. C. L. MEADER, of the University of Michigan.

Handbook of Latin Synonyms. By Dr. C. L. MEADER, of the University of Michigan.

History of Roman Literature. By Professors JOHN C. ROLFE, of the University of Pennsylvania, and JOSEPH H. DRAKE, of the University of Michigan.

Roman Constitutional History, from the Earliest Times to the End of the Republic. By Dr. JOHN E. GRANRUD, of the University of Minnesota. (*Ready.*)

Selections from the Elegiac Poets. By Professor B. LAWTON WIGGINS, Vice-Chancellor of the University of the South.

Topography and Archæological Remains of the City of Rome. By Professor SAMUEL BALL PLATNER, of Adelbert College.

———

ALLYN AND BACON, Publishers,

172, Tremont Street, 111, Fifth Avenue, 378, Wabash Avenue,
BOSTON. NEW YORK. CHICAGO.

A Latin Grammar.

By Professor CHARLES E. BENNETT, Cornell University. 12mo, cloth, 282 pages. Price, 80 cents.

IN this book the essential facts of Latin Grammar are presented within the smallest compass consistent with high scholarly standards. It covers not only the work of the preparatory school, but also that of the required courses in college and university. By omitting rare forms and syntactical usages found only in ante-classical and post-classical Latin, and by relegating to an Appendix theoretical and historical questions, it has been found possible to treat the subject with entire adequacy in the compass of 250 pages exclusive of Indexes. In the German schools, books of this scope fully meet the exacting demands of the entire gymnasial course, and those who have tried Bennett's Grammar find that they are materially helped by being relieved of the mass of useless and irrelevant matter which forms the bulk of the older grammars. All Latin texts for reading in secondary schools, recently issued, contain references in the notes to Bennett's Latin Grammar.

Professor William A. Houghton, *Bowdoin College, Brunswick, Maine.* The Grammar proper is admirably adapted to its purpose in its clearness of arrangement and classification, and in its simplicity and precision of statement, giving definitely just what the pupil must know, and not crowding the page with a mass of matter that too often disheartens the young student instead of helping him. I trust it will come into general use, for I think for the reasons just given, and because of its moderate compass and attractive appearance, students are likely to get more practical grammatical knowledge out of it than they generally do from the larger grammars.

John F. Peck, *Oberlin Academy, Oberlin, Ohio :* Bennett's Latin Grammar was adopted as a text-book in Oberlin Academy in 1897. It is proving itself a very satisfactory text-book and increasingly popular. The teachers of Latin in Oberlin Academy are thoroughly satisfied with the book and find it exceedingly helpful in their work.

The Critic, *Feb.* 29, 1896. The book is a marvel of condensed, yet clear and forcible, statement. The ground covered in the treatment of forms and syntax is adequate for ordinary school work and for the use of freshmen and sophomores in college.

Appendix to Bennett's Latin Grammar.

By Professor CHARLES E. BENNETT, Cornell University. For university work. 12mo, cloth, 246 pages. Price, 80 cents.

THE purpose of this book is to give such information regarding the history and development of the Latin language as experience has shown to be of service to advanced students.

The subjects treated are the Latin Alphabet, Pronunciation, Hidden Quantity, Accent, Orthography, The Latin Sounds, Inflections, Adverbs and Prepositions, and Syntax. Of these subjects, those of Hidden Quantity, Inflections, and Syntax receive special attention; and the results of recent investigation are set forth fully and clearly, but in compact form.

Professor Edouard Wölfflin, in the *Archiv für Lateinische Lexikographie und Grammatik.* February, 1896. Auf geringem Raume ist viel wissenswürdiges zusammengedrängt, und zwar mit praktischem Geschicke; zwei längere Listen geben die lateinischen Wörter von bestrittener Quantität und Orthographie, wobei die Ansätze von Marx oft berichtigt sind. . . . Die deutsche Wissenschaft wird sich nur freuen dass das amerikanische Schulwesen ein so brauchbares Hilfsmittel gewonnen hat.

Professor Hermann Osthoff, *University of Heidelberg:* Steht auf der Höhe des heutigen Wissens.

Professor Harry Thurston Peck, *Columbia College, N.Y.:* It is no exaggeration to say that so compact, helpful, and practical a collection of indispensable information cannot be found elsewhere in any language whatsoever. Even in Germany, the home of classical enchiridia, nothing has yet appeared that is so satisfactory. Professor Bennett seems to divine by instinct just what questions arise in the mind of the student, and he here answers them in advance in a delightfully lucid and simple fashion. . . . Everywhere the best authorities are cited; and it is certain that to many teachers, as well as students, the mere perusal of this little manual will open up many new vistas, and will put them in touch with the most scholarly doctrine of the day. In fact the book is one that no progressive instructor can afford to be without, as it summarizes an immense amount of information that is of the utmost practical importance.

Complete Edition.

BENNETT'S Latin Grammar and Appendix in one volume. 12mo, half leather, 282 + 246 pages. Price, $1.25.

College Latin Series.

ODES AND EPODES OF HORACE.

Edited by Professor CHARLES E. BENNETT, of Cornell University.
12mo, cloth, 464 pages.   Price, $1.40.

SATIRES AND EPISTLES OF HORACE.

Edited by Professor JOHN C. ROLFE, of the University of Michigan.
12mo, cloth, 458 pages.   Price, $1.40.

COMPLETE WORKS OF HORACE.

Edited by Professors BENNETT and ROLFE.   12mo, cloth, 922 pages.
Price, $2.00.

In these volumes each poem is preceded by a careful analysis
giving in a line or two all necessary information regarding the
subject, date, and metre.   Each volume is prefaced by a scholarly
discussion of the life and work of Horace, his metres, and language.   The commentary is concise, accurate, and eminently
judicious, in all cases telling the student all he needs to know,
and never telling him more than he needs, or more than he will
understand and appreciate.

THE DIALOGUS OF TACITUS.

With an Introduction and Notes by Professor ALFRED GUDEMAN,
12mo, cloth, 201 pages.   Price, $1.00.

THE AGRICOLA OF TACITUS.

With an Introduction and Notes by Professor ALFRED GUDEMAN.
12mo, cloth, 198 pages.   Price, $1.00.

THE AGRICOLA AND GERMANIA OF TACITUS.

With Maps, Introduction, and Notes, by Professor ALFRED GUDE-
MAN.   12mo, cloth, 366 pages.   Price, $1.40.

In the *Dialogus* is a scholarly discussion of the authorship of
the treatise.   The Introduction of the *Agricola* covers the " Life
and Writings of Tacitus," " The Literary Character of the Agricola," and " The Style and Rhetoric of Tacitus."   This introduction is reprinted in the *Agricola and Germania*, which contains
also an introduction to the *Germania*, and two valuable maps,
one of the British Isles, for the *Agricola*, and the other of Europe,
with both ancient and modern names, for the *Germania*.

College Latin Series. *Continued.*

THE ANDRIA OF TERENCE.

> With Introduction and Notes by Professor HENRY R. FAIRCLOUGH, of Leland Stanford Junior University. 12mo, cloth, 266 pages. Price, $1.25.

The introduction deals in a thorough yet concise fashion with the Development of Roman Comedy, the Plot of the Andria, the Characters of the Andria, Dramatic Entertainments, the Division of Plays into Acts and Scenes, Actors and their Costume, the Theatre, Prosody, Metres and Music, and the Language. The notes are carefully adapted to college and university work.

THE CAPTIVI OF PLAUTUS.

> With Introduction and Notes by Professor H. C. ELMER, of Cornell University. 12mo, cloth, 231 pages. Price, $1.25.

Professor Elmer's introduction is a brief but comprehensive survey of Plautus' life, his writings, metres, and language, Roman dramatic performances, and the history of the text of the *Captivi*.

SELECTED LETTERS OF PLINY.

> With an Introduction and Notes by Professor J. H. WESTCOTT, of Princeton University. 12mo, cloth, 326 pages. Price, $1.25.

The Introduction contains a Life of Pliny, a discussion of Pliny's Style, and a brief bibliography. The Chronology of the *Letters*, and a critical treatment of the text are given in the Appendices.

HANDBOOK OF LATIN INSCRIPTIONS.

> By W. M. LINDSAY, M.A., Fellow of Jesus College, Oxford. 16mo, cloth, 134 pages. Price, $1.25.

The author states very clearly some of the principles of form changes in Latin, and gives a collection of inscriptions by way of illustration, from the earliest period down to Imperial and Late Latin.

ROMAN CONSTITUTIONAL HISTORY.

> By Dr. JOHN E. GRANRUD, of the University of Minnesota. 12mo, cloth, 306 pages. Price, $1.25.

The political institutions of Rome are treated historically so as to furnish collateral reading for students of Latin, and provide an admirable introduction to further study of the subject.

Livy, Books I., XXI., and XXII.

With Introduction and Notes by Professor J. H. Westcott, Princeton University. 12mo, cloth, 426 pages. Price, $1.25.

AN attempt has been made in this volume to present in simple and convenient form the assistance needed by young students making their first acquaintance with Livy.

The editor's experience in the class-room has led him to annotate the text copiously. On the other hand, that fulness of illustration which apparently aims to supersede the function of the teacher has been carefully avoided.

Professor James H. Dillard, *Tulane University, New Orleans, La.:* I should like to say that Westcott's Livy is the most satisfactory text-book that I know of. Other works may put on a greater show of learning; but when one comes to every-day class-room use, the editing of this text is found to be exceptionally satisfactory.

Professor Charles E. Bennett, *Cornell University, Ithaca, N.Y.:* It seems to me an excellent book. The notes are exceedingly fresh and scholarly; they call attention to the right things in the right way. This edition is superior to any similar edition with which I am acquainted.

Fifty Stories from Aulus Gellius.

Edited for reading at sight by Professor JOHN H. WESTCOTT, Princeton University. 16mo, paper, 81 pages. Price, 30 cents.

THIS is a collection of interesting stories, which form excellent material for sight-reading. The Notes, which are quite full, are at the bottom of the page.

One Hundred and Twenty Epigrams of Martial.

Edited by Professor JOHN H. WESTCOTT. 16mo, paper, 81 pages. Price, 30 cents.

THIS selection is intended for rapid reading, or even for sight-reading with students of sufficient ability. For the sake of convenience and rapidity in reading, the notes have been placed on the pages with the text.